One Man Crime Spree

TIM "MURPH THE SURF" MURPHY

Edited By:

Name of Editor

Printed By:

Company Name

Printed in the United States of America

First Printing Edition, 2025

I S B N 0 - 0 0 0 0 0 0 0 - 0 - 0

Table of Contents

Author's Note

"The Charge of the Light Brigade"

by Alfred, Lord Tennyson

Memorializing Events in the Battle of Balaclava,

October 25, 1854   Written 1854

Half a league, half a league,
Half a league onward,
All in the valley of Death
Rode the six hundred:
'Forward, the Light Brigade!
Charge for the guns' he said:
Into the valley of Death
Rode the six hundred.

'Forward, the Light Brigade!'
Was there a man dismay'd?
Not tho' the soldier knew
Someone had blunder'd:
Theirs not to make reply,
Theirs not to reason why,
Theirs but to do & die,
Into the valley of Death
Rode the six hundred.

Cannon to right of them,
Cannon to left of them,

Cannon in front of them
Volley'd & thunder'd;
Storm'd at with shot and shell,
Boldly they rode and well,
Into the jaws of Death,
Into the mouth of Hell
Rode the six hundred.

Flash'd all their sabres bare,
Flash'd as they turn'd in air
Sabring the gunners there,
Charging an army while
All the world wonder'd:
Plunged in the battery-smoke
Right thro' the line they broke;
Cossack & Russian
Reel'd from the sabre-stroke,
Shatter'd & sunder'd.
Then they rode back, but not
Not the six hundred.

Cannon to right of them,
Cannon to left of them,
Cannon behind them
Volley'd and thunder'd;
Storm'd at with shot and shell,
While horse & hero fell,
They that had fought so well
Came thro' the jaws of Death,
Back from the mouth of Hell,
All that was left of them,
Left of six hundred.

When can their glory fade?
O, the wild charge they made!
All the world wonder'd.
Honour the charge they made!
Honour the Light Brigade,
Noble six hundred!

This poem, including punctuation, is reproduced from a scan of the poem written out by Tennyson in his own hand later, in 1864. The scan was made available online by the University of Virginia.

*https://nationalcenter.org/ncppr/2001/11/03/charge-of-the-light-brigade-by-alfred-lord-tennyson/

The British did conscript Irish troops which were significantly present in the Charge of the Light Brigade; of the approximately 673 men who took part, 114 (nearly 20%) were Irish. These soldiers were part of the general British Army regiments, with one regiment having a specific Irish designation. Irish soldiers made up a substantial portion of the entire British force in the Crimean War, with some estimates suggesting as many as a third of all British soldiers there were Irish. Irish soldiers were distributed across the five regiments that comprised the Light Brigade. There was one regiment in the Charge of the Light Brigade that was officially an "Irish" regiment: the 8th (The King's Royal Irish) Hussars. The other regiments in the Light Brigade had Irish soldiers within their ranks, but the 8th Hussars were the only one with a specific Irish designation and history. This regiment was formed from Protestants in Ireland in the late 17th century and had a long history of being stationed there, gaining its formal Irish title in 1777. It had the most Irishmen of the five regiments in the Light Brigade, with one officer and twenty-seven other ranks participating in the charge itself.

I had quoted the three highlighted lines for the majority of my adult life, never knowing their origin until investigating the Murphy Family Lineage.

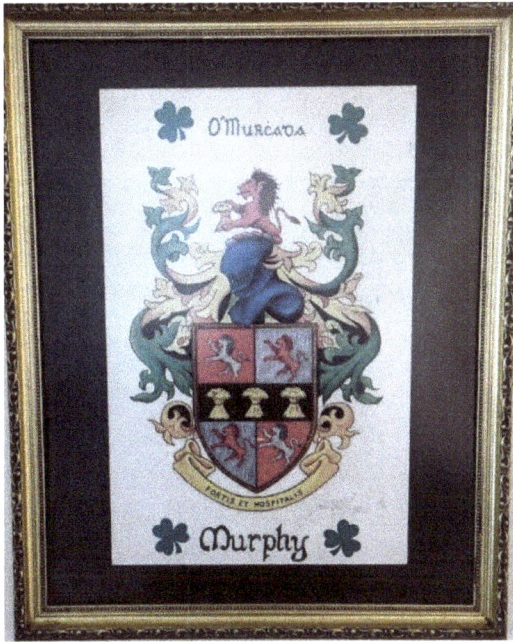

Original seven-color silk screen done by my brother, Patrick William Murphy, 5/10 copies for all Murphy Clan Members.

A couple of years ago, while touting On Clifton Hill Karaoke in Niagara Falls, Canada, after coming off the Stage of my good friend "KJ Jeff," an elderly Gentleman on vacation from the Emerald Isle came up and asked me to write my name down. I obliged with Timothy Patrick Michael Murphy; for Michael was my Catholic Confirmation name. He asked, "Do you know where your people are from? To which I replied: Dungarvan County Waterford. To which he stated: Oh, that explains it...you're the outbred of Vikings who came and raped our Irish lasses and left you Murphy bastard children so no one would ever conquer Ireland!

To which I retorted, "God invented alcohol so that the Irish didn't conquer The World!

There is much Truth in both statements, and it's borne out in the Murphy Family Name and History- NAME in Gaelic - O'Murchadha [Descendant of Murchadh meaning "Sea Warrior"]

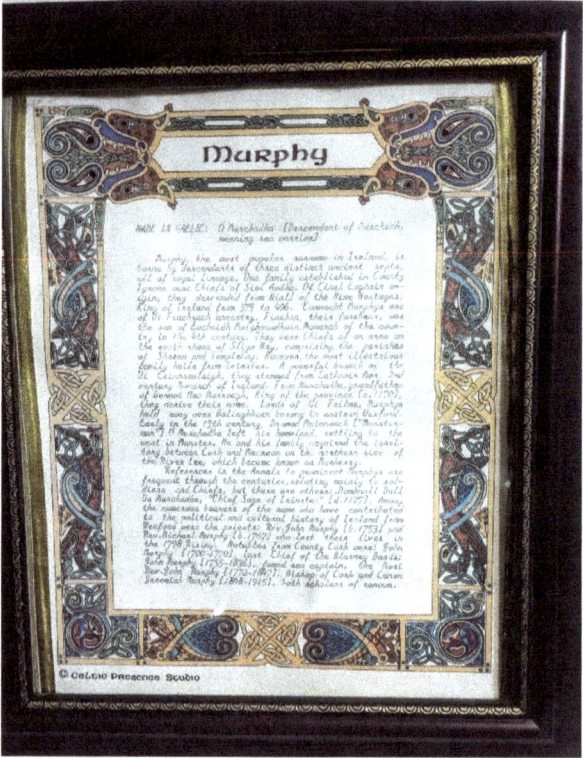

There is a truth to that...There is a Spirit of The Isle... One that seeks to protect those who can't! I will always choose to defend the underdog. I am known in Canada as "Murph the Surf-Robin Hood to the Homeless" because I care for everyone I meet and go out of my way to do so. Canada is my second home as I just learned through my oldest brother John Perry "Jack" Murphy, that my Great Grandfather, John Jeremiah Murphy,

1859 - 1929 {Loretto Rest, Syracuse, NY} was born in Canada (English) in 1859 ... and I am going to pursue dual citizenship for my love of Canada and owning a summer home in Sherkston Shores Ontario, Canada for 30 years.

This spirit is not unique to me. It lives in a breed of Irishman who feels led to protect those who cannot, to the downtrodden, the disadvantaged, and the disabled, which led me to adopt my departed wife, Laura Lynn Sorce Murphy's son from her first marriage, Justin Thomas Murphy, who has Spastic Quadriplegic Cerebral Palsy and is wheelchair bound. Laura brought him in to meet me in prison upon my request after finding out about him after months of her writing, accepting my prison calls, and visiting me in the joint before finally telling me. When I lifted that little 4-year-old, 32 pounds out of his collapsible wheelchair...God's Reclamation Plan on my life began... And continues to this day... Because I hope He's not done...because I am not complete! I am a Sinner! In need of, as my Mother, Donna Mae Krill Murphy Barczak, once put it, "Crawl on my knees Repentance Every day!"

I have made every effort in this book to tell the truth, which may be painful for some to hear. I also made an effort to protect the families I love...And not just my family. I changed the name of a beloved family because, for a period of time, they truly were my family. They treated me as such, and I rejoiced and grieved all their experiences... and still do.

To all others: If I offended you...The truth usually does hurt. If you want to talk about it, we can... But under JR's Rules... No Witnesses! We can go anywhere you want...But also know this:

"I am afraid of NO MAN on this Earth! What are you going to do?

Kill ME? Do me a favor...But if I get up...You ain't going to see me coming! I don't have a death wish... I just know who made me... And I ain't going anywhere until he calls me Home! And always remember this; 1 Corinthians 15:10 ... "But for the Grace of God...
I AM WHAT I AM!!!" I didn't make me this way... He did! Blame Him!

Timothy Patrick Michael "Murph the Surf" Murphy, October 9, 1958 – Till He calls me home! Come get it!

Foreword

Some stories ask to be told, and then some stories demand it. *One Man Crime Spree* belongs to the latter. It is not a memoir in the traditional sense; it is a reckoning, a confession, and a survival map drawn in blood, silence, and defiance.

Timothy Murphy, known to many as "Murph the Surf," lived a life that defied containment. From the steel bars of Attica to the shadows of Erie, Pennsylvania, his journey was marked by chaos, loyalty, and a code that didn't come from any law book. He didn't just survive the system; he stared it down and walked through it with his fists clenched and his mouth shut.

In 1985, Murphy's grief exploded inside a prison cell after the death of his beloved Mary Ellen DeSanto. The guards expected a riot. What they got was silence. The extraction team, trained to subdue the most violent inmates, backed off. A guard, then a counselor named Robert Alexander, who would later become a judge, witnessed it. In twenty years at Attica, he had never seen that team retreat. That night, they did.

Years later, Judge Alexander met Murphy at a men's ministry in a snow-blown warehouse. Murphy stood before a crowd of ex-bikers, ex-cons, and the kind of souls Jesus never gave up on, and told his story. The judge recognized him instantly, not from his face, but from the force of his truth.

Murphy's story isn't just remembered, it's felt. Judge Robert Alexander, who spent two decades inside Attica, recalled the moment vividly. The guards had suited up for a cell extraction, expecting violence. What they found was blood, grief, and a man who had nothing left to lose. Murphy didn't flinch. He didn't beg. He backed into the corner of his cell and asked one question: *"Who's gonna be the first motherfucker through that gate?"*

They backed off.

That moment burned into his memory. It was the first piece of a story that would take decades to tell.

Murphy's story didn't end in that cell. It unraveled across decades, stitched together by scars, silence, and survival. Judge Alexander, who had once run the infamous coal gang inside Attica, remembered the chaos well: wild prison cats eating severed toes, inmates crafting necklaces from bone, and guards dodging homemade hooch-fueled brawls. Murphy wasn't just another inmate. He was a force. A man who could turn a riot into a reckoning... He was a thinker...That's why he was on the team!

There were moments of horror, a young man slitting his own throat in fear, another mutilating himself to become a female. There were moments of absurdity, like the inmate who rode ten tons of coal down a chute and walked away grinning, "Boss, what a rush." And there were moments of grace, like the night Murphy brought his son Justin, wheelchair-bound and radiant, into Judge Bob's courtroom. The judge gave him the bench. Justin gave him justice. That night, 108 people went home not guilty.

This book doesn't sanitize the past. It doesn't ask for sympathy. It demands attention. Murphy's story is told with the kind of detail that can't be faked, because it wasn't. From the inmate who rode ten tons of coal down a chute and lived to laugh about it, to the young man who slit his own throat in fear, to the prison doctor who treated pain with sarcasm and aspirin, every moment in these pages is earned.

One Man Crime Spree is not a redemption arc. It's not a cautionary tale. It's a ledger of choices, consequences, codes, and survival. Murphy didn't ask to be understood. He asked to be heard. And through this book, he is.

Judge Robert Alexander, who saw Murphy from both sides of the bars, offers this foreword not as praise, but as proof. Proof that Murphy's story is real. That's brutal. That's unforgettable. And that it belongs to a world most people will never see, but should.

This is not a story about New York City's La Cosa Nostra. It's about the undercurrent, the forgotten towns, the quiet wars, the men who operated outside the spotlight and beneath the radar. Murphy was one of them. And every time he walks into a room in Erie, Pennsylvania, someone says the same thing: *"Murph the Surf, I thought you were dead."*

He wasn't. He isn't. And now, he's speaking.

CHAPTER 01

BORN INTO THE GAME

I should not be alive. And to this day, I question why I am.

They used to call me *Murph the Surf.* Not because I ever caught a wave, but because the name stuck. It started as a joke and turned into a label, one that followed me through bars, cells, and every bad decision that somehow didn't kill me. People said it with either a grin or a warning, depending on which side of the story they were on.

When I think of it, the only reason I'm still breathing is that I kept my word and lived by a code. That's it. I stayed under the radar for forty years, and nobody ever did a minute because of me. *You break the rules, the rules break you.* I learned that early.

My grandmother and grandfather Murphy ran the city of Erie during Prohibition. Grandpa Murphy had a tugboat on the Erie, Pennsylvania, dock, and he had modified it. He put in an extra gear set so he could kick all the low-end power to high-end speed at night. That thing could make it from Erie, Pennsylvania, to Presque Isle, to Long Point, Canada, in no time. If you look at a map of Lake Erie, you'll see two peninsulas in the middle of the lake. Presque Isle sticks out from Erie, Pennsylvania. Long Point is a peninsula in Canada. The distance between them? Only 27 miles across Lake Erie.

Grandma Murphy's stories were something else, and my oldest brother confirmed one of the wildest, that Eliot Ness was actually after them during Prohibition. He told me they had a payroll of $400 a week. I wasn't very impressed, but he emphatically pointed out that this was when "an Irish cop made $5 a week, and a city councilman made $10, and they had every one of them on the payroll."

Ness was a revenue officer from Cleveland, Ohio. A revenuer is basically like an IRS agent; they went after moonshiners and bootleggers for tax evasion. They had Buffalo shut down, Cleveland under control, and Detroit was Al Capone's turf. But the Canadian whiskey kept coming.

One of Erie's finest came to Grandma Murphy one night and told her that Perry couldn't make her run that night because there were revenuers in from Cleveland watching the dock. They had to put off the run that night to do some thinking, and that was Grandma Murphy's forte... Back then, the only other navigable point between Long Point, Canada, and the US shore was Barcelona Harbor, which had a lighthouse just north of Westfield, NY.

The Million Dollar Baby told Grandpa Perry to bring the load back to the Barcelona lighthouse, where she would have the truck waiting to offload the top-shelf Canadian whiskey. But that wasn't good enough for Grandma; she was concerned the revenuers would still track the load down. So once the whiskey was loaded onto the truck, they turned off the truck so it wouldn't run and pulled the wires on the spark plugs. Then Graham Murphy contracted a wrecker tow truck to drive to Barcelona and pick up the truck with the load on board. That way, the only one who would get busted was the poor son of a bitch tow truck driver who knew nothing about it.

They towed the truck back to Erie and offloaded it in the basement of Jack Paris Steakhouse on the corner of 6th and State, which was my grandmother's Italian partner for distribution. She was a genius. Maybe that's where I get it from... always thinking... can't stop thinking!

Let me make it clear: my grandparents weren't bootleggers; they weren't making bathtub gin...Although Grandma told me she had to resort to that to survive the year Grandpa took off to Chicago to modify Al Capone's tugboats. NO...They were Rum Runners. That meant they brought back top-shelf Canadian whiskey, prime liquor during Prohibition. People paid top dollar because they were used to rotgut and moonshine.

Erie, Pa., was one of the most treacherous little towns, stemming from its underworld roots and its location, basically 100 miles from Cleveland, Pittsburgh, and Buffalo. Because of the geography it was agreed a long time ago that Erie would be a neutral town and if any one city tried to take over the other two would come against it, That coupled with Erie being one of the best kept secrets for its waterfront and beaches and the fact that if anyone got too hot in their hometown they could come and lay low on the lam in "quiet little Erie"' This led to one of the biggest collection of a den thieves, gangsters, safe crackers, bank robbers, hoodlums, extortionist, arsonists, thugs, drug dealers and murderers. At one time, probably one of the most corrupt cities per capita in the United States, including the cops.

I graduated from high school in 1976. Grandma died in 1979. In that three-year window, I went to her at least half a dozen times to ask for money. She'd go, "Shh, don't tell your father," and reach behind picture frames, under carpets, out of pillows. She'd pull brand-new hundred-dollar bills—1927 silver certificates, never bent because she rolled her money in coffee cans at least twice a year. Each bill was worth ten grand today. I'd get a friggin ounce of dope and throw a kegger for the high school. That was 1976.

My grandparents' influence went far beyond Prohibition. They ran an illegal card game right across from the Erie police station for nearly thirty years after Prohibition. Finally busted when the Irish mayor, Tom Flatley, who was getting kickbacks from Grandma, got caught. He, the police chief, the head of the city council—all removed from office. Documented evidence. While in office, Flatley became enmeshed in a major corruption investigation linked to illegal gambling, bribery, and the "numbers racket" in Erie.

On or about April 10, 1954, a meeting took place in the mayor's office involving Flatley, a police inspector (Jack Martin), and others concerning collecting money from gamblers ("numbers" operators).

The investigation—led by the Erie County District Attorney—resulted in indictments against about 40 persons: 12 were tried and convicted, and 18 pleaded guilty.

In the case of Stanley M. Schwartz (an associate in the scheme), the Court described: "For nearly a year Martin, the Mayor, and appellant met once a month, often in the Mayor's office ... they equally divided the money collected ... about $1,500 was collected each month by Martin and appellant."

Flatley admitted in his signed statement that he received about $500 a month from Schwartz and Martin, though he maintained he did not receive money directly from gamblers.

Legal outcome: He pleaded guilty to charges of conspiracy and violating his oath of office as mayor. On December 15, 1954, he was sentenced to one to two years in prison and fined $1,000. He resigned or was removed from office in 1954 due to the scandal.

After Flatley's removal, George J. Brabender served as acting mayor from December 14, 1954, until January 5, 1955, and then Arthur J. Gardner became mayor (1955–1962).

The scandal is considered a pivotal moment in Erie's political history — marking the end of a specific era of local Irish political-machine influence and paving the way for reformist impulses. Some commentators labelled Flatley's story as "a tragic tale" of a once-beloved local politician who fell via corruption.

Even though he served time in prison, his case remains a frequently cited example of mid-20th-century municipal corruption in Pennsylvania.

Grandma's card games were legendary. She was known as the Million-Dollar Baby. Drove a gold Cadillac convertible, always dressed to the nines. When she walked into a bar, you'd better have a black velvet and Coke on the rail before her ass hit the stool, or the owner would hear about it. Half the people in the bar owed her money.

Her funeral in 1979—I was twenty years old—was something else. Standing at her casket, I looked around. Every Irish cop, city councilman, Italian gangster, hoodlum, and mafioso in Erie was there.

There are some generational stories, not just with my grandparents. My father flew off the USS Enterprise during World War II. He was shot down in the middle of the Pacific Ocean, flying nighttime missions over Japan. One night, he and I were in Akron, Ohio. He was a functioning alcoholic. He was teaching me how to be a functioning alcoholic. And how you do that is, he told me..."The first time you miss a day of work because of a hangover, you have a drinking problem! You can go to work, suffer and get paid, just as easy as staying home and not get paid!" I interpreted that as long as I didn't miss a day of work, I didn't have a drinking problem... I never did!

Once in 1976, months away from graduating from Academy High School in Erie, Pa., by the skin of my teeth, I'm sitting in homeroom and over the P.A. system I hear the principal, Don DeNardo, say: "Is Tim Murphy in that classroom? Send him down to my office, NOW!" Holy shit, what now? I was already on the hot seat and got kicked out of Band and Orchestra by Bill Burger, who was trying to hold my diploma because of my sophomore caper, where I fell on the sword for the senior drummers in the drum line with me when we stole all the cymbals from Sherman NY high school after we did the final concert of my sophomore year. To let the seniors graduate, I took the wrap! Then here in my senior year, I was accused of the big chocolate Easter Bunny caper where "someone unnamed" found a case of the band's fundraiser Choclate Easter Bunnies that had fallen off the back of the truck, or had been stashed in the tunnels underneath the Academy Band room and was underselling the band members on the Black locker market....(Of course, I didn't know anything about that.)

As I rounded the corner to peek in his door, there, seated next to him, was my grandmother, who had no legal reason to be there. My parents had divorced when I was eleven, and their best friends got divorced and switched couples, remarried. That's messed up enough, but in 1969, it was unheard of, even in Peyton Place. I lived with my mother and stepfather, and Grandma Murphy had no authority to be there—but she didn't need any. She had things well in hand. She said, "Yep, that's him, and I need him right now. It's an emergency."

Don DeNardo wrote out the pass for the day, and as we walked out of school, she said, "I need you to drive me to get your father." Until the day she died, the "Million-Dollar Baby" drove a gold convertible Cadillac Coupe DeVille. She could go anywhere around Erie—from bar to bar, club to club, and if she had a wee bit too much to drink and got pulled over, they'd give her a ride home. Over forty years after Prohibition, she was still well respected, a Grand Dame.

She wouldn't take the Caddy on the highway, though. One of the first times I asked her why, she told me it was because of my father. After World War II, she drove across the country to the San Diego Naval Hospital to pick him up, her only son, and now we were doing it again. We had to drive from Erie to Ashtabula, Ohio, to bail him out for DWI. He always drove from his business in Akron to Erie on the weekend to visit us kids, back Sunday night. But this one weekend was cut short, and he had a significant meeting with Lee Iacocca at Chrysler Corp on Monday afternoon. Grandma was going to make sure he didn't miss it.

She said, "I don't know what they did in that war, too, but they didn't send back the same boy I sent to them." My father flew off the USS Enterprise, doing the first blacked-out, all-instrument night bombing raids over Japan. One night, he was shot down and adrift in the Pacific Ocean for over seventy-two hours before being rescued by what turned out to be my uncle's uncle, but that's another story. They took him back to the San Diego Naval Hospital with "battle fatigue" (that's what they called PTSD then).

While hospitalized, he witnessed two Naval hospital orderlies mistreating a patient, and my father nearly killed them both. Grandma Murphy drove across the United States and got her boy out of a U.S. military hospital, no charges filed. She said that when he got home, he went out for a night on the town in his dress Navy blues. His travels took him to a fine Irish bar on the corner of West Fourth and State Street: Scully's. When they refused to serve him because he was too drunk, he said, "When I was over there fightin' and dyin' for you, you were over here partying and having a good time. Well, I'm havin' a drink." He then jumped over the bar and smashed every piece of glass, bottles included—a waste.

Instead of calling the cops, the owner called Grandma Murphy, who lived a few blocks away. She showed up, took a look around, and thought a group of Navy seamen had gotten in a brawl with a bunch of Army guys. She asked, "Jack, where are your friends?" The owner whispered, "It was only him, Mrs. Murphy." She took another look and said, "Clean this mess up... I'll pay ya for it in the morning," and she did. She said he was never the same after that, and he never really was. I suppose I wasn't either.

My father was one of the smartest men I've ever known. Fantastic mathematician, tool and die maker, draftsman, mold designer, self-made engineer, and pool shark, but he struggled with alcoholism and rage his entire life.

Until the day my grandmother died, she remained a well-dressed, independent woman with her own means. I'd go to her in high school, ask if I could borrow some money, and she'd pull out brand-new 1920s-era Silver Certificate hundred-dollar bills, never bent. I'd spend it partying with kegs of beer and pot.

Standing at her casket, I felt a hand on my shoulder, and a voice said, "I loved the old gal." I looked over and saw a man I had vaguely known, married to my oldest brother Jack's best friend's sister. He knew me better than I knew him, knowing I was doing stupid kid stuff and getting in trouble.

He said, "You know what, kid? I don't recommend this for a lifetime career, but if you're gonna do it, you're gonna do it right. They ain't got your prints yet, kid, and until they do, you're a virgin, and you're with me."

That was it, my introduction to Jimmy "JR" Russell, one of the most notorious gangsters from Lackawanna, New York. He spent over 27 of his 57 years in prison because he would never rat. I drove him for almost 10 years, and he taught me how to punch, peel, and burn safes, as well as how to work alarm systems. I was ahead of my time as "the Kid" with police scanners.

This is the story that led us to a life of crime, and oh, what a life it was while it lasted. But nothing lasts forever, does it now? "That's the way it goes, first your money, then your clothes!" he used to say.

"JR" not only knew my brother and Grandma, but he also knew my father. They were both pool players who faced each other in local billiard parlors and bars, eventually becoming friends, partners, and hustlers at times. Both were professional-caliber players and two of the smartest men I've ever known. My father stayed pretty much legit; JR was the opposite end of the spectrum but just as brilliant.

"JR" would get a percentage of a score to "consult." He'd tell people where they'd screw up and get a cut just for that. He used to say, "The most treacherous part of any score is cutting up the money afterward, you've already broken a few laws, a few more won't hurt." That's how he allegedly got involved in a multi-million-dollar armored car robbery outside Detroit in the early eighties, the last thing he went to prison for, but I get ahead of myself.

I quickly got into the tech side of things. I started out shoplifting from one of my favorite electronics joints at the time, Radio Shack. They had everything: walkie-talkies, handheld scanners, crystals for every band, and the grand prize, a National Radio crystal frequency manual that read like a nationwide phonebook. It lists emergency broadcast frequencies state by state, county by county, city by city, and township by township. I used that thing like a bible. It let me plan getaway routes and alternatives. Back then, handheld scanners only had six channels, so you had to know where you were going and how to get out—same rules as a bar.

I learned a trick with the higher-end walkie-talkies: transmit and receive crystals were standard. Flip the two crystals in a set, and you effectively encrypted the set — only those two could talk to each other. No one else could listen in. It was like our private line. JR started farming out my services across the country after he saw what I could do.

The JR consulting business was simple. He'd get a cut for pointing out where a crew would screw up. He'd lay out what-if scenarios and force people to think about alternatives. Part of the package was pre-programmed scanners. A buyer would tell us the area of the score and how they wanted to get out. With only six channel choices, you had to be right. JR never let on that his "kid" was doing the programming or getting the crystals. That little secret became lucrative for both of us. I'm sure I never got a full share, but he took care of me enough that I didn't complain.

After a while, the piecemeal work felt slow. I decided to go wholesale. I picked a Radio Shack outside of Erie — too hot in town — scoped it, planned the timing, and worked the alarm. Back in the hard-wire days, the systems were simple if you knew how to prepare them: take a bathroom window, slip the sensor screws, and keep the circuit loop closed with a paper clip. The system thought the door stayed shut. For the outside ringer boxes, you could spray some foam into the housing, let it set, and the alarm would never sound. The foam would muffle the bell just long enough.

I hit the store at night. Took the inventory I needed, left no prints where it mattered, and got the goods to JR contacts. That one score taught me more than any lesson book. The planning, the timing, the little tech hacks — that was my school.

I started traveling with JR. He drilled his rules into me from day one:

1. The answer to any question is always... I don't know!

2. Always plan your getaways with as many right-hand turns as possible...Right-hand turn on red!

3. Always have a good Plan B...Know your way in and your way out!

4. Watch something 3 times. Once you see it the same way, it's ours! We Own it!

5. The most treacherous part of any score is splitting up the money after...You've already broken a couple laws...a few more won't hurt!

He hammered those in until they were muscle memory. Some of it was common sense; some of it was what kept us alive.

That period made me worthwhile. I became the kid who could program a scanner in the back of a car and rig a set of walkies that no one else could hear. I could show a crew where the cops were going to pop, how the alarm would behave, and how to get out.JR clients liked the edge. They paid for silence, precision, and a straight exit. I got paid in cash and lessons.

If you asked me then whether I'd end up where I did, I'd have said no. But you learn fast when survival is the curriculum and pride is the tuition.

Grandma Ethel Mae Murphy, circa 1923, Erie, Pa.

Grandpa Perry Murphy, circa 1927, Chicago, IL.

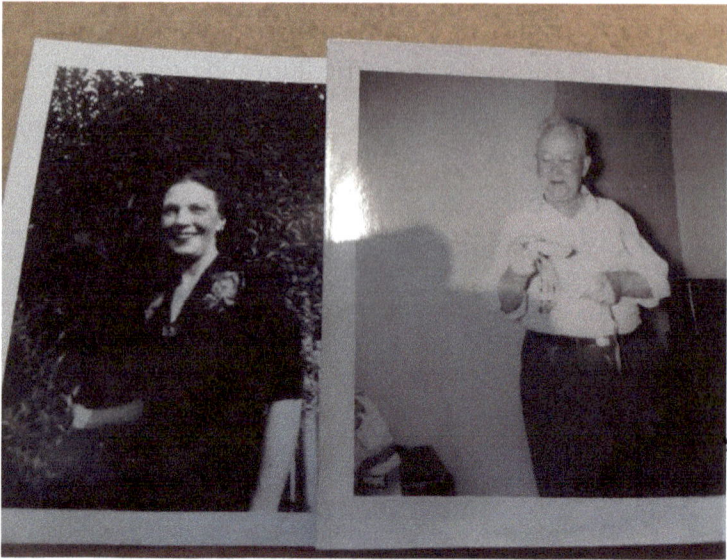

Grandma and Grandpa Murphy – As I knew them.

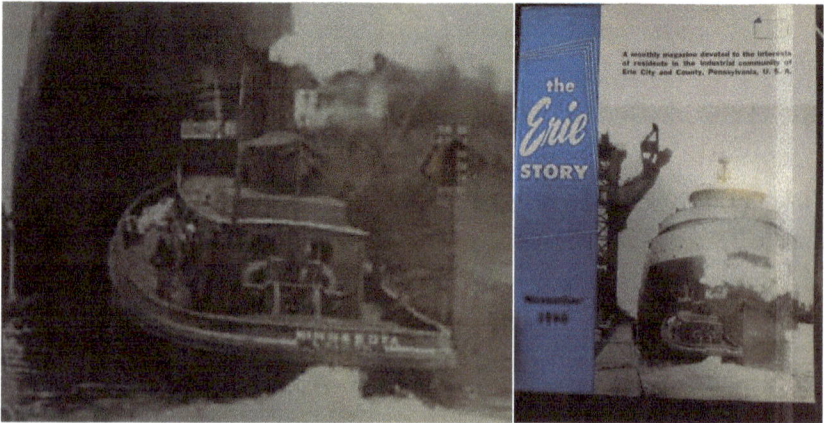

Grandpa Murphy on the deck of his tugboat – The Erie Story

– circa: November 1956

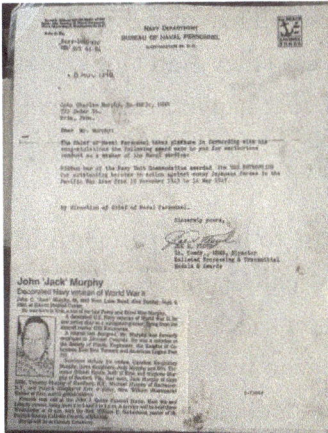

My Father John C. Murphy   Jack Murphy – Pool Hustler

Circa, 1946 on US Brig Niagara   circa: 1980

John Charles Murphy   Jimmy "JR" Russell – Mastermind –
Ribbon Bar of the Navy -   – Thief circa: 1979?
USS Enterprise – August 8, 1946

CHAPTER 02

BEWARE THE IDES OF MARCH

How the hell did I end up in this shit hole? I got busted up in little Lackawanna, New York, in a hot car from Pennsylvania, "outfitted for police usage" because I had police scanners wired into the car's power. That made it a felony on top of my being a "fugitive of justice" since I was on parole in Pennsylvania and crossed the state line.

Oh, there was one other minor detail: "possession of a defaced weapon." My little .25 Browning semi-automatic had the serial numbers machined off, and the barrel was threaded for a silencer. That pissed them off, because they couldn't find the silencer. Thank God they didn't look up the tailpipe of that hot car shoved up there on a coat hanger. If they had, I could have been doing life the hard way.

At the time, a piece with a silencer was 25 years to life; no parole. And I was flirting with "The Big Bitch"—the Habitual Criminal Act. Three strikes, and you're out. I narrowly missed that on a technicality, thanks to my good Jewish lawyer in Erie, Pennsylvania, who had me sentenced for my two felonies there on the same day, which under Pennsylvania law only counted as one felony. Thank God for technicalities.

New York State was trying to bank me for life. But it wasn't just me they were after; it was who I knew, who I ran with, who I'd done crimes with. That's what they were really after. But I never gave them up. My man had taught me well: "Keep your mouth shut, kid." And I did.

"JR" had sent me up to Buffalo with BJ DeSanto to get him out of town. Things were too hot in Erie, especially after the Feds grabbed "Fat Sam" Esper. Never trust a fat man; they have no self-control, and if they talk, it's over. BJ was a partner with Fat Sam, basically doing all the dirty work, so getting him out safely was critical.

I stole a car from a dealership by lifting the keys off the rack and making duplicates. That night, I picked up BJ, and we took off for Buffalo. I had a lifetime of JR's friends there; he was a legend in Lackawanna, NY, Buffalo, and back home in Erie. I was always known as "the kid" because I protected my identity. "Always watch the quiet ones," he used to say. "You don't have to worry about the loudmouths. You know the direction they're coming from." I became the quiet one, the observer, ready for anything.JR drilled into me: always have a Plan B, always an exit strategy.

Julian "Butch" Hallaby, JR"'s lifelong friend, owned the Checker Cab Company in Lackawanna and South Buffalo. As soon as BJ and I arrived, he put us up in his stepdaughter's apartment while she was out of town. Butch had been planning a score for months and needed two out-of-town faces to pull it off. He had tracked the weekly bank drops from a local supermarket. Cash was king; the store held $50,000–$60,000 in cash weekly.

Our plan was meticulous. I made a net of stainless-steel mesh to catch the money if the drop slot gave us trouble. BJ would wait in the bushes with a sawed-off shotgun I'd prepared. I had modified the shells with bookie "flash paper" to create a loud but non-lethal distraction if needed. JR always taught: avoid confrontation, if possible, but be ready for everything.

When the day came, I followed the store manager to the bank drop. BJ froze. The extra person with her threw him off. The money bag couldn't drop because the slot was jammed—perfect. We had 10–15 seconds to grab it. I almost ran up, but BJ didn't act. The manager and her companion got spooked and drove off. I screamed at BJ: "WHY didn't you GO?" He muttered, "I didn't know if they were armed." All I could think: Them's the rules—watch it three times, plan every angle. Break the rules, and the rules break you.

We drove back to Butch's stepdaughter's apartment. I was livid, needed a drink. BJ went inside, and I hit the streets. I started bar hopping, pool shooting — my favourite pastime, taught by my father — and terrorizing and intimidating bars—it was entertainment, power, and survival all at once.

But Lackawanna's finest were on me fast. Stopped me at Ridge Road and Community Drive. I should have run, thrown the gun out, anything. Hot car, stolen plates, scanner hard-wired into the car, defaced Browning with a threaded barrel. Thank God they didn't check the tailpipe. I was booked into the Lackawanna City Police lockup.

"JR" had always said: If you get jammed in Buffalo, ask for Bob Murphy. Robert Murphy was one of the highest-powered attorneys in Buffalo and represented JR early on. I requested him, and even at 2 a.m., Murphy personally responded. He stood in front of my cell in his high-priced three-piece suit, no tie... Hilarity ensued when he appeared... thinking I was his son Timothy. "Murphy's Law!" He said, "I can't take your case right now, I'm in the middle of a trial. But I'll send a guy from my office. He eventually got me connected with "BOND"... Not James, but Bill, Bill Bond from Murphy's office, who almost got me off on a technicality regarding the weapon.

After being held in Lackawanna, I wasn't going anywhere fast. They wanted me to flip on people back in Erie, but I kept my mouth shut. Bill

Bond put up a solid defense, but the system wanted its pound of flesh. I ended up in downtown Buffalo at 10 Delaware Avenue, Erie County Holding Center—a pit of dead time—ten months of nothing but counting days and doing 1,500 pushups a day while playing cards for repetitions. By the time I was moved upstate, I could do handstands against walls and clip off fifty upside-down pushups in a row. I was ready for anything.

Sentenced, but not as a habitual career criminal—thank God. I appeared before Judge Penny Wolfgang in the New York State Supreme Court. She looked over my pre-sentence investigation and, after reading through my FBI jacket, stated, "Well, Mr. Murphy, on paper, you appear to be a one-person crime spree! Hope you brought your toothbrush; you'll be needing it in the New York State penal system for 2 to 4 years." My break sent me to Wende Maximum, Attica reception, 85C0177—the 177th person taken into Wende C.F. for Attica Reception in 1985—Hell on Earth.

Then came the personal blow. A letter from My Mother that reads..." Timothy, my Son, I wish I were with you right now to put my arms around you, for the Love of Your Life, Mary Ellen DeSanto, overdosed and left this Earth last night! The grief hit harder than anything I'd experienced.

I kept saying to myself! WHAT, WHAT DID SHE JUST SAY! NOOOOO! FUCKIN NOOOOO! WHY GOD? WHY DID YOU TAKE HER, YOU BASTARD! I WILL SERVE SATAN THE REST OF MY LIFE!!!! FUCK YOU! FUCK THIS WORLD! FUCK ME! I'm going to find out who gave her the drugs, and when I get out, I'm going back to Erie, Pennsylvania and going to be Judge, Jury, and the Angel of Death all in one night, you BASTARD YOU! I started beating the steel walls of my cell, my hands looked like Hamburg bloody to the bone, blood was strewn all over my cell, all over my body, I was covered with my own blood and screaming like a wild man...

There was no other sound in that prison! No One dared until there was a sound, the sound of a Roman Legion marching down the galley, Crunch, Crunch, Crunch, CRUNCH! Crunch, Crunch! The cell extraction team: 8 guards in full battle array, dressed in orange jump suits so the other guards don't shoot them, yeah, how well did that work when Rockefeller ordered them to open fire….the poor bastards! But now they're coming for me, full battle shields, full body armor, helmets with face shields and full weighted batons to thump your skull! Crunch, Crunch, Crunch until they stopped at my cell. The scene must have looked like Hannibal Lecter, because I saw fear in some of their eyes as soon as they saw my cell. I backed my ass into a corner, looked them all in the eye, and said: "You guys are going to kick my ass tonight! I only have one Question…WHO…is going to be the FIRST Mother Fucker through that gate !!! Something in my eyes or my fury made them hesitate. They looked at each other for a few seconds, and then, through the Grace of God, they backed off.

Fortunately, that night there was a cool black Lieutenant in charge of the prison that night, and he came walking up to my bars and said, "Mr. Murphy, I have had calls about you from all over the county tonight. There are people very worried about you, worried you're going to hurt yourself or others. Really, I just don't want my men hurt. Why don't we take a walk down to the Infirmary tonight? I'll set you up with a real bed, a color TV and call down to the kitchen and get you anything you want to eat. Quite frankly, Mr. Murphy, I just don't want the paperwork on my shift." I looked him in the eye and said, "You Got That !"

He walked me down to the Infirmary and took care of me. Seventy-two hours on death watch to make sure I didn't hang myself. When I returned to the yard, no one tested me. Fear had earned me respect—or at least wariness. Mary's death may have saved me in a twisted way. Nobody messed with me at Wende.

Even later, almost 20 years after giving my testimony at a Men's Christian group in Darien, NY, a man waited for me in the parking lot. He was Judge Robert Alexander, Judge of the Village of Corfu, NY, where Darien Lake Amusement Park is. He had also retired from the New York State Department of Corrections... did 25 years in Attica, the hard way, 8 hours at a time. He introduced himself, then said, "Murph, in 25 years I only saw that crew back off one time...that night with you!" Thank You, Lord! That was not me! Fear, control, and survival, lessons I'd learned from JR and hardened through every run, job, and close call, were now in full effect.

Time in Wende and Attica hardened me, but I never lost focus. I kept my head down, observed, and kept my body ready. Every day, I followed the rules I'd learned from JR: loyalty, silence, respect, and having a plan. Pushups, handstands, and constant vigilance weren't just exercise—they were preparation. I didn't just survive; I built presence.

Outside support was crucial. My lawyer, Bill Bond, remained a lifeline. When the system tried to box me in, he found every technicality, every loophole to keep me from being railroaded. Later, Bill had to hand me off to another lawyer in his office, John Michalski, who had connections and later became the Honorable Judge John Michalski. The Honorable Judge John Michalski was a great guy and a great Lawyer.

He had been the Amherst Town prosecutor for years and would handle my tickets. He was then appointed to the New York State Supreme Court. He helped save my son, John Michael Murphy. RIP, December 21, 1989 – December 26, 2016, member of the 27 club with Janice Joplin, Jim Morrison, Jimmy Hendricks, Kirk Cobain...and on and on...from doing a lot of time as a youthful offender. John was a great guy. He used to schedule my appointment for the last of the day to help me out at work, but mostly John just wanted to hear a good mob story...He would close his office door and shut down the clock once I started telling him a story.

John committed suicide in April 2022. His second attempt was 2 years after he had walked out onto the train tracks in front of a moving train, all caught on camera and shown on the Buffalo News and 4 WIVB. That's another story, but he wasn't afraid of the mob; he was afraid of the Federal and State prosecutors who were trying to make him testify in the local trial of Peter Gerace, who owned Pharaoh's Gentlemen's club and is the nephew of alleged Mafia Boss of Buffalo, Joseph Todaro, JR. The charges stem that Gerace attempted to bribe a Drug Enforcement Administration (DEA) Agent Joseph Bongiovanni and allege Drug-trafficking and Sex-trafficking, and is leaving a string of bodies in its wake, but the most recent one of Gerace's former exotic dancer employee, Crystal Quinn, in a suspicious drug overdose, is still under investigation.

Even in prison, I kept an eye on the bigger picture. Who was coming after whom? Who was scared, who was loyal? The ARM, the Buffalo mob, JR's old network—these weren't just names. They were lines on a map, and I knew where I fit. Fear and respect went hand in hand, and I used both to navigate each day without incident.

The lessons from chauffeuring JR, planning every move, weren't just street skills anymore. They were survival tactics in a place where one misstep could cost everything. By the time I was released, I wasn't just ready to walk out—I was ready to operate, with everything I had learned sharpened to a knife-edge.

***

But it wasn't always like this. Before Lackawanna, before those bars and the extraction team and counting down days in a six-by-eight cell, I had a rhythm. A structure. Not an everyday life—nobody in this game has that—but it was mine. Back in Erie, working for JR, things made sense. There was a code, a way of doing business that kept you breathing and kept you earning: the careful planning, the drives where every second counted.

I was building something—trust, skills, a reputation that mattered in the only world I knew.

That's what made the fall hurt so much. I wasn't just some punk kid who got caught. I had something. I was part of JR's operation, part of a network that stretched from Erie to Buffalo to Cleveland. I knew how things worked. I had proven myself a hundred times over.

And when you lose that—when you're sitting in a cell wondering if you'll ever get it back—you realize what it was worth. That's what I was thinking about in Wende and Attica. That's what I was fighting to get back to. Not just the money or the action, but the life I'd built under JR's wing. The respect. The belonging.

Let me take you back to how it really was, before I screwed it all up in Lackawanna.

***

Back in Erie, I slipped right into the rhythm. It started slow—just running errands for JR, chauffeuring him to meetings, picking up what he needed. Mostly, he didn't want to drive himself. But things picked up fast.

The ARM ran quietly. Too quiet. They flew under the radar, exactly as Don Stefano wanted. The only family not called by the Patriarch's surname. Some called it respect. Don Stefano "The Undertaker" Magaddino called it stupidity.

JR couldn't be made—part Irish—but he'd been raised around made men in the ARM. He soaked up their ways and rules and passed them down to me. From day one, he hammered in: always have visible means of support. I worked in maintenance and machine shops, and I built his custom orders. Napkin sketches? No problem. Rules first. Work done right. Survive.

JR's words stuck with me: "Loyalty is worth more than gold. Silence keeps you breathing"... "Loose lips, Sink ships!" You can lose money, a job—but not your name. Once it's gone, you're done."

He drilled the same rules into me he was brought up on: never rat, never steal small, never steal from your friends! Respect was everything. If you said you were going to do something, you did it, even if it cost you. "Say what you do...Do what you say!"

He'd say, "It's not about being tough, it's about being smart. And actually, Tony Cangiano gave me the recipe for being tough"... "Murph...Murph... being a tough guy ain't that hard... 98% of the time you live just like anyone else...Just live your life... 2% of the time...You have to do what is required! How it's required! When it's required! It's just that easy, Murph!"

Those rules carried me across states, through tickets, errands, and every unpredictable moment of the life I was living. By the time I was fully entrenched, chauffeuring, planning, observing, I wasn't just a kid with a car anymore. I was part of the machinery, where trust and loyalty mattered more than guns. The lessons JR drilled? Survival. Plain and simple.

One of the first times I really proved myself? JR called me at one o'clock in the morning. He had to get to Lackawanna, New York... fast. His father was passing. I streaked across Erie, picked JR up in his Cadillac, and hit the highway. I set the cruise control to a hundred miles per hour. Eighty-nine point nine miles from Erie, Pennsylvania, to Lackawanna, New York, done in just over an hour—city streets included.

We pulled into Our Lady of Victory Hospital. JR went in; I waited in the car, like usual. A couple of hours later, he came out. I could tell it wasn't good. I'd never seen him dejected like that. His father had passed. But he was grateful he made it in time to say goodbye. That moment endeared him to me. He always loved me, but after that, he trusted me. He never questioned how I was going or how I was gonna get there. I got him where he needed to go, every single time.

That night was more than just a drive. It was my first taste of what JR demanded: speed, precision, and reliability under pressure. From that moment, I was his shadow. Wherever he needed to be, I got him there. No excuses. No mistakes. That trust—that bond—it was everything.

Monday nights became something else entirely. Not just because of the game, but because of Monday Night Football on nationwide TV. Back then, it was the equivalent of Netflix, Google, or Amazon launching today. Huge. Every bookie, every odds-maker across the country was paying attention—especially every La Cosa Nostra family.

The Philly family caught on first, led by Angelo "The Docile or Gentle Don" Bruno. But in the period between 1980 to 1982, the Philly Mob went through three Bosses of the Family: Bruno led until his assassination in 1980. Philip "The Chicken Man" Testa became boss after Bruno's death. Testa was killed by a nail-bomb at his home on March 15, 1981... "Beware the Ides of March." And the worst was yet to come: Nicodemo "Little Nicky" Scarfo, who was brutally violent and embarked on what's often called the "Second Philadelphia Mafia War."

They came up through the North Eastern Pennsylvania crime family of Russell Bufalino. Absolute genius, the way they took the old Italian daily numbers and flipped them on their heads. They printed Monday Night Football tickets with five-digit numbers. The winning number? Based entirely on game stats printed in Tuesday morning papers: total yards rushing, total yards passing, return yards, yards penalized, and total score. Add them together, take the last digit of each sum, and you have a unique five-digit winner worth five thousand bucks.

Tickets were folded and sewn shut at the ends so that you couldn't peek. They printed 100,000 tickets a week, numbered 00000 to 99,999, $2 apiece. That was a weekly take of $200,000, paying only a $5,000 winner and maybe a couple thousand spread out to lower winners if you hit three or four digits. Money funneled back to Philly—one dollar per ticket. JR got fifty cents a ticket, bar owners got a cut, and I ended up getting a quarter per ticket just for driving him around.

Tuesday mornings, we went all over Erie. On Wednesdays, we'd head to Buffalo via the Seaway Trail along Lake Erie, with regular stops along the way. My chauffeuring duties had really taken off by then. But it wasn't just about the money. At every stop, we picked up information—who had money, where it was. Information was power. The only reason JR or anyone else got tied up with "Fat Sam" was that he had a way of digging up intel. JR was the chess master. Every detail had to come from him. No mistakes, no outside fabrication.

That's how I got schooled early in the art of observation, logistics, and planning—the stuff that separates a kid with a ride from a player who survives in the game.

Tim "Murph the Surf" Murphy, Collins-NYS CF–1985

Mary Ellen DeSanto, and Tim Christmas@ at Dad's house, final time

Mary Ellen DeSanto
– circa:1980
"The first of the three Great Loves of My Life"

CHAPTER 03

SHOULDA BEEN A POSTMAN

Guess I gotta go back a bit. I did manage to graduate from high school, barely. Passed by the skin of my teeth. I had a little hustle going back then, called it Wax-A-Million. Nobody else had thought of it. It was an Auto detailing business.

I learned the ropes from my after-school job washing and waxing limos and hearses at the auto livery across the street from my mother's house. That place taught me plenty. I'd "borrow" one of those limos after hours, take my friends out partying, and have it back by eleven. Wash it up, make it shine, like nothing ever happened. If I missed curfew, my stepfather Joe-B would make damn sure I remembered next time.

The livery had a morgue annex, Erie County's. It was just a cold room with one cooler, where they brought in accident victims during the night. That was my first introduction to death up close. Didn't bother me after a while. Maybe that's not something to brag about, but it toughened me up early. I learned how to stand in the same room with death and not flinch. I'd need that later, more than I could've imagined.

When I finally graduated, I had plans, or at least I thought I did. I was gonna enlist in the Navy. My old man and my brother both had served, and my mother agreed to sign the papers so I could go in at seventeen.

My brother Jack gave me some advice that stuck. He said, "When you sign up, tell them you wanna be a postman."

I laughed. "A postman? What the hell for?"

He said, "Because on a ship, the postman's got it made. He controls not only the mail, but he's also the paymaster. Electricians keep his air-conditioning working, cooks feed him steaks, and everyone looks out for him. Do twenty years, retire with a Navy pension. Go back home, get a job at the post office, do another twenty, and you're double-dipping, full pension from both by the time you're fifty-seven."

That was the grand plan. Sounded solid. Simple. Smart. But life had other ideas.

So, I took the bus from Erie, Pennsylvania, to the Naval Induction Center in Buffalo, New York. When they asked what occupation I wanted, I said straight up, "I wanna be a postman."

They looked at me like I'd lost my damn mind.

One of them said, "But you qualified for the Nuclear Program. Less than two percent pass that test. It's a six-year commitment, two of those years underwater on a submarine."

I told them, "I don't think I could handle two years locked in a metal tube under the ocean." Funny thing, I found out later in life, I could've handled it just fine, ask the New York State Department of Corrections.

They wanted me to stay another day, talk to a Lieutenant Commander. I refused to be sworn in and said, "Just give me my bus ticket back to Erie."

They wouldn't. Instead, they stuck me in the Hotel Lafayette in downtown Buffalo, which, in 1976, was long past its glory days. The place had gone to hell. Hookers, junkies, and drifters filled the halls. That's where the United States Navy decided to lodge me for the night.

The next morning, a Navy Commander took me out for breakfast. He tried to talk me into the program, told me again how rare it was to qualify. I said, "Look, I really just wanna be a postman."

He looked ready to blow a gasket. "You can't be a postman in the United States Navy!"

"Why not?" I asked.

"Because you can't get a security clearance, you've got a shoplifting charge from when you were thirteen."

I stared at him. "Wait a damn minute, I can get clearance to work around nuclear weapons, but I can't get clearance to deliver mail?"

He didn't think it was funny. I said, "Then give me my ticket back to Erie."

And they did.

Maybe the worst decision of my life.

I went back to Erie, Pennsylvania, back to my mother's house at 314 East 32nd Street. Same block, same memories, same rules. She acted glad to see me at first, but I think she'd already pictured me following my older brother Jack into the Navy. My coming home wasn't part of her plan. Within a week, she told me I had to move out and live with my father in Akron, Ohio. Said it straight, "You just remind me too much of your father."

That cut deep. I didn't argue. I knew she had her reasons. I remembered the last night of their marriage, the sound of his fists pounding the bathroom door in a drunken rage, and how I swore I'd never be like him. Years later, I came damn close to doing the same thing.

One night, I tried to sneak into the house after having a few beers with the boys. I hadn't made it two steps inside when I saw her standing in the dark doorway, her silhouette waiting.

"You're drunk," she said.

"No, I'm not."

"Yes, you are."

There was no way she could've smelled it from across the room. Then she said, "You know how I know? Your left eyelid droops just like your father's when you've been drinking."

That shut me up. She was right. To this day, my left eye still droops after a few drinks. The biggest problem was that she had told my late wife, Laura Lynn Sorce, before she married me on April 15, 1989. She never forgot...Or let me forget... She would call it out... "You know what your Mother told me..." Busted Again! But I always made it to work the next day...So I didn't have an alcohol problem...

Another lifetime lesson learned the hard way. It hurt when she told me to leave, but I couldn't hold it against her. She'd already carried enough. She worked every day to keep seven kids together, and somehow did it with grace.

It was late summer of 1976, and I moved to Tallmadge, Ohio, a suburb of Akron. I moved in with my father and his third and fifth, Sylvia... She definitely counts twice because she took him worse the second time. In fact, the first thing he would say about the second divorce to her was... "She even took the toilet paper!" That's low.

The woman he'd left our family for—Joe-B's ex-wife, Florence, had gotten cancer and died a few years into their marriage. After that, he changed. They told us he'd had a heart attack when he quit coming around for a while, but I think something worse happened inside his head. Maybe a breakdown. Maybe something he never told anyone.

Still, I was grateful to be there. After the divorce, I'd always wanted to move back in with my father. It'd been one of those daydreams you swear you won't say out loud, but you hold onto anyway. Through his job, he hooked me up with a mold maker/machinist apprenticeship and a trade school. I didn't finish the four-year program, but I put nearly two years into it while working with him every day.

Dad taught me the trade: how to read blueprints, run every machine in the shop, work to a thousandth of an inch. No slop. Mill, lathe, grinder, you name it, I ran it. He drilled precision into me the hard way. "Right on, Bugs Nuts!" or somebody could get hurt. You miss a spec, a part fails, people lose work, worse, someone could end up dead or in prison. That kind of discipline stuck. It wasn't flashy, but it made you reliable. And in this life, reliable meant something you could hang your whole future on.

It was around that time when the evening news out of Akron and Cleveland started buzzing with talk of bombings. They said a mob war was breaking out, and Danny Greene, the so-called Irishman, was trying to take over from the Italians. Their boss, John Scalish, had just died, and things were blowing up, literally. Every few weeks, another explosion would hit the airwaves. Between '76 & '77 there were 36 bombings in Cleveland, Ohio, trying to "Kill the Irishman"... just watch the movie. That stuff got under my skin. I was proud of my Irish blood and couldn't help thinking how wild it would be to be part of something like that. The only problem was, I was new in town and didn't know a soul.

Back then, stories like that didn't get plastered everywhere like today, when one man with a gun can make world news. You might catch a few clips on the local stations, maybe a mention on the Huntley–Brinkley Report if it was big enough. One night after trade school, the National Tool and Die and Precision Machinists Association, I decided to find the latest bombing site myself. No GPS, no Google. Just a Cleveland map and a half tank of gas. I didn't find it that night, but next time one went off, I tracked it down. It turned into a strange little hobby. I'd finish up classes, get out of the shop, then take a cruise to see what the Irish mob had done this time.

When I wasn't chasing mob explosions, I was shooting pool with my father. He was a master at the table. Angles, spin, bank shots, all of it. He'd point to the spots on the rail like they were landmarks on a map. "Right speed with the right feed," he used to say, worked for pool, worked for machining, worked for life. He'd been teaching me since I was about eleven, back when my brother Jack somehow hauled a ten-foot regulation table into the attic of his house in Meadville, Pa. Those were the early lessons: control, patience, and when to strike.

We got good, too. Used to hustle partners' pool now and then. We'd walk into a bar separately, pretend we didn't know each other, then he'd point at me and say, "I'll take that kid over there." Nobody expected the kid to sink balls. We'd clean up and laugh all the way home.

But not every hustle goes smoothly. One Friday night, Dad wasn't with me, and I took every penny off a guy wearing an "Akron Scrap Yard" shirt—big mistake. At the end of the night, I went out to my little Ford Pinto, opened the door, and before I knew it, fists were flying through the gap. He'd waited for me, came running up, and started swinging. I couldn't even move. Tried to crawl across the seat, thinking maybe I'd slip out the passenger side, but he met me there, too. I threw my shoulder into the door and knocked him down just as the bar owner, a friend of my dad's, came out with a baseball bat. That was the end of it. I learned something that night: never hustle a man who works at a scrapyard on payday.

One of the only other things I had going on at the time was hitting the local discos. Disco ruled the world then, and Ohio had one significant advantage: you could drink at eighteen. They served what they called three-two beer, three parts beer and two parts water. It was weak, but I didn't care. After coming from Pennsylvania, where the drinking age was twenty-one, I thought I'd found paradise. I could dance too; that part I got from my father.

One night, after cruising Cleveland looking for the latest bomb site, I stopped at a place called The Carousel for a couple of three-twos. The place was nearly deserted, with maybe five or six people scattered around. I started talking to this guy who looked like he might know the scene. Figured I'd ask if he could score some pot. I thought I smelled it on him. He gave me a hard stare and said, "You a cop?"

"No way, man," I said. "I just moved up from Erie. Don't even know where to score yet."

He didn't buy it. Started grilling me like he was the one wearing the badge. I could see it going south fast, so I pulled out my Pennsylvania driver's license, my NDTPMA trade school ID, and my father's business card. That seemed to calm him down a little. Then he asked what I'd been up to that night, and I told him I'd been driving around looking for the latest bombing site.

He squinted at me and said, "Why the hell would you do that?"

I said, "Because I'm Irish, and I want to get into it."

That did it. He laughed, ordered us both a beer, and the night took a turn.

That was the night I met Fast Freddie. I never knew whether that was his real name... And I never asked a second time, and that's what I always called him. He turned out to be one of the biggest local drug dealers around and had ties to Danny Greene's mob. I had no idea then that if I'd gotten in with them, I would've been on the losing side and crossed paths with Ray Ferritto, who almost became my brother-in-law later on when I moved back to Erie.

Fast Freddie was "the connection"..."The Plug!" I started slow with him. He gave me a joint that first night, and things took off from there. Pretty soon, I was buying lids, and over time, he started liking me because I was from out of town and nobody knew who I was. That helped.

We built a relationship, one I kept even after I moved back to Erie. Freddie didn't just deal weed; he had everything. It all started with Black Beauties, those little speeders everyone was on back then. We loved them because you could party all night and still show up to work in the morning. But then moved to uppers, downers, all arounders... including eventually "Mason jars" – 10,000 hits of "Orange Sunshine," "Purple Barrell micro-dot acid ... all the way to a four-ounce tincture of LSD-25. Lysergic acid diethylamide with United States government markings, manufactured by the CIA for mind control experiments on most lifetime incarcerated prisoners. There is documented evidence that the CIA conducted extended experiments on prisoners for over 70 days at four times the usual dose. And we wonder why we have maniacs on the streets.

I lived entire summers off of the "shake" of the micro-dot and another summer off the LSD-25...oh what summers they were...but like the 60's & 70's... if you can remember them... You weren't there!

I kept buying from Fast Freddie—weed, Black Beauties, whatever he had—and started dealing to some of the guys at my father's shop. Meanwhile, I was still learning the mold-making trade. My father didn't give me a single break. It didn't matter that I was the boss's kid; I had to put in my hours on every machine, no shortcuts.

My old man used to say, "The first time you miss a day of work because of drinking, you've got a drinking problem." I twisted that in my head to mean, as long as I make it to work, I don't have a drinking problem. So I went to work every damn day. That logic stayed with me a long time, and it was dead wrong. I had plenty of problems, but I didn't figure that out until much later.

Eventually, I got to the bench. That was the final stage, ninety days of pure boredom. That's where molds get finished and polished, no room for mistakes. You work with sandpaper and custom tools, and for clear parts, use diamond dust polish until you get a mirror finish. Every mark had to be gone. Every edge perfect. That kind of work taught patience. Precision. But outside the shop? I was learning a whole different kind of discipline.

For ninety days, I rubbed on those molds, day after day, getting more and more disenchanted with the trade that made my father who he was. He was a self-made engineer who learned everything the hard way, working two or three jobs at a time to support seven kids. I still remember his drafting board down in the basement back in Erie before the divorce.

He taught himself to draft and designed toys that were sold to companies like Fisher-Price and Mattel. "Happy Apple," "Hoppy Frog," those were his. Still in production today. But the one that really made his name was a seamless, egg-shaped mold that left no parting line in the plastic. That was the original Weebles. Remember "Weebles wobble, but they don't fall?" That was his design. If he'd kept the rights, we'd have been millionaires. At one point, there were more Weebles in the U.S. than Americans, and we could've had a piece of everyone.

We'd have been set for life… if he hadn't married six times. Though numbers three and five were the same woman. She took him to the cleaners both times—especially the second go-round.

Anyway, I kept rubbing those molds, bored out of my mind. Sitting still all day wasn't me. On the ninetieth day, my father came out of the office and said, "Alright, what machine do you want to work on next?" I didn't have the heart to tell him I wanted out. But I'd been staring at an old engine lathe on the other side of the divider partition for three months, and hadn't turned once the whole time I'd been there.

I said, "Dad, what I'd really like to do is fix that lathe."

He looked over at it, then back at me, and said, "Alright, you can fix it, but if you take it apart, you're putting it back together. So you better damn well keep track of it."

My heart jumped—finally, something with a pulse. I tore into it right away. When I opened the covers, it was like a Swiss watch inside, perfect little pieces of precision and patience. I laid out every part I pulled on a 4x8 sheet of plywood, marking each one with a magic marker so I'd know how to put it back.

After a couple of weeks, I found the problem: a follower pawl worn down to a nub, which wouldn't stay engaged. I traced it on paper, guessed what it must've looked like when it was new, machined it, ground it, heat-treated it, and put the whole damn gear train back together.

I went back into the shop and told my father to come out to the floor, like I had a question about the machine. He never cut me any slack, but he never passed up a chance to teach. We stood there by the lathe, and I hit the power button. The motor came to life; I pulled the lever to engage the head, and the turret started turning. You should've seen both our faces. I disengaged it, hit stop, and we just stood there watching the machine like it had a mind of its own.

My father finally said, "Well, know this about yourself, if you can fix this, you can fix just about any machine there is. They don't get much more complicated than this. So, what do you want to do next?"

The time had come. I didn't want to break his heart, but I knew mold-making wasn't for me. And by that time, October 6, 1977, Ray Ferritto had blown up Danny Greene in his dentist's parking lot. That ended any fascination I had with that scene, at least for a while. The mob war I'd been romanticizing from a distance was over, and the Irish side had lost. Whatever dreams I'd had about being part of something like that evaporated with that car bomb. I said, "Dad, this isn't for me. I want to move back to Erie."

The disappointment on his face said everything. He looked away, took a long pause, and then said, "Well, I've worked in over twenty mold shops in my life, sometimes two or three at a time. When the job ain't goin' like you think it should, you gotta have enough confidence in yourself to close up your toolbox, roll it out the door, and roll it to the next shop down the street, and you'll do the job there, no matter what it is."

That line stuck with me. Another rule from one of the greatest men I've ever known. So I closed my toolbox and headed back to Erie.

Leaving Akron felt heavier than I expected. My father didn't cry often, but his eyes watered enough to make me look away before he changed his mind about letting me go. For nearly two years, I'd been doing that same run between Akron and Erie every weekend. I knew every crack in the pavement on I-271, every billboard on I-90, and every fast-food exit where the fries always tasted stale.

Mentor, Ohio, became my unofficial pit stop. Nothing fancy about it. Just a strip mall with a RadioShack that felt like Disneyland for a guy who liked gadgets more than souvenirs. I'd walk in pretending I wasn't broke, staring at the newest toys like they were calling my name. That year, they rolled out a slimline six-channel scanner. Sleek, small, looked like it should've come with its own theme music. The only catch was that it needed police crystals for frequencies, and each one had its own number. Not phone numbers—actual frequency codes. A whole catalog of them. A book thicker than the town's phone directory.

I asked the sales associate if I could use the restroom. Standard move. You always ask politely. In the restroom, I spotted an alarm sensor sitting in a spot that told me the installer was either lazy or overconfident. I stood there thinking, A paperclip might just laugh at this thing. Not that I planned on doing anything right then. I just noticed everything. That habit became one of the biggest tools in my life—know the layout, know what's protected, know what's not.

Out on the sales floor, the crystals were kept in a small drawer display case. Nothing locked. Nothing watched. Just sitting there like they were begging for someone curious to open them up. And the catalog? Right next to it. A full list of the frequencies for every police department, fire station, EMS crew, and even airport channels. The kind of information you could use for a dozen different reasons, depending on your intentions—and your imagination.

I didn't take anything that day. Didn't need to. The real thing I walked out with wasn't a crystal or a scanner. It was the realization that noticing the weak spots, the overlooked details, became the difference between failing and winning in every part of my life.

I went back out to my car, my 1972 Oldsmobile Delta 88. I called it *The Loadsmobile* because the thing looked like it ate smaller cars for breakfast. It also shook like it was complaining about every mile past 100,000, but it still pushed 100 on the highway without blinking.

I dug around the front seat and the floorboards until I found a paperclip that looked like it had already lived a rough life. Good enough. I headed back inside, acted like I forgot something, and slipped into the bathroom again.

The window alarm sensor had two exposed terminals sitting there like an invitation. I straightened the paperclip, touched both terminals, and the light on the alarm panel never even flickered. Jumped clean. That meant the window could open without the system noticing. I unlatched the window, pushed it open just a little, and walked out of the store before anyone had reason to wonder why a guy spent so much time in the restroom.

I grabbed supper at the diner in the same strip mall—nothing fancy—just a meal, a booth, and time to think. I waited for the place to close and the parking lot to go quiet. When darkness settled in, I drove around to the back of the building and found the bathroom window.

I slid it open just enough that it should've set off the alarm. It didn't. That told me the paperclip was doing its job. I didn't crawl in right away. I didn't even move. I drove back to my car and parked far enough away to watch without looking suspicious.

I waited fifteen minutes. No patrol car. No mall security. Nobody is even slowing down to check the doors.

I said to myself, *Alright, time to see if this works.*

I went around to the alley behind the strip mall, opened the bathroom window, climbed in, and pulled it shut behind me so it wouldn't be obvious anyone had come through. The place was silent—no motion sensors. No surprises. Just the hum of whatever cheap lights they kept running at night.

I headed straight for the display with that Slimline scanner. That was the whole point of the night, and there it sat, brand new and practically glowing like it knew it was coming with me. I picked it up without a second thought.

Then I turned to the drawers holding the police crystals. There were rows of them—tiny plastic drawers, hundreds of them. If I tried grabbing one at a time, I'd be there till sunrise, and if I tried pulling the whole case without securing it, the drawers would scatter across the floor like I kicked a hive. That wasn't happening.

I looked around and spotted a roll of three-inch shipping tape sitting near a counter. Perfect. I wrapped the entire crystal cabinet with layers of tape until it looked like a cocoon. The case was broad and tall, packed with crystals. There had to be thousands in there.

Then came the surprise I didn't even realize I was walking into, the FCC crystal frequency handbook. A thick catalog listing every frequency in the country, broken down by state, town, and jurisdiction. Police, fire, EMS, everything. I didn't know it then, but that book would bankroll moves I hadn't even dreamed up yet and turned out to be more valuable than the scanner and the crystals combined.

I gathered the scanner, the taped-up crystal cabinet, and that handbook—my future playbook—and moved them all into the bathroom. The cabinet was the real problem. It was heavy, awkward, and barely fit when I sized up the window—looked like I had maybe an inch on each side. Tight, but doable.

Everything was staged. All I had to do was pass it all through the window and load it into the car.

Then a thought hit me, I should take another look around the store. There might be something else worth grabbing.

I started strolling through the store, taking my time. Then I spotted a pair of walkie-talkies. I could use those, and they ran on the same crystals I already had in the stash I'd taped up. So into the bathroom they went.

I took one more slow turn through the aisles, just to be sure I wasn't missing anything. When I turned around, I froze. A full case of Slimline six-channel scanners sat there on a low shelf. Twenty-four units, still strapped shut in the original shipping box. I didn't even have to open it. It felt like the store was handing me a going-away gift.

I slid the case into the bathroom, lined everything up, and started passing the boxes out the window one by one. Set them on the ground below, quiet and clean. When the last piece was out, I climbed through, shut the window behind me, and walked back to my car as I'd just stepped out of a laundromat. No rush, no nerves. Slow is invisible.

I loaded the trunk, eased out of the lot, and headed toward Erie in the old Delta 88. That car never complained. It just swallowed whatever I threw at it and kept rolling.

Once I got to Erie, I needed a spot to stash everything until I figured out how to move it. Luckily, the year before, I'd helped Joe B build a garage with a loft. I'd used that loft to keep some of my Wax-A-Million gear. It was perfect. I hauled the scanners, the crystals, the whole score up there and tucked it away.

Before auto detailing shops were even a thing, I had my own little setup. Learned the trade, taking care of the limos at Rupp's all through high school. I cleaned for regular clients too, and I was smart enough to offer pickup and delivery. That meant I drove a different car almost every week. High school kids called it luck. It was just a hustle.

My mother, whom I hadn't lived with for almost two years, let me move back in. My younger brothers, Patrick and Michael, were thrilled to have me home. Three Murphy boys again: Timothy, Patrick, and Michael. Fine Irish brothers. Joe-B wasn't exactly throwing a parade, though. First thing he said was, "Well, you'd better find a job if you're gonna live in this house."

Joe-B was tough, but he stepped up for a family that wasn't his own. Remember that wife-swapping mess I mentioned? My father had an affair with Joe-B's first wife, which broke up Joe-B's marriage. Joe-B turned around and married my mother after my father divorced her. Instead of letting bitterness consume him, he raised seven of us Murphy kids like we were his own. He had one son from his first marriage, but he treated all of us the same. He taught me plenty, too, especially about building. We started with a tool shed, then built a family room addition, and eventually a two-and-a-half-car garage. I ran my side hustle out of that garage, Wax-A-Million.

But he was serious about me having a full-time job. My father helped one more time. I applied to a new frozen foods plant opening in Erie, where the HR manager had previously worked for my dad. I got hired as employee number six at Van de Kamp's Frozen Foods.

I worked the line processing frozen fish, which is probably why I still can't stand seafood to this day. If you ever saw how it was processed, you'd think twice before putting any of it in your mouth. But that could be said for most food, really.

After about six weeks at the new plant, the first production line was finally up and running. Then one day, the stainless-steel conveyor belt just stopped dead. When the line stopped, everyone stopped. It wasn't long before the new plant manager came storming out, trying to troubleshoot the problem with the maintenance crew.

They figured it out quickly enough. The head maintenance foreman told the manager it was a stripped drive sprocket, and they'd need a new one. Said it would take a couple of days to get the part. This was long before Google and overnight delivery, so that meant a couple of days with the whole line down. Nobody was working till that sprocket came in.

I overheard the whole exchange and walked over to take a look. The plant manager was laying into the foreman for not keeping spare parts in stock. I cut in and said, "Why don't you just make one yourself?"

Both of them turned and looked at me like I had two heads. The plant manager barked, "And how the hell do you think we'd do that?"

I said, "Well, you've got a brand-new lathe and milling machine back there in the maintenance shop, why not turn one up?"

They looked at each other, realizing they didn't even have a machinist yet. I said, "I could do it."

The manager said, "Well, go ahead, let's get started."

I looked right at him and said, "That depends."

He squinted. "That depends on what?"

I said, "That depends on whether this safety helmet turns from blue to yellow."

See, the regular production workers, guys like me, wore blue bump caps and made just above minimum wage. Maintenance guys wore yellow bump caps and made about five bucks more an hour.

I think it took about three seconds for the plant manager to tell the foreman, "Get him a yellow bump cap." Just like that, I was a maintenance mechanic.

The foreman was furious. I'm pretty sure he had someone in mind for that job, maybe family, but timing wasn't on his side. He handed me the yellow cap and led me back to the maintenance shop. The machines were brand new, hadn't even been run yet. He was probably waiting for me to screw up.

They'd already pulled the bad sprocket off the conveyor and laid it on the bench. I remembered my brother Jack once telling me how he made a new drive sprocket for his Honda the night before a race. Jack raced that weekend, and his sprocket had spun. He took a piece of flat steel, drew out a bolt-hole circle matching the diameter of the motorcycle's sprocket, laid out the holes along that circle, and drilled them one at a time. Once the holes were done, he used a bandsaw to cut from hole to hole, creating teeth on the sprocket. The new sprocket changed the gear ratio, which helped him win the race and several more after that. This was back in the sixties when Jack was winning trophies left and right.

The owner of the Motorcycle shop, Menzel himself, came up, saw what Jack was doing, and said, "You are the Master of Crude." The name stuck. Even after Jack went into the Navy and later became the master troubleshooter for Otis Elevator, the nickname stuck; he could fix anything. He was a Murphy.

I followed his method, more or less. Made a replica of the sprocket out of stainless steel, which is a real bastard to machine, but it worked. and fabricated a new stainless-steel drive sprocket. By that afternoon, the conveyor was running again. From that day on, I was officially a maintenance man who could fix just about anything.

The next morning, the line was running again.

I had a dark blue uniform, a yellow bump cap, and a new title: maintenance mechanic. It marked the beginning of the next decade of work, where I learned on the go and fixed everything they threw at me. But the truth was, I never felt satisfied. I was good at what I did, but I wanted more. I just didn't know what that "more" was yet.

It was during this period that my grandma Murphy passed away. Around the same time, I was about to make a life-changing acquaintance, someone who would show me what to do with the RadioShack boxes I had stashed away and set me on a path I couldn't have imagined.

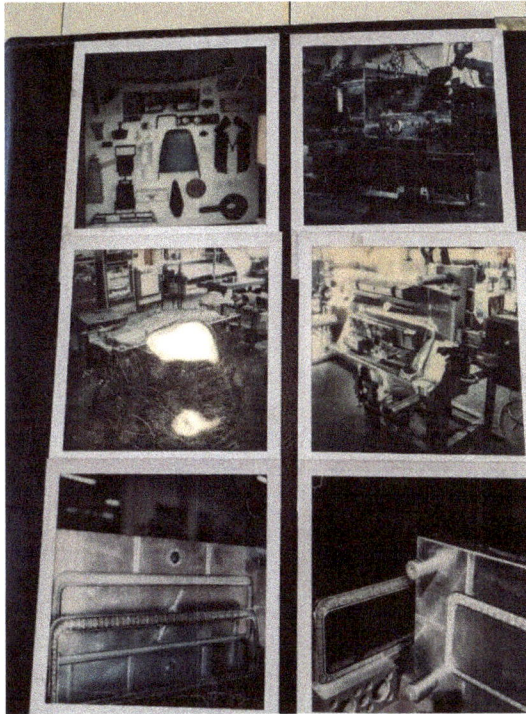
Buffalo Molded Plastics Mold & Die Division, Tallmadge, Ohio, One of the 1ST Automated Plastic Injection Molds

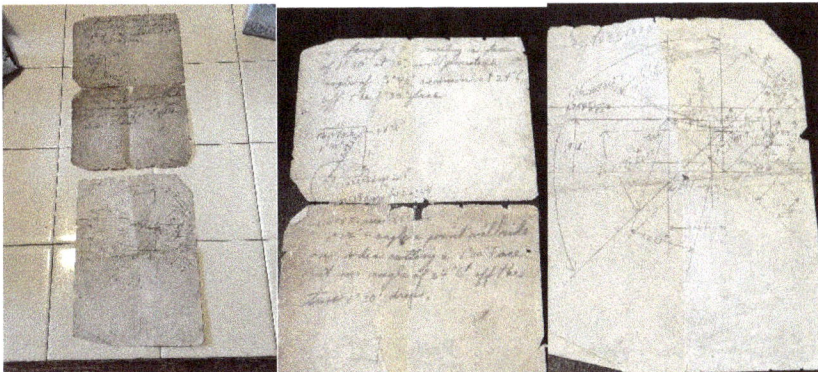
John Charles Murphy's Trigonometry calculations & explanations

CHAPTER 04
JIMMY J.R. RUSSELL AND THE KID

Jimmy Russell, the original JR and the original "OG." Where do I begin with him? Well, first off, just let me say I loved the man. He was a father figure to me as much as my own father, Jack Murphy, and even my stepfather, Joe B. But as I had to discover, as with all men, he was just a man with all his fallacies and faults.

I had to learn this first with my father; that same night, he showed me the picture of the men on the deck of the U.S.S. Enterprise. He sat there looking at that picture, then said, "You know, I had it all. I had a great life, a great wife, a great family, a great home and livelihood... and just couldn't see it."

That struck me like a ton of bricks. It was at that moment that I had to knock down all the fantasies I had built up in my mind about my father since he had left our home in Erie. I had to knock him off the pedestal I had put him on and realize he was just a man, with faults like the rest of us.

And just as I learned with my stepfather, Joe B—Mr. B, because I would not call him dad—but there is always a reason. I would learn that much later in life, after I had repeated the destruction of my own family, just as my father had.

One morning, I called my mother to talk to her before I went to work. Joe B answered the phone, and I just felt the spirit led me to say, "Joe, if I never told you before, thank you for raising us kids and keeping the seven of us together. I know I was no day at the beach to live with, but you were a pretty tough guy yourself."

There was a long pause of silence when he said, "You know, Tim, I don't have one happy memory as a child. My parents were right off the boat from Poland. They were both alcoholics and beat each other every day of my life."

It was at that moment that my attitude about him changed. Everything became clear about why he was the way he was. He was a man with all our faults—he was a good man.

But that may be why I was always searching for that father figure. And there he was: Jimmy JR Russell. I realized later in life that he was just a man and had used me for his own purposes, as I knew he had probably also done with his brother Bobby and with his brother Peter, my best friend in life, but we had asked for it, wanting the fast life. We went in eyes wide shut. But I just recently learned he also used my brother Jackie in the same way that may have boosted JR into national recognition.

"JR" had used Peter over a decade before I had met him to do his bidding, and then, when Pete got older and went on his own, I took over.

One of the stories JR and Pete used to tell from back when they worked together was the job that landed both of them five years in the pen. Sounds serious, and it was, but hearing them tell it, we'd be laughing until we cried. That's the thing about those guys — they could make the worst nights read like a vaudeville act.

Technically, it was a kidnapping, although nobody was ever held hostage or really threatened. JR was the brains, a mastermind; he planned everything so we could avoid contact with the victims whenever possible.

Violence was a last resort. If it was necessary, his rule was simple: no witnesses.

"JR" had learned the K-mart manager's routine. Every Sunday, the manager would make a weekly bank drop—usually over $50,000. JR scoped the job for months and studied the rhythm of the manager's life. He found out the manager's wife hosted a ladies' card party every Sunday afternoon, their little alone time while he did the counting and the drop. JR timed everything like a Swiss clock.

When the day came, Pete went to the house. He cut the phone lines and then parked down the street to watch, making sure nobody left and that the cops didn't show. The whole point was to isolate the target without any confrontation. JR loved plans like that — surgical, tidy, minimal mess.

There was another man involved, the one with the original information. His job was to make the call to the manager at work, the guy counting the money, and tell him his wife had been kidnapped. The message was simple — if he ever wanted to see her again, he'd take the bank drop and leave it at a specific location. The only thing JR didn't set up was the drop spot. He didn't know the area that well, so he left that to the other partner.

The partner makes the call and tells the manager to leave the money at St. John's Church, or they'd kill his wife. That last part wasn't part of JR's plan. The manager was told to make the drop and return to K-mart, where he'd get another call with directions to find his wife. It was supposed to take less than an hour. He was even told he could call home — just not the cops, or he'd never see her again.

The manager said he'd do it. Everything was set. Pete was watching the house, JR was watching the manager at K-mart, and the partner was watching the drop spot. Everything started smoothly. The manager left K-mart with a box full of cash. This was long before cell phones, so JR" used a phone booth near a bar to call his partner and tell him the manager was on his way. Everything looked tight. Pete waited down the street, outside the house, while the plan played out.

About forty-five minutes later, the bank manager came back — no box. JR called the partner to pick up the money, but the guy said the manager never showed. JR said, "You sure? He just got back." The partner called the manager again, this time threatening his wife's life — again, not part of JR's orders — yelling, "Where the hell is the money?"

The manager swore he had left it and begged for his wife. JR told the partner to check again, but like JR always said, "No money." The partner called the manager again, asking exactly where he dropped it. That's when it all fell apart. The one detail JR left to someone else—the drop spot—St John's Church. Turns out, the partner was Roman Catholic and the manager was Lutheran. The partner sat watching St. John's Roman Catholic Church while the manager left the money at St. John's Lutheran, about a mile away.

By the time they figured it out, JR sent the partner to the right one. But the pastor of St. John's Lutheran had already found the box by the back door. At first, he thought God had answered his prayers. Then he called the cops. By the time the partner arrived to pick up the box, the police were waiting. They caught him on the spot.

He rolled over on JR and Peter right away. They were picked up within days, and each got a nickel in the joint. Years later, when they told the story, we'd be laughing so hard we'd cry. "The gang that couldn't shoot straight," JR would say, and we'd be rolling. I used to think, how can you laugh about losing five years of your life?

"JR" told me later, "If you don't laugh, you'd cry."

He wasn't wrong. That was the last time he ever let someone else handle the details.

With me, things started slowly. I was running errands for JR, mostly small drop-offs in a bag. I never looked in the bag. Maybe I told myself it was plausible deniability, maybe I didn't want to know. Either way, I knew whatever was in there wasn't legal, and I loved it. It was what I'd been looking for. I can't blame JR for using me because I was using him too, to get what I wanted, or what I thought I wanted.

We'd meet almost every day at the Ole' Monte Club, *Mousie* DeAurora's place. That was our hangout. Mousie Sr. was a great guy, but his son, *Mousie JR.* —Mikey D.—ran the day-to-day operations. The DeAuroras were cousins with the DeSanto family, so we all became one big happy family... at least for a while. Until the walls fell in and the rubber met the road.

Sometimes we'd meet early in the morning. One time, when Mikey was late opening the joint, JR picked the front door lock in seconds, and we went in and served ourselves. When Mikey finally showed up, we scared the hell out of him. We were sitting at our spot, the little short section of the bar at the end by the service walk-through. It was like our own private four-foot bar, and no one else dared sit there when we were around.

Mikey started cursing at us for "breaking in," until JR stopped him cold and snapped, "You better be here on time to open your joint. And by the way, we didn't break in, we picked it. There's nothin' broken, asshole." That was JR. And I loved him for it.

Then he took me to the next level. That's how it's done—they groom you, step by step. They start you with small things, test your reliability, and see if you can keep your mouth shut.

Things were getting a little hot in town. JR worried the cops might pull him over for some minor traffic violation and try to jam him up with a bogus charge. He didn't need that, so he came up with a solution: he wouldn't drive anymore. That's when I became his chauffeur.

I'd worked at a limousine rental since I was fourteen, washing the limos and hearses every day after school. I'd park them, back them in, and make sure each tail fin lined perfectly with the red line on the wall. My boss, *Butch*, had every model year of Cadillac from 1970 through 1976, six hearses and seven limos. Every year, he'd sell the oldest and buy the newest, so I got to know every detail, every design change.

Even on days they didn't go out, I'd wipe them down with a clean white towel dipped in water and wrung through a wringer. Butch had one prized personal limo that rarely went out unless the place was busy—a 1966 Cadillac Fleetwood Brougham Seventy-Five Series, one of the original factory-built stretch limos. It had the extended back doors, the fold-down jump seats, and a power privacy window that sealed the driver off from the passengers. I loved those cars. I learned to drive in one of them, threading it through tight spaces like it was nothing.

So when JR said he wanted me to drive his *Caddy*, it felt like a promotion. And what a car it was—a 1970 Cadillac Fleetwood Brougham, loaded with every option Cadillac offered that year. Nineteen feet long from nose to tail, painted *Lucerne Aqua Firemist* with a black vinyl roof and black leather interior. It was gorgeous. And it was mine, at least to drive.

Every day, I'd drive my car to JR's house, then switch to his Caddy and take him out to do business. I loved that car. Eventually, it became mine. JR and I made a deal: when he went to prison, I'd buy it from him. I'd drive him to the joint myself, drop him off at the door, hand him cash to go in with, and he'd sign over the title. Even if I didn't have all the money upfront, I'd send payments to his commissary account.

He loved that setup too. He'd always say, "Don't give me the cash till I'm at the door." He wanted that steady flow of money coming in while he was inside—and he got it. I never missed a payment.

I loved that guy.

It started slow, like I said—just running errands here and there for JR, mainly because he didn't want to drive. But then things picked up, and it all came down to Monday nights—*Monday Night Football* on nationwide television. That show was a phenomenon. Back then, it was the equivalent of the rollout of Netflix, Google, or Amazon today. It was massive, and it became the biggest shot in the arm for every bookie and odds maker across the country—especially for every La Cosa Nostra family.

The first family to really understand its potential and capitalize on it was the Philadelphia family, led by Angelo Bruno, portrayed later by Harvey Keitel in *The Irishman*. The Philly Mob was even more treacherous in the early 80s than any of the five Families in New York City, as they went through 3 bosses in less than 3 years. Angelo "The Gentle Don" Bruno was the boss from 1959 to 1980; the family enjoyed an era of peace and prosperity.

There was a territory beef with some in the New York City Genovese Family that led to his murder in 1980. Bruno was succeeded by his loyal friend Phillip "The Chicken Man" Testa, but within a year, he was killed with a nail-bomb explosion in 1981. When the dust settled, Nicodemo "Little Nicky" Scarfo emerged as the boss and was a paranoid, homicidal maniac who led the family into a highly dysfunctional era that ultimately destroyed the Philly family.

The *Monday Night Football* tickets came up from Philly through the Northeastern Pennsylvania crime family of Russell Bufalino, whom Joe Pesci played in the same movie. But this wasn't the movies; this was real life, and it was genius.

They created a variation of the old Italian daily number and took it to an entirely new level. They started printing *Monday Night Football* tickets, each stamped with a five-digit number. The beauty of it was that it couldn't be fixed. The results were based on stats printed in the Tuesday morning paper.

Each ticket was folded and sewn shut on both ends so you couldn't see the number until after you bought and opened it. The winning number was made by taking both teams' total yards rushing, total yards passing, total yards on returns, total yards penalized, and total points scored—adding them all up and using the last digit of each sum to form one unique five-digit number. That number was worth $5,000.

It was an incredible setup. Every week, they'd print 100,000 tickets, numbered 00000 to 99,999. They sold for two bucks apiece, bringing in about $200,000 a week. Only a $5,000 winner and maybe a couple of smaller payouts—four or three matching digits, cut from that. The rest? Profit.

The money funneled back to Philly, but only a dollar per ticket. JR got fifty cents a ticket, and he'd give the bar owners we distributed through a piece of the action. Eventually, he started giving me a quarter a ticket as I drove him around Erie every Tuesday morning. On Wednesdays, we'd head to Buffalo along the Seaway Trail up the Lake Erie coast, hitting our regular stops. That's really how my chauffeuring job with JR began.

It was a gold mine. But every stop we made wasn't just about money—it was about information. We learned who had money and where it was. And information, as JR used to say, was power.

The only reason JR—or any of us—ever got tangled up with "Fat Sam" was because that man had a way of getting information. But JR was the real chess master. He could figure out every detail himself and never let anyone else handle the thinking again.

One of the first times I really proved myself to JR was the night he called me at one o'clock in the morning. His voice was tight. He said he had to get to Lackawanna, New York—fast. "Get here," was all he said. His father was dying.

I tore across the city of Erie and pulled up at his place. He was waiting with that look that said, "Don't waste time." I picked him up in his Cadillac and hit the highway, setting the cruise control at a hundred miles an hour. We covered the 89.9 miles from Erie, Pennsylvania, to Lackawanna in just over an hour—city streets were the only thing that slowed us down.

I pulled up at Our Lady of Victory Hospital. JR went in, and I waited in the car like always. When he came back out a couple of hours later, I could tell it wasn't good. I'd never seen him that quiet. His father had passed, but he was grateful he'd made it in time to say goodbye.

That ride sealed it. He already liked me, but that night he trusted me. From then on, he never questioned how I was getting him anywhere—he just knew I'd get him there.

The next time we had a family emergency, it was his brother Bobby. JR called him "RJ." Bobby was a habitual gambler. After Don Stefano "The Undertaker" Magaddino passed away in 1974, Buffalo was wide open for a while. It was like the OK Corral.

The Buffalo ARM—officially the Niagara Falls/Buffalo Family—had been under the control of Stefano Magaddino, an old-school Sicilian from Castellammare del Golfo, Sicily. He wasn't just any boss. He was the senior-ranking Sicilian in the entire United States. After Lucky Luciano was deported, Magaddino became the head of all five families in New York City. He was the man at the top of the Commission. New York City never wants to admit it, but old-school Sicilians respected seniority to a tee.

The FBI has documents to prove it. There's even a picture in the September 1, 1967, edition of *LIFE* magazine showing Stefano Magaddino crowned and sitting on a throne in Buffalo, though it really should have been Niagara Falls.

In 1957, Magaddino told Joseph Barbara to host the American Mafia summit at Barbara's ranch in Apalachin, New York. Barbara didn't want to do it. He had reservations about holding it there, but Magaddino pushed it, and Barbara gave in. That meeting turned out to be what everyone now calls the Apalachin Conference. Russell Bufalino, whom Magaddino originally made, helped organize the whole thing. He was the go-between, contacting the delegates, handling food and hotel arrangements. But the meeting got raided by New York State Police, and it blew up in their faces. The Apalachin Fiasco, that's what it became known as. It was a major blow to organized crime's secrecy across the country and destroyed Barbara's reputation. That humiliation pushed Barbara into retirement by 1958.

After that, Russell Bufalino became the de facto street boss of the Northeastern Pennsylvania crime family. When Santo Volpe died in 1958, Bufalino officially took over. From 1960 through the 1970s, he spread out—gambling, bootlegging, labor rackets, you name it. By the seventies, he was one of the top men in Cosa Nostra. Then he tried to move back into Buffalo, looking to take over loan sharking, the numbers, the rackets...

Bobby was into them for ten large — ten grand — and he couldn't pay. They were threatening to break his legs. When he called his older brother, JR, there was panic in his voice. JR called me right after. Said we had to get to Lackawanna, again. Then he said, "Bring the mellon-thumper."

The mellon-thumper was a MAC-10 automatic machine pistol with an eighteen-inch silencer. "Suppressor" is the polite term, but it doesn't change what it is. I grabbed the mellon-thumper. On the way there, he filled me in: Bobby owed Bufalino's men, and they weren't waiting much longer. JR said we were going to meet them man-to-man.

We pulled into the Crown Club on Electric Avenue, which is now Big Al's, Cagney's, and C2s. JR told me to park a little down from the bar, facing toward Ridge Road. He said a Cadillac was going to pull up across the street, and he would walk up to the back window to have a little discussion with them. We waited in our Caddy.

The black Cadillac pulled up as scheduled. JR walked up to the back window and pounded on it. It rolled down. Before he left, he told me, "If, when he's walking away, he hits the street... that I was to spray that black Caddy with the MAC-10 with the 18-inch suppressor—the 'melon-thumper."

Well, I heard a little of the conversation. Then all I heard was, "I will wipe out you and your family name!" Oh my God, my throat hit the pit of my stomach.

I was ready to jump out and spray that Caddy, but JR came walking back and then walked into the bar. I waited for the black Caddy to pull off and made sure they were gone. Then I came into the Crown Club. We ended up calling Bobby and telling him things were taken care of. We drank there till closing at 4 a.m.

I went out to start the Caddy, but when I turned the key, nothing happened. Deader than a door nail. Had the OK Corral broken out there, we would have been stranded with no way out. It turned out that we had to sleep in the Caddy that night.

"JR" called a friend of his down on Ridge Road to come to us and put a new starter in the Caddy that morning. He fell asleep in the back seat. I sat up all night with that Mellon-thumper lying across my lap, not knowing what was going to happen. Had anything happened, we would have been stuck there and may have been dead. Once again, but for the grace of God, we walked away.

"JR" started trusting me with more because I was picking things up fast and figuring out a few tricks on my own. I was learning about walkie-talkies and police scanners. I started with shoplifting from one of my favorite electronics boutiques at the time, Radio Shack.

They had everything you wanted: walkie-talkies, hand-held and base scanners, a complete selection of all the crystals needed for the different bands available, and the grand prize: a National Radio crystal frequency manual that read like a nationwide phonebook, listed state by state, county by county, city and township of every emergency broadcast frequency. It was always kept right next to the crystal drawers. I used this extensively as I planned getaway routes and alternatives.

You had to be selective because, before programmable scanners made everything easy for novices, you only had six channels available on handheld scanners. You had to know where you were going and how you were going to get out, same rules for a bar. I learned some tricks of my own. With the higher-end walkie-talkies, there were standard transmit and receive crystals. I found that if I swapped the two walkie-talkies in a set, it effectively encrypted them so only those two could communicate and blocked anyone trying to monitor those channels. It was effective. It was like our own private line that no one else could listen in on, even if they wanted to. It was a nice feature and a selling point because JR began farming out my services across the country.

We only did so much locally because that would have brought too much heat on us, so he would often be contacted for his unique consulting services. He would get a piece of the action to tell people where they would screw up. He would present all kinds of what-if scenarios to prompt people to consider alternatives and plan for them. As part of this service, he would offer pre-programmed scanners where they would have to provide what area the score was in and how they wanted to get out. They only had six choices, so they had to be right.

Of course, JR never let on that his "kid" driver was the one doing all the programming, getting the scanners and the desired crystals. This became very lucrative for both of us as our service came in demand. Of course, I'm sure I never received a full share, but he always took care of me, and I was happy.

After a while, the piecemeal approach became a bit cumbersome, so I decided to go wholesale. I decided to take off a Radio Shack store and relieve them of their inventory. I had scoped out Radio Shacks in surrounding cities and found a prime target within a couple of hours of Little Erie, PA. It would have been too hot in Erie. After selecting my target, I knew I would have to get past their alarm system, which Radio Shack sold to the public. It wasn't going to be that difficult. I used my old trick of going in during regular business hours and preparing the system for re-entry after hours.

Back in the day of hard-wired systems, it was often quite simple if you could access an entry point, often through a bathroom window. You could bypass the system by simply inserting a paper clip into a window or door sensor. Just adding it across the two screw terminals of the sensor would keep the circuit loop closed and the system set when you made an entry and exit. For good measure, the outside ringer box, which was often the extent of the system, could be defeated by adding some "Great-Stuff" spray foam insulation and allowing it to set for a half hour or so. It would harden up inside the ringer box and prevent the alarm from sounding or being heard—just for good measure.

I went in that evening and, just as planned, it was a piece of cake. I relieved them of all the walkie-talkies they had, almost a full case of their six-channel hand-held scanners, the entire crystal drawer case—which I had to duct-tape shut—and the pièce de résistance, the National Radio crystal frequency manual. That was gold, because we could now supply a scanner set up anywhere in the country.

"JR" started marketing us everywhere, and word spread quickly through his circles. We became very much in demand. He used to get into the back of his 1970 Cadillac Fleetwood Brougham and say, "Wake me up in Pittsburgh, wake me up in Detroit, wake me up in Chicago, wake me up in…" and I would. He never revealed that it was me setting these up, as a way of protecting both him and his golden goose. He knew what he had.

I found out many years later—actually just a few years ago—that I wasn't the first Murphy whose services he tapped. I'm sure he used my father's machine shop on certain occasions before I was even involved with him. I found out that when my oldest brother, Jack, got out of the Navy as a Chief Petty Officer and an Electronic Technician, JR came to him in the early 1970s and asked if he could develop a device to detect whether a phone line was being tapped. Jack told him that if the tap was already on the line, that would be nearly impossible to tell, but if the line was clean, he could install a device that basically worked as a meter monitoring the phone line.

"JR" took my brother Jack down to Florida—Tampa or Hollywood, I believe. Once there, JR took him to an unnamed man's house, and this man asked him the same question. Jack gave him the same answer and installed the monitor on the phone line. Once it was installed, Jack liked what he saw on the meter and marked a line on the display. He told the man that if the needle of the meter strayed off that mark, someone was listening in on the line. The man was quite pleased, as far as I understood, and they left and returned to little Erie, PA. That was the last time Jack did anything for JR. On the ride home, he got spooked and never did anything else with him to my knowledge.

He worked for Otis Elevator for 40 years and became their top elevator technician. He was the troubleshooting contact for the western half of Pennsylvania during the last half of his tenure there, earning the title "Master of Crude" for his ability to fix anything, no matter how old it was. They always called Murphy!

The last thing I knew my brother did, which may have approached illegality, was during the early '90s. Jack was way ahead of the curve with computers, and this was before the internet really exploded. He was the elevator serviceman at Carnegie Mellon University in Pittsburgh. While repairing an elevator, a man walked up to him and asked, "Are you Jack Hack?" to which my brother answered, "Well, it depends who's asking!" The man turned out to be the head of the Computer Science Department at Carnegie Mellon—a very prestigious university. He said, "My students tell me you're one of the best at getting into programs. I've been trying to get into this program for over a month."

That was all my brother needed to hear. He said, "Where's your terminal?" He had a challenge in front of him and couldn't resist. This was a time before hacking was really a thing, and the only computers on what would become the internet were at universities and military research sites. The professor had to sign in to the system, which allowed Jack to record the username and password. He then went to work trying to get into the program that the Computer Science professor couldn't access. In less than an hour, he cracked it. The professor was grateful and told my brother he could use the system whenever he needed. Jack made a mental note of that.

A few years later, he was reading one of the first books on hacking. He decided to give it a try himself. At the time, he lived in a very rural area of central Pennsylvania and thought he would use the system to locate my baby brother Michael, who had followed Jack's footsteps into the Navy. Jack thought he would try to use the military network to locate him, since Michael was out at sea on the U.S.S. *Stump* as an electronics tech and fire control officer, handling nuclear weapons.

Jack started letting his fingers do the walking, leapfrogging through the system, and actually found out Michael was doing war games in the middle of the Atlantic Ocean off the coast of Brazil. Suddenly, a warning message popped up requesting authentication. Jack panicked, thinking he was about to get traced. Quick on his feet, he ran to the main junction box on his telephone pole and used alligator clips to jump across nearly every other phone line in the box to throw off any trace they might have been running. He said it scared the hell out of him, and he never did it again.

That's our gift from God; we can take apart and fix anything. It became my reputation too once I got out of prison and started working legally for Dunlop Tire Corporation, General Motors, Delphi Thermal Systems, and Goodyear Tire and Rubber. My reputation was: *"If Murphy can't fix it, we're all in trouble!"*

As for JR, I believe this little service is what elevated him into national prominence for his skills. He was a man who got things done—and he did.

James P. Russell Family Man

-circa:1980

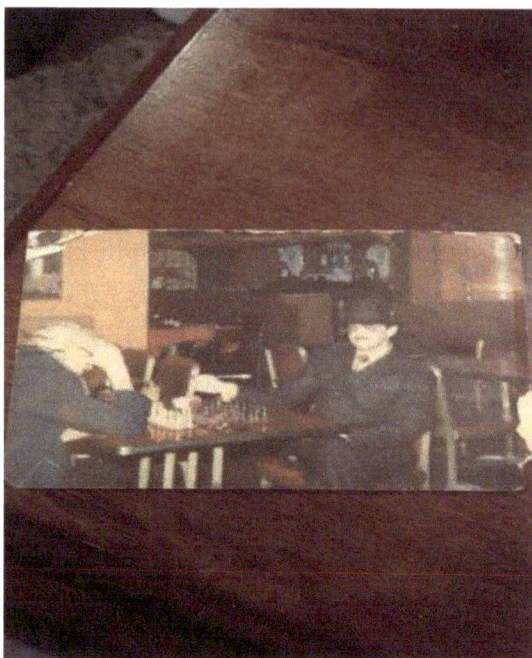

James P. Russell Family Man

-circa:1980

"JR"'s 1970 Cadillac Fletwood Brougham (Lucerne Aqua Firemist) with a black vinyl roof and black leather interior. My "Starship Enterprise"

CHAPTER 05
PETER "DR THE DOCTOR" RUSSELL

Peter "Dr. the Doctor" Russell was JR's youngest brother and the closest in age to me, though he was still almost a decade older. He felt like a big brother to me. I remember the first time we met. JR called me to his house, and when I walked in, a guy was pacing back and forth until JR introduced us. He didn't trust me at first, even though I'd been with JR for a couple of years. He didn't trust much then; he was hot.

"JR" told me I had to follow him to Pete's place, help stash his car, and bring him back. Pete had other requirements and was sizing up my driving skills. "Can this kid fuckin' drive?" he asked. "He can drive," JR replied. "Well, I want you right on my ass, so close no cop can see the plate on this thing!" He had an early 1970s Plymouth, an unmarked New Jersey State Police cruiser, and the plates were bad. It was fast. He needed it home and stashed, just like JR said.

He took off in the cruiser, and I was right behind him in my 1972 Olds Delta 88. I stayed within three feet of his rear end the whole way. When we arrived, he pulled the car behind his house, got out, and pulled the plate. I had a tarp and some bungee cords in my trunk. Pete gave me a look when I pulled them out and started covering the car. We rode back to JR's, and when we walked in, Pete said, "The kid can fuckin' drive!" JR replied, "I told you he could fuckin' drive, don't doubt me, asshole!" I took it as a compliment. Pete and I were in right then.

Within a week or two, he was so hot he couldn't go back to his place, and he ended up moving in with me at my apartment. I had to keep a low profile because I was holding the regular shipments of bales of Colombian coffee in my attic. When we got the bales, I'd bring them up to my apartment. I had a huge living room with two couches along each wall and an eleven-piece sectional set forming a big U. I'd drape a 20-by-30 piece of plastic over the furniture and throw a fifty-pound bale in the middle. I'd break it open with a meat cleaver and start bagging and weighing on a triple-beam scale in one-pound zip-lock baggies. After they were weighed, we'd bring them up to the attic and line the rafters with the best insulation available.

It was quite a production. I'm sorry to say I used my two younger brothers to help bag and weigh. On payday, they'd help me count the money. I had to maintain a steady cash flow to JR so he could keep the supply coming. It was perfect for several years.

Now that Pete was living with me, we were into everything. He had the main connection for coke—kilo, 2.2 pounds. We were rollin'. We had so much cash it was a pain in the ass. You think you'd never have that problem, but this was the late 1970s, and moving product and cash discreetly was its own headache. We always kept some legal job as cover; that was one of JR's rules from the ARM, the Niagara Falls/Buffalo crime family that Stefano Magaddino ran for decades after Lucky Luciano got deported.

The ARM operated in total silence. Don Stefano insisted on it. They were so low-key that they were the only family not known by the patriarch's last name, unlike all the other five Commission families and most others across the country. In Life, that kind of anonymity was considered an insult by some, but to Don Stefano "The Undertaker" Magaddino, it was smart business.

"JR" could never be made because he was part-Irish, but he was raised by made men in The ARM and carried their rules like scripture. He drilled them into my head. The first rule: always have a visible means of support. I worked as a maintenance mechanic at a manufacturing plant. It wasn't glamorous, but it gave me access to a full machine shop, where I could build JR's "special orders." He'd sketch the design on a napkin, and once I had it memorized, that napkin was gone—literally eaten to erase any trace.

"JR" landed Pete a bartending job at the PP Club—the Petrola Peligna Society—one of the hottest spots in Erie's Little Italy. You couldn't just walk in; you had to get past old Pasquale at the door. Pete worked one of the front bars, dressed sharp in his three-piece suit like the rest of us. That's the night I met the DeSanto girls.

Pete was seeing Patty D then, a knockout Italian beauty in a black, low-cut dress. She was at Pete's bar getting a drink when her ex-husband came in with a few friends. He was wearing a jean jacket and had a bad attitude. "Well, you look good tonight," he said. Patty smiled politely. "Well, thank you, thank you."

Pete caught that and was already moving down the bar. Her ex kept going. "You never got dressed up like that for me." Patty didn't miss a beat. "Maybe you never gave me a reason to." That's when the idiot sealed his fate. "You look like a fuckin' whore."

Pete came flying over the bar and hit him so hard he nearly dropped before he hit the floor. One of the guy's friends tried to pull Pete off, and suddenly the whole front bar exploded. Patty's brother Elmer jumped in, then Billy, and now it was on—us in our three-piece suits, cracking heads with bikers in denim. It was chaos.

Then, out of nowhere, a rock glass came flying across the bar and smacked Merck—who hadn't even joined the fight yet—right in the temple. He dropped like a stone. The whole place froze. Everyone turned to see where it came from.

At the far end of the L-shaped bar sat this gorgeous Italian girl with a grin as she'd just won a bet. JR stormed over. "What the hell are you doing?" She looked up, all innocent. "Well, everyone was fighting, and I just wanted to help." JR barked back, "He was on our side!"

That was the night I met Mary Ellen DeSanto—the girl who became the love of my life. I fell for her right then and there.

She wore a silver velvet, low-cut jumpsuit that caught every eye in the room. Pete introduced us, and she walked straight up to my table and asked me to dance. The song was Michael Jackson's "Rock With You." I was in heaven. She was stunning, and every head in the place turned to watch.

She came home with me that night, fell asleep on my sectional couch, and I never laid a hand on her. I treated her like a lady, and I think that surprised her. We started seeing each other after that, and before long, we were inseparable. That night tied it all together—DeSanto, the Russells, and me, the smart Irish kid who could figure anything out.

While Pete and I lived together, we hustled nonstop. Between moving weed and coke, we were always chasing the next score. We didn't go after civilians — too much heat. We went for the ones who wouldn't be quick to call the cops: bookies, dealers, and certain businesses that preferred to stay off the radar. Coin-operated machine routes were perfect; quiet cash, steady flow, and no paperwork.

We got word about a guy who fit both categories — ran a coin-op business and booked bets on the side. Saturday night was the jackpot: weekend collections and betting money in one place. It was cold enough to make your breath hang in the air, and everything went exactly to plan. The owner was at a card game in the back room of a private club, the kind that lasted till dawn. We were in and out in under an hour, back home with two heavy canvas bags full of cash before midnight.

The snow was fresh and crisp, squeaking under every step. One of the cardinal rules before a job: empty your pockets. Nothing that could identify you. No wallet, no keys, no loose change, no comb, nothing. So there we were, standing at the door of our apartment after a perfect score, both of us grinning like idiots until Pete says, "You got your keys?"

I look at him. "I was about to ask you the same thing."

He'd taken the spare set and never put it back. Two professional thieves, locked out of their own place — the Gang That Couldn't Shoot Straight, starring Murphy's Law.

Pete decides he'll climb the drainpipe and get in through the living room window he'd left cracked open. He scales the pipe easy at first, gets one foot on the ledge — then I hear it: *crick... crick... CRACK.* The whole thing tears loose from the wall, and Pete rides that pipe straight down, landing flat in a three-foot snowbank.

I ran over to check on him. He was hurting, but laughing between curses. I ran around back, climbed up the rear stairwell, and let us in through the kitchen door. By the time I got him upstairs, he had one swollen ankle and one busted ego. To make it worse, one of his bags had been packed with quarters instead of cash, and when he hit the ground, they went flying everywhere.

We must've looked like lunatics, laughing through the pain, quarters half-buried in the snow. When spring came, and the snow melted, you could hear kids out on the block yelling every few minutes, "Found another one!" There must've been twenty of them scouring the sidewalks for quarters.

The Gang That Couldn't Shoot Straight, alright, but we never missed the laugh.

The New Year's Toga Party at Patty's house was strictly "toga or no entry." Twenty-four wine glasses laced with LSD sat ready, and cocaine and Dilaudid moved through the night like currency. Pete handled the cash, but by morning, when I asked him where he had hidden it, he couldn't remember. Every one of D's brothers and sisters tore through Patty's apartment looking for that money. No luck. We finally wrote it off, figuring someone at the party must've lifted it.

Patty got her name because she was born on March 17—St. Paddy's Day—so a few months later, we were back in her apartment for her birthday. This time, we mixed a massive punch bowl of "Peppermint Patty's:" half a gallon of green Crème de Menthe, half a gallon of white Crème de Menthe, and half a gallon of white Crème de Cocoa. It tasted just like a Peppermint Patty, and after a few batches, it could hook you quick.

Pete eventually had to sit down to catch his breath and plopped himself on the corner of the table just as Mary walked into the kitchen. The leg snapped, the punch bowl slid off, smashed to the floor, and the sticky green flood spread everywhere. Mary slammed into the stove, which banged against the wall. Then the wall clock fell, cracked open on the stovetop, and out popped twelve thousand dollars Pete had hidden and never told me about.

Once again—The Gang That Couldn't Shoot Straight.

But oh, what a party it was.

We loved to party. One Halloween night, I was driving, Pete riding shotgun. He sat there, clenching his fist, saying, "I can feel it, Timmy." "What the hell are you talking about, Pete?" I asked. He had someone who owed him money for coke he was going to collect on. "I can feel a cue stick in my hand. We have one of two choices tonight. We can stay in Erie and track this motherfucker down, or we can go to Buffalo and have a good time." That was all I needed to hear. I hit the gas and took I-90 East toward Buffalo.

We started in his old stomping grounds of Lackawanna and South Buffalo, at an old friend's bar, Kenny and the Poplar Inn on South Park Avenue. Kenny and Pete were biker buddies, riding "in the wind" together. They'd been in a bad wreck — Kenny lost a leg below the knee, and Pete's leg was busted so bad his foot turned pigeon-toed when he drank. You could always spot him.

We sat at the bar with Kenny. A couple of Halloween partygoers were in full rubber latex masks at the far end of the bar. Those masks had just hit the market, and they drove Pete nuts. He went up and offered them twenty bucks to try on the masks. They wouldn't take them off. He offered to buy them. They refused. He threw two fifty-dollar bills on the bar. Still no dice. That only made Pete more determined. "Oh, we have to do this. We have to get a couple of masks and go into some bars and not take them off, no matter what!" he said.

We said our goodbyes and hit the streets in search of masks. It was nine or ten at night, not many shopping options. We stopped at Wilson Farm's convenience store looking for even a kiddy mask and found nothing until

Pete spotted a rack of black stocking caps. He grabbed one, asked the cashier for scissors, pulled the cap over my head, and started cutting out eye holes. The cashier looked stunned. While Pete cut the second hole, an off-duty Buffalo city cop working security walked out of the back room. I said, "No matter what you do, don't do anything stupid. There's a Buffalo cop right behind you." He slowly turned and said, "Really? We're just making a Halloween costume." He wasn't buying it.

I saw a rack of mirrored aviator sunglasses. I shoved a pair into the eye holes and said, "We are going as the Invisible Man." The cop half-smiled. We paid, grabbed another pair, threw money on the counter, and took off.

Pete was already cooking up our first stop. We'd been coming up to Buffalo every week, collecting on jewelry fenced to Butch Hallaby. Butch had invested some of it in remodeling a restaurant called the Old Pony Post. Pete wasn't happy about that, so every weekend we drank up a bar tab until Butch made good. That made the Old Pony Post a perfect target for our new costumes.

We went in, had a couple of drinks, and started making people uncomfortable. I got uncomfortable. "Let's find somewhere else to go," I told Pete. We finished our drinks and headed out to the car. As we pulled out of the parking lot, a Hamburg Town police car pulled into the drive. We yanked the stocking caps off just in time and drove right by. That didn't slow Pete down. It hyped him up. "Oh, we gotta find another place to go. I got it. We have to go to Cuffy's, the Park Grille in the First Ward of Lackawanna." Anthony "Cuffy" Caffero owned the Park Grille, sat on the city council, and was one of Pete's old friends and business partners.

As we pulled up, the scene outside was almost surreal—people in costumes everywhere, partying in the street. One young lady was dressed as "Tim the Enchanter" from *Monty Python and the Holy Grail*, complete with ram's horns on her headgear and flash paper that sent flames shooting from her hands. It was wild.

Pete grinned and said, "Oh, this is great, Timmy. We have to go into this place like we're taking it off. When we walk in, I'm going to head straight to the owner. You stay at the door with your hand in your pocket like you're holding down the joint."

He marched up to the front door and kicked it open. The door slammed against the wall beside the jukebox, which skipped straight to the end of the song. The whole place froze—perfect silence except for the collective gasp from everyone staring at the two thugs who had just stormed in.

Pete walked right up to Cuffy, who was behind the bar. He stepped onto the bar rail, leaned over, and barked, "You got thirty seconds!" Then he leaned in close and whispered, "To guess who I am—or we're drinking all night for nothing."

No one heard that second part, including the girl dressed as a gold Tin Man who was standing at the bar with her back to me. Her friend kept trying to get her attention, saying, "Mary, Mary, Mary..." until she finally turned around.

Her face was painted gold, but I could tell she was a knockout blonde. Her eyes went wide when I said, "Mary, where have you been all my life?"

She stammered, "Do I know you? I don't think I know you. And my girlfriend says you guys look like the type that's going to make everyone take their clothes off and rob them!"

That was actually a pretty popular crime at the time. I told her, "She's right!" and she almost lost it. I had to reassure her I wasn't going to make her strip—though honestly, that would've been a nice touch.

Meanwhile, Pete was whispering sweet nothings into Cuffy's ear, probably convincing him we weren't really knocking off the joint. We ended up drinking for free for hours. Pete got drunk enough that his right foot started to turn pigeon-toed, and that's when Cuffy finally looked down and said, "Peter Russell, you son of a bitch!"

Cuffy and Pete went way back. They'd done plenty of business together, and I'm sure Pete took care of whatever a politician needed to stay in office. Years later, I asked Cuffy why they never cleaned up the old Bethlehem Steel Plant—still an eyesore on the eastern shore of Lake Erie. It had once been a massive source of income for the City of Lackawanna, but was now just a rust-belt skeleton.

He said, "There's a multitude of sins buried out there."

From the sound of it, he didn't just mean the environmental kind. I'm sure there were others.

As the night wound down, neither Pete nor I ever took off our masks—though I was tempted to for the Gold Tinman. When we were finally heading out, I said to Cuffy, "You still don't know who I am," and we made our escape without ever paying for a drink.

The following week, we had to make our regular trip from Erie back up to Buffalo to collect the money being fenced by Butch. We were still running a bar tab at The Old Pony Post until that bill was paid in full. After getting our payment and knocking back a few rounds, Pete said we had to stop in at Cuffy's joint — The Park Grille.

As we pulled up, I told Pete, "You gotta let me walk in by myself and talk to Cuffy."

I walked in alone, straight up to the bar. "Hey, Cuffy, how ya doin'?" He gave me a hard look, suspicious, and said, "I'm sorry, I don't believe I've made your acquaintance."

Right on cue, Pete came walking through the door.

Once again, Cuffy yelled, "Peter Russell, you son of a bitch!"

I grinned and said, "Yeah, but you still owe me a drink."

A while later, Pete had to take a two-year vacation at Mercer Correctional Facility, halfway between Erie and Pittsburgh. I drove down to pick him up on his release date. We took I-79 back north, stopping off for a few drinks along the way, and eventually bar-hopped across Erie, half terrifying everyone who saw the two of us back together again.

We ended up at one of our old stomping grounds, The Ole Monte Club. As the night went on, we pulled two stools together at the bar and ordered a round. Pete got his "C.C."—a shot of Canadian Club. I got Grandma Murphy's favorite, a shot of "B.V."—Black Velvet.

Right as we were about to raise our glasses, Pete asked, "Timmy, the whole time I was in there, was Patty a good girl? Did you ever make it with Patty?"

I looked down at my shot of B.V., gulped, thought for a second, then slammed it down and said, "Well, Pete, would you like to answer that same question about Mary?"

Pete looked at his C.C., slammed it back, and said, "On second thought, let's forget I ever asked that question."

We were that tight of friends. We shared everything —everything. We were closer than brothers. We were partners. Partners in crime.

Pete was planning to skip court, but his mother had signed over her house to the bail bondsman and would lose it if he didn't show up. I was reading over his bond paperwork and noticed a clause that said they couldn't take her home in the case of "apparent death."

I told him he could stage his own suicide. So, he wrote a note, tucked it into his Bible along with a few personal items, and rode his motorcycle to Shade's Beach, near the Pennsylvania-New York border. Then he disappeared for over ten years.

When they finally found him in California, he was brought back, sentenced to prison, served his time, and then did it all over again for another decade.

The Erie Times-News captured it best:

Peter Michael Russell, convicted of two high-profile Erie burglaries decades ago, faked his suicide to avoid prosecution in 1984. He was found after 10 years, sentenced to prison, and released. In 2003, he disappeared again in yet another attempt to outrun the authorities in Erie. Russell, once described in court as a "soldier" in a local organized-crime faction, has turned up once more. He is now 61 years old, alive, and still wanted by the law.

Erie police on Friday arrested Russell in two outstanding cases -- a forgery investigation from December 2002 and a hit and run from July 2002 --

after police in Las Vegas apprehended him there on Jan. 12, officials said. The Las Vegas police picked up Russell on a bench warrant that Erie County Judge Michael E. Dunlavey issued in 2003 over a probation violation in a prior burglary case, Erie County Chief Deputy Sheriff Jon Habursky said. The Las Vegas police encountered Russell after responding to a call for a domestic disturbance at a residence on Jan. 12, said Officer Laura Metzler, a police spokeswoman. She said the police filed no charges over the reported disturbance, but checked the records on Russell and arrested him on the warrant from Erie County. Erie County sheriff's deputies flew to Las Vegas to get Russell two weeks ago. Once he was at the Erie County Prison, the Erie police arrested him for the forgery and hit-and-run cases.

Russell, who was on the Erie police's most-wanted list for some time, was arraigned by Erie 2nd Ward District Judge Paul Urbaniak and ordered held at the Erie County Prison on $10,250 bond. Russell remained there on Tuesday. His preliminary hearings in the 2002 cases are set for Monday.

Russell was a well-known fugitive in the past. On Sept. 10, 1984, he was to appear on the first day of his trial on charges that he burglarized a home on East 12th Street of $29,000 in cash and $500 to $600 in silver coins in 1979. Instead of showing up, Russell faked his suicide by leaving behind a pile of clothes, a Bible, and a bogus suicide note at Shades Beach in Harborcreek Township.

He eluded authorities until police in San Bernardino, Calif., near Los Angeles, arrested him in 1994. Back in Erie, Russell pleaded guilty to the East 12th Street burglary and another heist that netted $65,000 from a residence on Royal Avenue in 1982. Police said the high-profile cases were related to an organized crime investigation in Erie, including the involvement of Samuel "Fat Sam" Esper, a purported racketeer who entered the federal witness-protection program. Russell's past came to light at his sentencing in the burglary cases in Erie County Court in January 1995. His lawyer, A.J. Adams, then an assistant public defender, described Russell as a "soldier" for an organized-crime faction.

"He has spent the last 10 years of his life looking over his shoulder for either the government or organized crime," Adams said in court. Erie County Judge Stephanie Domitrovich sentenced Russell to two to five years in state prison and ordered him to perform 10 years of probation, including 500 hours of community service. Russell was paroled in May 1997, according to the Pennsylvania Board of Probation and Parole.

Five years later, Erie police charged him with the hit-and-run and forgery cases. He disappeared before the police could arrest him. Police accused Russell of leaving the scene of an accident at West 18th and Sassafras streets in June 2002. In the other case, according to court records, police accused Russell of forging five checks and conspiring to forge two others that an Erie convenience store cashed in late December 2002. The police said the checks totaled $1,167.

Russell, his latest foray as a fugitive over, is now facing another prosecution, 17 years after his long-awaited court appearance in January 1995.

"All I remember is that he faked his own death," Adams, Russell's former lawyer, said on Tuesday. "I wish I could remember more. But 17 years — there are many clients in between."[1]

Copyright 2012 - Erie Times-News, Pa. McClatchy-Tribune News Service

---

[1] *Pa. Fugitive Who Once Faked Suicide Found Again," Erie Times-News,* Feb. 22, 2012

That was my best friend Pete, and even though we lost touch for more than thirty years, once my brother Jack forwarded me that article, I went looking. I found Bobby and learned where Pete was doing time in Pennsylvania. We reconnected for the last few years of his life, and it was like we'd never missed a beat. We were always partners, and he proved the point: that kind of bond doesn't end.

When Bobby died in May 2016, Pete came up to Buffalo and stayed with my wife and me for about a week. He met my whole family and made a connection with my son Johnny that I didn't even know about. When Pete went back to Pittsburgh, he and Johnny stayed in touch on Facebook. John even created a Facebook profile under the name "Casey Russell," another Russell brother. Johnny was known around town and in the drug circles as "Casey Buffalo Jones." He was pretty well known in the local bar music scene, the festivals, "festies," he used to call them, and in the drug game. He wasn't some punk. He had a direct line to the regional plug who lived in Rochester and controlled most of the product in the region. This guy sold products to anyone moving weight, from organized crime to biker gangs. He fronted, on consignment, over five thousand dollars' worth of cocaine, acid, molly, and other drugs to push in the Buffalo area. I didn't know about this until after the fact, after John missed some payments.

I ended up driving John to the plug's house and walking right up to the door to make it clear: if he fucked with my son, he'd have to go through me. Johnny had told the plug about my reputation. I told him right up front that if he wanted me dead, he better do it then and there, because I wasn't calling no cops and he wouldn't see me coming. We left with an understanding: I'd straighten things out, and he'd leave my son alone.

On the ride home, I asked John how he had blown the deal. He told me he'd fronted most of the drugs to a local trap house, a place full of transients coming and going, always wheeling and dealing—rookie mistake. I was furious, but it was done.

Less than a week later, Pete called and said he had to come to Buffalo to attend to some business. I told him he always had a place to stay. He showed up the next day and, without the usual small talk, said, "We have to go see Johnny." I was surprised, but on the drive, Pete explained he and John were Facebook friends under the assumed name "Casey Russell." John had told him everything about the plug and the trap house, and Pete was there to make it right.

We picked up John, and Pete wasn't joking. "Where's the drug house?" he asked. John took us straight there. Pete turned to Johnny in the back seat and told him to go in and bring the main dude back out to the car. John did what he was told. Pete and I slipped back into old roles, doing what we did best.

We waited in a funeral home parking lot across the street from the trap house. A few minutes later, John came out with the dealer. Pete was standing outside the car using a cane. I didn't know how far gone he was, but he was doing this one last job for his old partner. The guy walked up to the car, and Pete flipped back into the gangster I'd known. He told the guy he was going back in and bringing out any drugs and money owed to John, and if that didn't happen, we were going to take everything and leave no witnesses. He made it plain he'd come back from Pennsylvania and not leave anyone standing. The dealer understood. He went in, grabbed the stash and the cash, and brought it back out. Pete made it clear the dealer had better pay John weekly or he'd be back, and there wouldn't be any introductions next time.

They straightened things out with the plug. That's a partner.

I traveled to Pittsburgh several times to see Pete after they told him he had prostate cancer. One of the last times we sat at a table together, he said, "Did I ever thank you for blowing up Crazy Bobby's car in Patty's driveway?"

I was caught off guard. I had forgotten about that for almost four decades until the memory hit me. After Pete was sentenced for one of his many felonies and was in prison, I was driving by Patty's house at two or three in the morning when I saw Crazy Bobby's car in her driveway. There was an unwritten rule: respect a man's wife or girlfriend for a decent amount of time, then be discreet. There had been no waiting period and no discretion.

I pulled the car down the street. I had an old sheet and a gallon of gas in the trunk. I stuffed the sheet into the gas tank filler tube, doused the car and interior with gas, and lit the sheet. The car burned to the ground right in her driveway. The next day, a picture and a headline appeared in the local paper. We used to cut those pictures and articles out and mail them to the right people with no return address. The message was always received. That trick had been used before, and it worked.

Pete never forgot. He always knew who had his back. Partners. I was with him when he died in Pittsburgh, just like I had been with JR when he died in Our Lady of Victory Hospital decades earlier. I miss you, bro. In the wind. Partners to the end.

Murph and Pete - Pittsburgh 2019

Murph the Surf Younger Days 1980

Peter "DR" Russell - Blasdell, NY

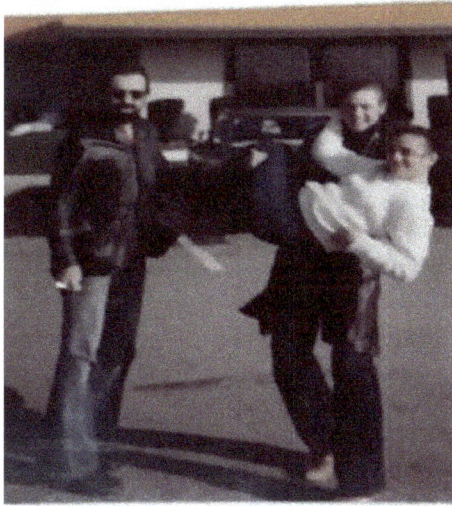

*Peter, Murph, Joi Blasdell, NY – 1980 - Our Secret Meeting - Place Buffalo
South Motor Lodge*

Peter, Mitzi, Murphy   *Peter feeling No Pain*   *Mitzi in Uniform*

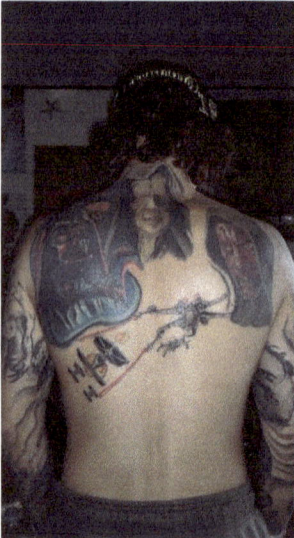

John Michael "Casey Russell" Murphy

December 21, 1989 – December 26, 2016 – Member of the 27 Club!
My Only Regret in Life is that I let him know about "Murph the Surf."
Every Son tries to outdo his Father!

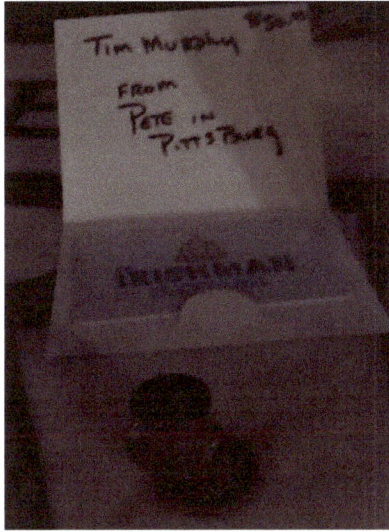

One last gift from Peter in Penna. In 2019, Pete sent this for my birthday. Sent from Pittsburgh to Williamsville, NY

This was mine and JR's Grifters' trick – A quarter, a nickel, and a dime balanced. JR worked the Grift... I worked out the physics! "There's a trick to every trick, and a hustle to every hustle." JR and I often drank for 40 cents a night. And I picked up more beautiful women by promising to tell the secret. Which JR made me promise to only tell beautiful women... It worked!

CHAPTER 06
BOBBY "R.J." RUSSELL

Bobby was the middle Russell brother. J.R., or Jimmy Russell, was the oldest. He was my mentor. Peter, Dr. Russell, the youngest, was my best friend. We lived together and shared apartments.

Bobby was between them in age. Both Peter and J.R. had come to Erie; they weren't from there originally. J.R. had been sent from Buffalo to handle collections and bring money to Westfield.

Peter had been living in New Jersey with Mitzi, the Playboy Bunny. Things got too hot for him down there, and he had to leave. That's how he ended up in Erie, where I met him.

Bobby Russell was the middle brother. He mostly stayed up in Buffalo. The Russells were from Lackawanna, a steel town outside Buffalo. Bobby ran two good restaurants there, the Boston Sea Party and the Passport, which comes into this story later. He always worked and always had something going on. But when things got rough in Erie, J.R. would call him for backup.

The code was "bring the cousins." The cousins were Smith & Wesson. Bobby had a .357 Magnum and a .44 snub nose, both chrome-plated. When he showed up, it meant things were serious.

He also ran a seafood business, hauling frozen shrimp and fish in a refrigerated truck from Buffalo to Erie once a week to supply local restaurants. But Bobby had one significant weakness: gambling. He couldn't stop.

One night, he called J.R. in a panic. "They're gonna break my legs," he said. He owed ten grand in gambling debts to the mob. That was the scariest night of my life.

After Stefano Magaddino died in 1974, Buffalo was in chaos. Magaddino had ruled the Buffalo mob — known as *The Arm* — for nearly fifty years. He wasn't just a boss; he was one of Lucky Luciano's original Commission members, the so-called sixth family. He was senior among Sicilians in America and carried more weight than anyone. When disputes broke out among the New York families, Magaddino's crew came down from Buffalo to settle it.

After his death, there was no clear successor, and that's when everything in Buffalo started to unravel. Russell Bufalino, the same man from *The Irishman*, began to move in.

There's *Kill the Irishman,* and then there's *The Irishman.* Two separate stories entirely. *Kill the Irishman* was about Danny Greene in Cleveland. *The Irishman* was about Jimmy Hoffa — his disappearance and his ties to the mob.

Hoffa's connection to organized crime started with Russell Bufalino. Bufalino was originally from Buffalo but was later sent to run the eastern part of Pennsylvania, the Scranton area. He wasn't just another mob boss. He served as a kind of counselor to all five New York families when there were disputes that didn't call for violence — the kind that didn't need Stefano Magaddino's muscle; they called in Bufalino to negotiate.

When Magaddino died, Bufalino came back to Buffalo and began taking over the rackets and gambling operations that had been left wide open. That's who Bobby Russell owed money to — the Bufalino outfit. They were heavy-duty, no joke.

Bobby called J.R. in a panic, saying he needed help. J.R. called me and said, "Bring the melon thumper."

That part, the melon thumper, is why I've been hesitant to write this chapter. I've even talked to my lawyer about it. I made a lot of money in my life doing two things: setting up scanners and making silencers. I was a machinist by trade. I worked a couple of years in Akron, Ohio, with my father in his machine shop, so I knew how to build things most people only read about. So JR would draw parts on napkins. He never told me what they were. I was a second-shift maintenance man at a small machine shop with a milling machine, lathe, and drill press, and I could whip up a silencer in a few hours. JR had gotten a MAC-10 machine pistol. If you scroll down through my video clips, you'll find two that feature a MAC-10; one even shows it with the factory silencer. They originally started MAC-10s for the CIA and Vietnam as assassin weapons. They took a 50-round magazine and could dump fifty rounds in two seconds. Put an 18-inch silencer on one, and you had a melon-thumper. With that suppressor on, what came out sounded like someone plucking a melon.

But I had just built this melon thumper. I'd machined it, and JR always gave me the honor of firing the first round out of a fuckin" silencer, which you could blow your hand off with if things weren't fuckin" correct. My stepfather had worked at a brass and copper mill foundry, and he had those large asbestos-like barbecue mitts used there. I took one of those mitts — it went all the way up to your elbow — and I cut a finger hole in it so I could stick my trigger finger out through the barbecue mitt.

Then you go to the corner of a concrete block building, stick your arm around the corner with the gun, and fire the first fuckin" shot. Get past the first shot, and you're gold. If you don't, it can be catastrophic. If the silencer and barrel aren't aligned properly, it could blow up in your hand. I'd finished this melon thumper a few days earlier and fired a couple of rounds out of it, but never an entire clip. That's another thing: when you go full automatic and empty a clip, the barrel gets hotter than a two-dollar pistol. I'd never done a full test fire on it.

Then JR called and said, "Bring the melon thumper, we're going up the Buffalo." I was like, Oh, fuck. I followed orders. JR and I drove down to Lackawanna, N.Y., and JR explained it to me. He said, "Now, you take the friggin Cadillac. You pull it around. You pull it a little bit down from the bar that we were going to meet Bufalino's men in, and you keep an eye on that front door. There's gonna be a big black Cadillac pull up, and I'm gonna walk right up to that car, and we're gonna have a little talk. If I turn around and walk away and walk back into the bar, you sit and wait till that black Cadillac leaves. But if I turn around and I hit the fuckin" deck, meaning lay flat in the freaking street, you empty that clip into that fuckin" car."

At that point in my life, I would have done it unquestionably. But believe me, I was shaking in my pants. It wasn't what you sign up for, but that's how this whole thing goes: things happen in front of your eyes, and you're in, or you're out. If you're out, they've got a place for you.

We were sitting there, and just as he said, the big black Cadillac pulled up. Bobby was inside the bar. JR was sitting in the Cadillac with me. JR gets out of the Cadillac before the guys even fuckin" get out of the Cadillac. He walks up to the back of that friggin Cadillac, and the first thing he does is pound on the window. I thought, holy shit. The back window rolls down a little, and I hear a discussion, not the particulars. Then I hear JR's voice say, "Do you know who the fuck I am in this town? I will wipe out you and your family name."

I'm holding my fuckin" breath. I do not know what will happen. JR turns and gives me the eye. The Mac-10 with the melon-thumper is lying across my lap, and my finger is on the fuckin" trigger. JR turns slowly and walks into the bar. The guys wait a few minutes, and then they drive off.

I throw the melon-thumper in the trunk of the Cadillac and go inside. Bobby and JR are drinking. We're partying, having a good time, and then JR starts on him: "You're a degenerate gambler. You gotta stop this. See what you make me do?"

We partied till four in the morning, which is when bars used to close in Buffalo. Four o'clock comes, and we're gonna roll, I'm gonna drive him back to Erie. Bobby took off in his car. I turned the key in the Cadillac, and it was as dead as a doornail. Had we gotten into a gun battle, we'd have been stranded. It wasn't just the battery; it was the starter. The car chose that moment to die.

"JR" says, "Looks like we're sleeping here till the morning." There were no cell phones then, no 24-hour service shops. He says, "We gotta wait till my buddy's garage opens up at eight o'clock. I'm going to sleep in the back seat. Wake me up at eight." I was still nervous that the black Cadillac was gonna come back. JR went to sleep in the back seat. I went to the trunk, pulled out the melon-thumper and laid it across my lap. I didn't sleep. I tried to close my eyes, but I sat up, vigilant, till sunup. At eight, I woke him; he gave me a number to call, and ten minutes later, a tow truck arrived. They hooked the Cadillac, put a new starter in it, and within an hour, we were on our way.

That was my first real dealing with Bobby Russell. Bobby had stories for days. Unlike JR and Peter, who were fearless, Bobby was cautious. JR and Peter ran at things; nothing intimidated them. Bobby was careful and precise. JR groomed people to do his dirty work, and the first person he groomed was Bobby, the middle brother.

Bobby eventually got cold feet. He and JR committed a burglary and got busted. They took all the money, but Bobby grabbed the change as well; the bag broke, or something, and that's what helped pin them down. Bobby and JR did a couple of years for that. After that, Bobby wanted out. He enlisted in the Marines for a four-year stint and became proficient with weapons. Bobby knew weapons. I think he joined the Marines to get away from JR. He thought it was his only way out.

"JR" started grooming Peter, teaching him how to crack safes and bypass alarm systems. Bobby was different from the other two brothers. He only worked with his brothers and me. I was the only other person Bobby would ever work with.

At one point, both Peter and JR were in jail, serving relatively short sentences, rather than being held for long-term charges. They were off the street. Bobby calls me up in Erie. He says, "Timmy, you've got to come down." He's in Buffalo, I'm in Erie. He's so paranoid he won't even talk on the phone. "No, Timmy, you've got to come down. I got to talk to you."

It was wintertime. I said, 'All right, I'll be down.' I drive down from Erie to Buffalo and meet Bobby. He's living in Raintree Island, a suburb in Tonawanda, outside Buffalo. At the time, he had a beautiful young girlfriend, way out of his league. She was strait-laced and didn't know what Bobby, JR, Peter, or I did.

Bobby gave me the address of a bar to meet him at, the Golden Pheasant in Tonawanda. I show up. It's a pool bar. I started shooting pool by myself. Soon, Bobby shows up, and we start talking while playing. Then the Kingsman biker crew walks in, the president, his old lady, the sergeant at arms, and a few others. They put a quarter on the pool table. I try to be polite. "Hey, the table's yours. We're just here having fun, trying to talk."

The president goes, "No, my old lady wants to shoot doubles. We're gonna shoot you guys doubles." I didn't want to play; I just wanted to find out what Bobby had to say. But they were insistent, so I said, "All right." Bobby and I were both good, so we agreed.

We rack the balls. Bobby breaks playin' eight ball. He makes two balls. Five of our balls are left on the table. The Kingsman lets his old lady shoot first; she misses. I step up and run all five balls in a row, calling every shot, exactly like I called it. Seven balls are left for them, plus the eight ball. I can't see a direct shot on the eight ball.

My father had taught me a trick when I was eleven: a four-cushion bank shot using the diamonds on the table. My father, a trigonometry genius due to his work in the mold shop, knew every angle. Those diamonds on the pool table were markers, and I knew how to use them.

I saw the shot—the path was there. I could make that four-cushion bank. I called it: eight ball in the corner, four cushions. I lined up, clicked the cue, bing, bing, bing, bing, clunk. The eight ball went in.

The place went dead quiet. You could cut the air with a knife. Bobby came walking up to me, his back to the Kingsman. I'm holding my cue, he's holding his. He leans in and whispers, "Whatever you do, don't let that fuckin' cue stick out of your hand. Because we may need it to get out of here."

He was worried they were gonna kick our asses. But the Kingsman president appreciated the shot. We didn't want to play; I'd come to talk to Bobby. The table's yours, I said. They ended up buying us a drink for winning the game. My friend and I slipped into a corner and talked.

Bobby had run two classy restaurants, the Passport and the Boston Sea Party. He no longer worked at them, but he still had the safe combinations. He said, "Timmy, I got these combinations, but we gotta check it out. We can't just use the combination. We gotta make it look like the safe was broken into." I said, Alright, give me the addresses. He gave them to me, along with the combinations. He thought I was joking because JR always said you watch something three times before moving on.

I went first to the Boston Sea Party, but it was closed due to blizzard conditions and impaired driving. So, I drove to the Passport. That building sat on Transit Road near the I-90 exit. The parking lot had only a few cars because of the storm. I walked in, sat at the bar, and ordered a Black Velvet and Coke.

There were four or five guys at the bar. I worked the room a little, charming the barmaid, and told her I was from out of town, my car was broken down, and I was waiting for a tow. She was doing last call because the weather was getting worse. She started walking the patrons out the back door. I said, "Honey, the tow truck isn't here yet. Could I use your pay phone before you kick me out?" She said, 'Sure,' and she let the last folks out and locked the door.

So there I was, the barmaid and me, locked in, the storm howling outside.

I put on my leather gloves before I went to the phone. I always carried that little .25 automatic with the barrel threaded for a silencer. I didn't have the silencer with me that night, but I had the .25. Bobby had given me the cousin — the .357 bullnose —, and I had that tucked down the back of my pants.

When I came out of the phone booth, she was locking up. I had the .357 in my hand — chrome plated, a monster of a piece. She almost shit. She went hysterical. I said, "Honey, I'm not here to hurt you. I'm not gonna hurt you at all." Then I told her the first thing we were gonna do was clean up the bar and wash all those glasses. My prints were on at least two of them, and probably on the bar, so I made her wash every glass and wipe down the bar with Windex until it was spotless.

"Now, honey, we've got to go back to the office," I said. "That's where the safe is." She was petrified. I kept reassuring her, "Honey, I'm not here to hurt you." I warned her again: Please don't look me in the eyes. She'd already seen my face; I didn't want her to memorize it.

In the back room was the safe, as big as a refrigerator, a two-door monster. A beautiful mahogany desk, a friendly office, and a black leather couch. I told her to lie down, face down on that couch. She probably didn't know if I was gonna kill her or fuck her. I threw a coat over her head so she couldn't watch what I was doing.

I hadn't only brought guns. I had burglary tools: pry bars, a chisel, and enough to make it look like the safe had been forced. I dialed the combination, opened the safe, then started beating the hell out of it. I broke the dial off, making it look compromised. I opened it up, and there was about $26,000 in cash. The owner wasn't just a restaurant owner; he was also a bookie. That's how we picked targets: people who couldn't call the cops. Drug dealers, bookies, anyone doing dirt. They couldn't go to the police, so we took their money.

I'd stuffed the cash into a canvas bag I kept inside the lining of a long leather coat. I still have that coat, with the right-hand pocket ripped out so a sawed-off shotgun could fit. I put the burglar tools in the bag, stuffed the cash in, and zipped it up. "Okay, honey," I said. "We're done here. You can let me out." She got up, eyes wide, thinking I was gonna kill her. I told her, "Just let me out, and you'll never see me again."

We walked to the back door, the same door she'd let the others out of. She unlocked it, still not believing I was actually leaving her alone. I think she was in shock. I turned to her and said, "Now, honey, I've been nothing but a gentleman to you all night. Would you do me one favor?"

She looked at me, confused. "What's that?"

"Would you give me five minutes before you call the cops?"

She laughed a little, then said, "I gotta go to the bathroom and have a pee. I gotta have a cigarette. You got a good 15 minutes."

"Thank you, young lady," I said, leaned over, kissed her, and left. The snow was blowing hard as I headed back to Bobby's apartment, knowing his girlfriend was there, straight as could be.

Back at Bobby's, I said, "Bobby, we gotta talk."

"We could talk," he replied.

"No, Bobby, we gotta go in the bedroom."

In the bedroom, I pulled the canvas bag out of my coat lining and plopped it on the bed, then pulled out the cash: twenty-six grand.

"What did you do?" Bobby asked, eyes wide.

"I told you if I saw it, I was gonna do it," I said.

"Holy shit, Timmy, what did you do?"

"I told you I was gonna do it if one looked right."

Immediately, he said, "Timmy, you gotta get out of town. You gotta get out of town."

"Bobby, it's a blizzard. I ain't going nowhere. I'm gonna get a stripper and a hotel room for a couple of days."

"No, Timmy. You gotta get out of town now."

I didn't know why he was so paranoid until two summers ago. I ran into a guy at a bar who'd been a maitre d for Russell Salvatore here in Buffalo. Russell Salvatore owns the finest dining restaurants, Salvatore's Italian Gardens, Russell Steaks, Chops and More, and he's known for putting TVs in every hospital room in Buffalo General and Mercy Hospital.

Apparently, the owner of the Passport was Russell's older brother, Anthony, who knew many mafiosi. I hadn't known that at the time, or I might've had second thoughts about robbing it. Two years ago, the maître d' casually mentioned that he used to work for Anthony at the Passport. That's when I finally put the puzzle together: that's who owned the Passport.

Bobby was losing it. He couldn't believe I'd actually gone through with it. Now he's shoving me toward the door, telling me to get the hell out and drive back to Erie. I'm thinking, *holy fuck.*

I get in my car, hit the I-90, and head toward Erie. By the time I reached Dunkirk, New York, halfway between Buffalo and Erie, the storms were brutal. Snow and wind are coming sideways. Then I see nothing but red brake lights ahead; the interstates were at a standstill. People are stuck in traffic on the I-90 for hours.

So, there I am, sitting in the car with a hot piece and thirteen grand—my half, stuffed beside me. It's a whiteout outside, dead silence inside. I remember telling you before, I've smoked weed just about every day for fifty years. I had some in the car, but nothing to roll it with: no papers, no pipe, nothing. The only thing in the ashtray was a crumpled Erie City parking ticket. I pull it out, flatten it, rip it into four strips, and roll four joints out of a parking ticket.

So now I'm sitting in the car, smoking those makeshift joints, nodding off in a snowstorm, when someone starts pounding on my window. I jump. It's this guy in a little four-wheel-drive truck yelling, "Hey, either pull over or join in—we're starting a caravan through!"

I yell back, "Man, I'm right behind you!"

He pulls out, I fall in line behind him, gripping the wheel, white-knuckled, crawling down the I-90 in his tire tracks. We move inch by inch, but at least we're moving.

Eventually, I see a road sign—Route 20. I don't even remember taking the exit; I must've followed his taillights right off the highway. That road runs between Buffalo and Erie, so I figure I'm okay. I start to get my bearings—

almost to Harborcreek, Pennsylvania, right near the state line. I'm about forty-five minutes from Erie. On a normal day, it'd be twenty, but this storm's chewing up the road.

I keep creeping along, trying to stay awake, when I see yellow lights behind me. Snowplows. Perfect. I think, *great, I'll let them pass and then follow them the rest of the way.*

I edge over, still rolling, and let them by. As they pass, they kick up a wall of snow that dumps right over my windshield, completely burying it. I can't see a damn thing.

My windshield wipers froze and couldn't even move. They stalled right out. I thought, ah, fuck, I gotta get out and clear the windshield. I step out to free up the wiper blades, and the moment I take my foot off the gas, the car dies. I try turning the key, but it's as dead as a doornail. Going so slow for so long had drained the battery. Now I'm in the middle of a blizzard, hot, with cash and a gun.

I grab the canvas bag from the trunk, take out the burglar tools, leave them in the trunk, tuck the canvas bag into my coat, and start walking along Route 20, looking for civilization. Down the road, a yellow light appears. I flag it down; it's a Red Cross vehicle. They're rescuing people because the power's out and folks are losing heat. Thank God they stopped for me. I hop in, and the driver says, "We're taking people to the local high school as a warming shelter. Hop in."

I sit up front, and in the backseat, there's a small family: a man, a wife, and two kids, huddled, shivering. I think, holy shit, I'm being rescued by the Red Cross. I'm along for the ride. We move down Route 20, and I'm not thrilled about spending the night in a high school gym. Then I see neon lights on the horizon, a bar sign. Fiddle Inn. Snow blowing, half a dozen snowplows in the lot. I figure someone inside might give me a ride to Erie. I tell the Red Cross driver, "Just let me out here," and he drops me off in the parking lot.

Inside, at least half a dozen guys are at the bar with the owner behind it. If you want a ride, the only way is to buy a drink. I do. I say, "Hey, anyone going to Erie tonight? $100, give me a ride." No takers. I even tried offering $500, but still no one. It's that bad out. Gradually, everyone else leaves, except for the owner and me. I had told him what had happened, how my car was stranded, and that the Red Cross had rescued me. He says, "Let me make a call." He contacts the local garage, tells me not to worry, and assures me that they'll tow the car in the morning, put it in the garage, and let it thaw.

Still hoping for a ride, I wait. The owner says, "There's a little inn down the way. I know the owner. I can call and see if she can give you a room, and I can give you a ride there." I agree. He calls the owner of the Rainbow Inn, a small highway motel with maybe a dozen rooms, and I get a room. No TV, just an AM radio, but I'm safe. I'm in the room.

I figured I was better off than where we were, any port in a storm. I decided to get some sleep, knowing I'd wake up in the morning and call the garage with the number the owner had given me.

Morning comes, and there isn't even a phone in the room. I have to go to the office. I open my motel door, and there's three feet of snow halfway up the door. I can't even make it to the office. I think, holy shit, I'm stuck here for a while. Fortunately, around lunchtime, the owner's husband clears a path and even brings me a hamburger and fries. I finally get to the office and call the garage. They'd already picked up the car that morning and were thawing it out, charging the battery, friendly little community.

I didn't get home for three days from when I originally left Erie. I ended up spending a second night at the Rainbow Inn. When I finally made it home, I was living with Mary Ellen DeSanto, the love of my life, who later died of an overdose while I was in prison. There were no cell phones back then, so I had no way to update anyone or call ahead.

I get back home, and she's pitchin' a bitch, going off about me going up to Buffalo and probably messing around with some stripper. It took me a couple of days to calm that down.

About a week later, I got a piece of mail at my house, addressed to me, with no return address. I open it and pull out an article from the *Buffalo News*—headline: *Kissing Bandit Strikes*, the story of the Passport robbery. Bobby had cut the article out and sent it to me in an envelope. We used to do that to each other after favors.

CHAPTER 07

JIMMY "ELMER" DESANTO

Jimmy "Elmer" DeSanto came with a name that already carried weight in Erie. He was the eldest son of the Frank DeSanto clan. Frank had his seat at the Erie Daily Times sports page for so long that people said he came with the building. The man always had the right tips, the right angle, the right pull. Folks pretended it wasn't power, but everybody knew better.

The family was already cracked when I showed up in their orbit and fell for Mary Ellen DeSanto. My first great love. The kind that makes you stop and look at your own life like you walked into the wrong movie.

Even with the parents long divorced, something held them together. It wasn't a perfect picture. It wasn't polished. It was something else that hit me harder than I expected. I wanted it. I wanted all of it. The noise. The routine. The comfort of people who didn't run from each other, even when they had reasons to.

Saturday evenings at the DeSanto' house were a whole event. Mama DeSanto would stand over the stove, turning out meatballs like she was feeding half of Erie. Pork and beef, mixed by hand. She'd sear them in a heavy pan, one batch after another, and the smell told you Sunday was already coming. That sauce would simmer low throughout the morning. Nobody rushed it. Nobody questioned her method.

By Sunday afternoon, everyone circled the pot as if it were a treasure. Bread dipped straight into the sauce. Meatballs disappeared before they ever hit a plate. Nobody stood on ceremony. If you didn't grab one, someone else would.

When the pasta finally landed on the table, the whole thing shifted into something loud and warm. A table full of people who didn't pretend to be perfect but somehow held together anyway. I used to sit there and study it, as if I were trying to catch a secret.

My own family had its bond, sure, but it didn't move like theirs. The Murphy clan had its own rhythm, but it never came close to the DeSanto pull. They had a way of making you feel like you stepped into a world where people fought hard, loved harder, and kept coming back to the table.

That was the doorway. That was the start. And that was what kept me in their orbit long before I understood the cost.

Our family came out of a night that could have wrecked anybody. My father, Jack Murphy, went through the bathroom door and almost killed my mother, Donna Mae Krill Murphy. I was the only one of the seven of us who saw it with my own eyes. My brother, Jack, was in the Navy and never wanted to accept that it had happened. My three older sisters, Judy, Margie, and Diane, stayed locked in the upstairs rooms until sunrise, as if they were waiting for someone to tell them the storm had passed.

I was downstairs in the little bedroom off the kitchen. Oldest of the three youngest boys. Timothy, Patrick, and baby Michael. That poor kid got it from us. Nothing cruel, just that rough brand of family humor where you jump on the youngest because he can't fight back yet. We weren't gentle with him, but it came from the same twisted love every family claims.

I was the only one bold or foolish enough to crack that door open when I was about eight or nine. That's when I saw Jack Murphy in full rage go through the bathroom door, as it offended him personally. I swear that moment flipped a switch in me. Little Timmy died right there, and something else moved in, something that didn't need much to set it off. The exact trigger my father carried.

My older brother Jack used to tell me stories about Dad and Uncle Bill. Uncle Bill's uncle had once rescued my father in the middle of the Pacific, so the two of them had a bond that most people wouldn't understand. They repurchased an old hearse in the day to haul ashes. The thing stalled in the middle of an intersection. Dad wore a new overcoat, heading to church. Uncle Bill was driving, and Jackie sat between them.

Dad got out and lifted the hood to figure out what was wrong. The engine backfired, causing a fire in the carburetor. Dad yanked off that new overcoat and smothered the flames. Right then, the car behind them honked. Not a smart move. Jackie said he saw it happen in Dad's eyes. That overcoat was ruined, and the man in the other car had just volunteered to pay the price.

Dad walked back slowly and steadily. The guy inside must have seen the same thing because he started rolling up his window. He didn't stand a chance. Dad snapped that window in pieces with his bare hands until there was nothing left to roll. Then he reached in, hauled the man through the opening, and beat him in the street until Uncle Bill dragged him off.

Grandma Murphy had to make another call to the mayor's office. Thomas Flaterly. They played cards together across from the Erie Police station, so she knew exactly who would pick up the phone.

That was the bloodline I came from. That was the engine under the hood. And I knew it early.

That night in World War II carved something into him, and I'm convinced it passed straight down the line. I carried the same hair-trigger. I could walk into a bar calm and walk out after turning the whole place upside down, and it happened more than once. JR used to look at me and say, "You know what I like about you, Kid? You got snapability." His words meant we could be sitting there, having a solid night, with people laughing, nothing tense, and then one fool would say the wrong thing, and the switch would flip. Dr. Jekyll and Mr. Hyde without the lab coat.

"JR" knew exactly how that switch worked. He kept me like a pit bull on a tight chain, and I did the jobs he aimed me at. He didn't need speeches or instructions. He pointed, and that was enough.

Another story my Grandma Murphy told me about my father came out during that long ride to Ashtabula, Ohio. She let it all spill. She said when he came back, "I don't know what they did to my boy, but he was never the same boy that I sent over there." Back then, it was called shell shock or battle fatigue. Today we'd call it PTSD, and nobody pretends it's imaginary anymore. She said that while he was at the San Diego naval base, he saw two orderlies roughing up a serviceman who was already down, and he snapped—nearly killed both men with his hands. The Navy tried to hit him with attempted murder because both of those guys ended up in the hospital.

My Grandma Murphy got in her Cadillac and drove from Erie all the way to San Diego with rolls of hundred-dollar bills, 1927 silver certificates, crisp because she kept them rolled in coffee cans. She showed up to rescue her son, something she did more than once for the only boy she had.

I swore I'd never drag anyone through that kind of madness. Then I turned around and lived out the same pattern almost perfectly when I caught my wife, Laura Lynn Sorce Murphy, cheating on me. My first thought was, "Can we call it even now?" because years earlier, I had been the one who crossed that line. I ended it cleanly, but forgiveness never arrived. Not once. Not as long as I stayed at Dunlop Tire, where my mistress worked. I put a gun to my head and forced myself to leave Dunlop for General Motors, hoping a fresh start would give me a chance, but that didn't change anything. She was a vengeful Sicilian with a long memory, and she kept a running scorecard.

It reminded me of that scene in *Goodfellas* when all the wives sit around swapping stories like it's just another Tuesday. That's how it felt with us. Nothing ever seemed out of place because everyone we ran with lived similarly. Lawyers on speed dial, bail money ready, someone always getting grabbed for something. That was everyday life. And in the middle of all that chaos stood James "Elmer" DeSanto, the ultimate Swiss Army knife of larceny. He had that Joe Pesci energy from *Goodfellas*—the guy who didn't just steal because he needed to. He stole because he loved the thrill of it. When a score was done, he'd hang out the car window, firing his .357 like it was part of the celebration.

Jimmy was one of the toughest men I've ever met. He and Carmen Fargo did a five-year bid down near Pittsburgh in their early twenties, and Western State Penitentiary was no playground. When he came home, nobody tried to tell him. Nobody tested him. He wasn't big—maybe five-eight, maybe one-seventy, but if I had to walk down a dark alley, he's the one I'd want beside me every single time.

His nickname alone said it all. Elmer didn't come from anything—wasn't a middle name, wasn't a family name. Yet he had it tattooed on his upper shoulder like a dare. He waited for someone to say, "Oh, Elmer... that's pretty funny, huh… like Elmer Fudd." He'd fix that stare on them and repeat, "That's pretty funny, huh." And then it would hit in a blur. He delivered one of the fastest, nastiest beatings I ever saw. I watched him take down bikers twice his size in seconds. That speed came straight out of Western State—no doubt about it.

He ripped off drug dealers like it was a sport. Mousie fed him information. One week, it was a six-month-old dog in the yard, and the next, it turned out to be a six-year-old Doberman. There was the wrestling coach who was moving serious weight. Nobody was supposed to be home, but an eighty-year-old mother was sitting right there. Looking back, I swear God had me in that house for a reason.

Jimmy was the ultimate booster. Professional level. Nerves like a steel cable. We once walked through Sears, and the six-foot screen at the top of the escalator was playing a VHS video. Jimmy unplugged the VHS player in one smooth move while the screen went fuzzy. I watched the whole thing with my jaw halfway to the floor while I ran for distraction. He didn't flinch. Didn't hesitate. Didn't even blink.

He even carried the title to his totaled Lincoln Continental Town Car, and he used to put it up in pool games against guys who had real, running vehicles on the line. He'd break, play like the devil was guiding his cue stick, and I'd hold my breath as he walked out of the bar with someone else's keys. I saw him do it twice—drive off in a car he didn't own thirty minutes earlier—while his Lincoln sat dead in a junkyard.

Jimmy "Elmer," Billy "BJ," Peter, & Murph the Surf ... Consulting & Drinking the $$$

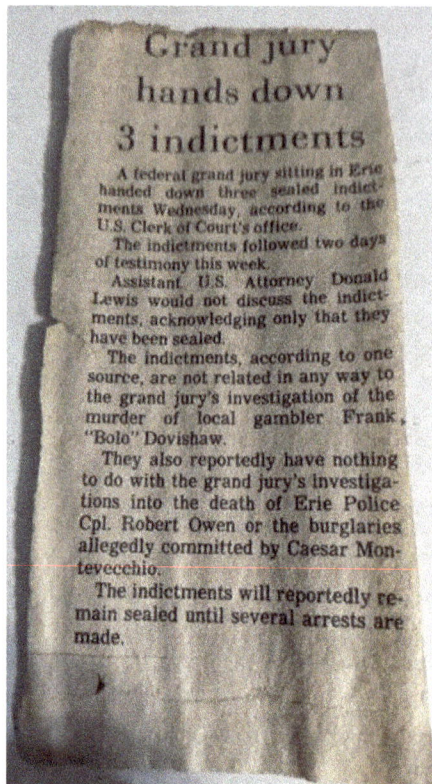

Grand jury hands down 3 indictments

A federal grand jury sitting in Erie handed down three sealed indictments Wednesday, according to the U.S. Clerk of Court's office.

The indictments followed two days of testimony this week.

Assistant U.S. Attorney Donald Lewis would not discuss the indictments, acknowledging only that they have been sealed.

The indictments, according to one source, are not related in any way to the grand jury's investigation of the murder of local gambler Frank "Bolo" Dovishaw.

They also reportedly have nothing to do with the grand jury's investigations into the death of Erie Police Cpl. Robert Owen or the burglaries allegedly committed by Caesar Montevecchio.

The indictments will reportedly remain sealed until several arrests are made.

The article that ended the Secret 7! It wasn't the murder of "Bolo" Dovishaw; It wasn't the murder of Cpl. Robert Owen or Ceasar Montevecchio... They had "Fat Sam" Esper... It had to be us they were coming for in the morning ...

CHAPTER 08
BILLY "B.J." DESANTO

I got a handful of stories about Billy DeSanto, and picking which ones to tell feels like sorting through contraband. You know you shouldn't admit half of it, but you also know these are the ones that show exactly who he was.

One night stands out. It turned into an acid party at Mama DeSanto's house, and she had no clue everyone was tripping. Jimmy and Billy were there. Peter and JR Russell were there. I was there, Patty and Mary DeSanto were there, and a couple of other girls were there. Jimmy's girlfriend was around, too. We were tripping hard, all of us. There was this big bowl of walnuts on the table. JR and I were on the couch, laughing at who knows what, while Billy was up dancing, as if the music was running through him. Then he started grabbing whole walnuts and eating them with the shells still on. No hesitation. No cracking them, just crunching through them like it was a bowl of popcorn.

That was Billy. Unpredictable. Wild. And somehow it always fit.

JR nudged me and said, "Every time he does something like that, I'm glad he's on our side."

I lost it. I laughed so hard I had tears in my eyes. I told him, "I gotta join you on that one," because those DeSanto brothers were nuts in a way only brothers like that can be. We were tight once, all of us moving through life like one loud, reckless unit.

I'm laying out a burglary in Billy's chapter because it threads right through him, me, and the whole twisted web back then. I burglarized a massage parlor controlled by wise guys, and I hated the owner. He's the same guy who later caused the Monday Night Football ticket mess. That place was his little kingdom. I couldn't stand him.

I first met Mary DeSanto in the P.P. Club, and back then, Peter Russell kept warning me. "She's gonna break your heart, Timmy." I fell for her anyway. I fell fast. She told me she worked in an office. I didn't question it. I didn't want to. Then my birthday rolled around, October 9th, 1980. Peter set me up with a massage for my birthday. And not the innocent kind. He made sure I knew exactly what kind of massage it was.

He arranged the appointment. He arranged who'd be doing it. He knew exactly what he was doing.

I went to that massage parlor for the first time, stripped down on the table, waiting. The door opened. The girl walked in. Gorgeous. And it was Mary Ellen DeSanto.

My heart dropped. Hers did too. We both froze. Peter had set the whole thing up as some twisted way of showing me the truth. It hit us both like a punch to the chest.

But I loved her, and I wasn't going to judge her. I told her, "Who am I to throw stones? I'm a thief. You do what you gotta do, I'll do what I gotta do. At the end of the night, we'll both take a shower, and I hope you end up in bed with me. If not, when you come home in the morning, take a shower, and I'll cook you breakfast."

That became our agreement. Even when we went out to Vegas, it stayed the same. We did what we had to do to survive.

But that massage parlor, FNG Corporation, crawled under my skin. Their checks listed FNG Corporation, and FNG stood for "Fun and Games." It summed up the whole filthy setup. I hated that place. I hated who ran it. And eventually, I got even.

I hated this motherfucker enough that getting even felt like a civic duty. I started by scouting the fucking alarm system. Took my time. Walked the perimeter. Found a window in the back that wasn't alarmed. That was all I needed. Measured the glass and had a piece of plexiglass cut to the exact size. Old-school precision without any blueprint.

When it was time, I taped the entire window the way we always did it. An X across the center, a border around the edges, smash the pane, and the tape holds the pieces so there's no crash echoing through the neighborhood. I climbed through, slid the plexiglass into the frame, and it looked untouched from the outside. Clean entry.

Inside the office sat one of those roll-top drop safes embedded in the concrete floor. The kind where you turn the drum and envelopes fall into the vault below. This one was buried about 18 inches into solid concrete. Whoever installed it probably thought it was bombproof.

I went at that thing with crowbars, chisels, splitting wedges, and a three-pound sledge. No subtlety. Just raw force. I broke it out of sixteen inches of concrete. Later on, the cops thought the safe had been blown up with explosives. It made me laugh because the truth was worse. I did it the hard way.

Once I got the safe loose, I realized I couldn't crack it there. The steel was too thick. No torch on me. So, I took the entire safe. Loaded it up and hauled it straight to Mama DeSanto's house. Me, BJ, and Elmer cracked it in the backyard. Took a couple of hours—loud, sweaty, ugly work. But we got in.

Once we were done, I told them we needed to get out of town and have some fun while things cooled off. I suggested Akron, Ohio. No plan, no strategy. Just distance.

I bought a '72 Cadillac Fleetwood Brougham. Medium green, white leather inside, white vinyl roof. Smooth ride, big enough for a parade.

Me, BJ, and Elmer drove to Akron to lay low and raise hell in equal measure. We checked into the downtown Holiday Inn. While we were at the front desk, I noticed the security monitors behind the clerk. The pool camera feed was out. It caught my attention immediately. Not because I was planning anything, but because once you live a certain life, details like that jump out whether you want them to or not.

We took three separate rooms. No sharing, no questions. Pulled the shades, settled in, and waited for whatever came next.

We hit Akron like we owned the place, even though we were only supposed to be hiding. That night, we headed straight to this monster discotheque called the Big Apple. The place could pack four or five hundred people. It had one of those new lit dance floors that everyone thought was the future.

Me, Billy, and Jimmy grabbed a table and kept the night rolling. Across the room was a horseshoe booth with six girls packed into it, all talking and laughing like they ran the building. Billy looked over and announced he felt like dancing. That was it. He stood up and walked straight to their booth.

He asked them to dance. He didn't have to say much. One must've nodded, because the next thing we saw made the whole table stop breathing for a second. He slid his hands under the table—this table holding six drinks, and lifted the entire thing the way a waiter carries a tray. He walked it out of the booth and set it down in front of them without spilling anything. Not even a drip.

It was one of those moments where you don't know if you're supposed to laugh or question what planet he came from. But that was Billy. Always doing something you couldn't unsee.

The girls were amazed, and the night tilted in our favor fast. We ended up with six of them from the University of Akron hanging out with the three of us. We partied right up to closing. When the lights came on, we asked if they wanted to come back to the hotel to keep it going. Three backed out. Three were all in.

We piled into my Cadillac and headed back to the Holiday Inn. I leaned over to Elmer and mentioned again that the pool camera was out. Figured we might get lucky and talk the girls into skinny dipping.

We asked if they wanted to swim. They said, "Oh, is the pool open?" We told them yes, even though I knew the camera was the only thing "open."

We got up there, and, of course, the door was locked. One girl said she thought the pool was supposed to be open. Elmer didn't blink. He turned around with that Cheshire Cat smile and said, "Don't worry, honey, you're in the company of thieves."

He reached into his pocket, pulled out a pick, and opened that lock in 3.2 seconds. When it went click, click, and the door popped, their faces said everything.

We walked in as we lived there. We told them we didn't exactly bring bathing suits. Nobody hesitated. All six of us jumped into the pool, skinny dipping.

It turned into a solid night. And that line of Elmer's stuck with me forever. "You're in the company of thieves."

Hard to top an introduction like that.

And then there was Billy with that table. This thing had to be thirty-six inches across, a full dinner table. He lifted it without spilling a single drop. Looked like a waiter showing off a giant pizza over his head, then brought it down soft enough that not one drop hit the floor. The girls stared at him like he was Superman working part-time in a disco. They could dance too, so the whole scene looked like something out of a movie none of us could afford to buy a ticket to.

That was just one story with Billy and Elmer. There are plenty more for Billy's chapter.

But the thing that still gets me is how the cops looked at that busted-out safe and swore it had to be blown with explosives. Let me tell you, there was nothing fancy about it. I hated the owner so much that I treated the job like it deserved. I just beat the thing out of the concrete and cracked it by brute force. No magic. No clever trick. No "knowing the model of the safe" or finding the sweet spot. Just rage, tools, and enough stamina to make a point.

You couldn't make any of these stories up. Had to live them. But by the grace of God, I did.

CHAPTER 09

BACK IN ERIE

Frank Fimonarri busted at the Pittsburgh airport, headed for Colombia to score pot directly from the Medellín Cartel with two million dollars in cash. Well, did he have balls? Because there was a million dollars in counterfeit cash interlaced with a million in real cash, which he had taken out and inserted. He was going to rip off the Pittsburgh mob for the cash while getting two million in pot to fly back. He had a pilot's license, and the plane would be loaded and ready for him to fly back once he landed. Man, that took balls, except someone blew him in, right at the boarding gate at the Pittsburgh airport.

When I met him, he'd been down in a Federal Penitentiary in Lewisburg for seven or eight years at this point. One night, I was showing him a little jailhouse ingenuity—how to brew coffee on the edge of a toilet seat with an aluminum pie tin suspended from shoestrings. The secret? A toilet paper "doughnut"—toilet paper rolled around your finger thirty times, the top and bottom tucked in, lit in the middle of the doughnut, set on the edge of the toilet. Instant coffee, ready to flush if a guard came down the hall. That was contraband innovation at its finest.

Frank was laughing the whole time, eyes shining like he hadn't seen a lifeline in years. He told me about the Pittsburgh bust, how he was moments from scoring the deal of his life and walking away with cash, pot, and a plane ride home. That was his kind of game—high stakes, high risk, and absolute balls of steel.

We'd sit in that cell, him teaching me the shortcuts, the tricks to survive the boredom and tension of federal time. Every little move was a lesson in patience, cunning, and knowing how far you could push the envelope without tipping off the guards.

And man, every story he told, from dodging the Pittsburgh mob to the aluminum pie tin coffee trick, made me realize how much guts it really takes to live like that and survive. You think you're tough? You haven't spent a night teaching someone how to brew coffee on the edge of a toilet while dodging the watchful eyes of the guard.

As we sat there cooking the coffee up, Frank said to me, "Boy, Murph, I feel just like a Boy Scout here. Back in the Fed joint, we have coffee urns right at the end of the galley. You walk up and get a cup anytime you want. I gotta get the fuck back there."

I took a bold step and said, "Well, what the hell are you doin' here now, Frank?"

You see, you don't ask anyone in the joint what they're in there for—not if you value your life—because you never know what the reaction will be. Some are only too eager to share their charges, while others just might fuckin' kill you for asking. I usually never ask. Just like whenever J.R. and I were delivering a police scanner or a silencer, I never wanted to know what it would be used for. If the person started talking about what they wanted to do with it, I'd stop them and say, "Excuse me, I really don't want to know any details because, God forbid, if anything goes wrong, I don't even want to be considered the weak link."

Some who wanted to brag might be offended, but most old-timers were usually impressed, and they told me so.

With thought, it was different. We had developed a good relationship ever since he hit the galley. Greg McMichael—Susan's second husband—came up to me and asked me to cell up with Frank. I initially said, "What the hell does he want me to cell up with him for? He's not a fag, is he?"

Greg said, "No, no, no. Just go talk to him. This guy's for real."

And he was. From the moment we started talking, I knew Frank wasn't just another lifer blowing smoke. He had a presence, a kind of intelligence and calm that cut through all the bullshit of federal time. He could size you up, read the room, and keep you laughing even in the middle of total boredom and tension. That night, sitting there with the edge-of-the-toilet coffee brewing, I realized Frank wasn't just a story—I was getting a front-row seat to how someone survives that life and comes out sharper, tougher, and still human at the core.

I walked up to Frank's cell, and Greg made the introduction. I said, "Why the hell do you want me to cell up with you?"

He looked me square in the eye and said, "I just got sent here from the Fed joint, and I don't want any knuckle-head or ass-hole getting moved in here. Greg says you're solid, so I want you in the top bunk before they move anyone else here."

I could accept that answer. I had some pull with one of the Prison Lieutenants, Dave Camino, who was a bouncer at the P.P. Club—the Petrolo Peligna Society, our private Italian night-club. I asked him to make the move before the new arrivals came up from the night-before arrests.

Once I was in the top bunk, Frank opened up. He started telling me about his first bust—drug trafficking, even though there were no drugs. But he couldn't explain the two million in cash, and he sure as hell wasn't going to rat on the Pittsburgh mob.

It wasn't until he had been held almost three months that the Feds discovered the million in counterfeit bills, interleaved with the real cash. They charged him with counterfeiting and threw the book at him because they knew what it was going to be used for—and he wouldn't say a word.

I asked, "Well, what happened with the real cash?"

He shrugged. "I gave it back... how do you think I'm still alive? Originally, they were going to kill me before they found out I was snitched on. I gave them most of the real stuff back before the Feds even discovered the fake stuff. They were actually happy. I saved 'em money, and I'm doin' this bid without saying a word. I'm gold with them."

I came back to the question I'd been holding, "So what the hell are you here for this time?"

He shook his head. "Well, the old lady and I were getting divorced, and she was selling the house. I can't really blame her, even though that's where part of the real cash went. The only thing I told her was to make sure you clear out EVERYTHING from the house. Well, the dumb bitch didn't listen. She never did. Left some boxes and an old suitcase in the basement. When the new owners came in and started cleaning out the basement, they opened it and found hundreds of credit cards and fake IDs in it. It was my getaway case for when I got back from Colombia because I knew I'd have to get the fuck out of Dodge. The Colombians would be hunting me, and so would the Pittsburgh mob. I wouldn't have lasted long if I had stuck around. I was gonna take off and buy my own private island. Had it all lined up... best laid plans of mice and men."

I nodded, letting it sink in. How many times have I heard that line in my lifetime? How many times? I'd always wanted to hook back up with Frank if, and when, we both got out, but I didn't know the outcome of his case, and there were a couple more stories waiting in my own life before I could catch up with him again.

CHAPTER 10

CASINO TIME

Susan knew half the hustlers in Vegas, but Geri McGee was in a league of her own. The stories about her and Lefty Rosenthal weren't rumors; they were blueprints for survival. Geri showed Susan the grind, Susan passed it to Mary, and Mary... hell, Mary took it to another level. She was young, she was gorgeous, she landed in Cosmopolitan under the headline "Sex for Sale in Las Vegas," and that magazine might as well have punched me in the chest. My Angel was a centerfold — literally —, and it stung every time I thought about it.

When I took her out there, I never let her out of my sight. She hustled chips from high rollers, drifting from table to table like she owned the place, while I hung back just far enough to watch her shoulders tense if anything went wrong. If a gambler grabbed her wrist, I stepped in. If she wandered too close to a guy with the temper of a rabid pit bull, I stepped in. But sometimes stepping in wasn't an option. Sometimes she had to go upstairs with them. Sometimes I stood there watching elevator doors close with my stomach in my shoes, reminding myself I wasn't exactly Saint Murphy. I was a thief. A damn good one. Judging her would've made me a hypocrite and an idiot in the same breath.

We had our deal. "You do what you gotta do. I do what I gotta do. If we land back in the same bed when the sun comes up, great. If not, I'll cook you breakfast while you're in the shower. No questions."

It worked. Not because it was romantic, but because it was honest.

Then came that night.

Mary was hustling some Arab millionaire — billionaire, more likely, loud, arrogant son of a bitch with more money than manners. In my head, he was every slur I could throw at him, sand n****r, raghead, whatever ugly word I could reach for out of anger and fear. He took her by the arm and dragged her from the table like she was a purse he'd misplaced. I was halfway out of my seat, ready to put a hole in him big enough to read a newspaper through, when I saw the two bodyguards behind him. Real bodyguards. Real turbans. Real guns under the robes.

Didn't matter. I was still ready to swing.

But Mary turned her head just enough to catch my eye, and she gave me this tiny look, an impression that said, *Don't. I've got this.* So I froze. Not because I agreed. Because she asked me to trust her.

I kept trailing them as they moved fast through the casino. They weren't heading for an elevator. They were heading out. Straight through the lobby. Straight past security. Straight to the fucking valet stand.

My pulse went into overdrive.

I bolted for my car and by some miracle spotted their limo right as it pulled up. I tucked in behind them, staying a couple of car lengths back, waiting for them to turn into the Mirage or the Sands or the Hilton. But they weren't stopping at any of them. They were cruising past every damn marquee on the Strip.

And that's when my gut started talking. Something wasn't right. Something was way off. And Mary was in the back of that limo with three men I didn't trust as far as I could throw Caesars Palace.

We were heading out of town, and I couldn't tell if they were driving toward Los Angeles or some dust-bowl gambling pit in the middle of nowhere until the limo took a sharp turn and rolled straight into McCarran Airport. Not the main terminal either — the damn thing glided around a side gate that went right to the tarmac. That's when my mind kicked into overdrive.

Who the hell is this son of a bitch?

The limo eased up beside a private Learjet like it was pulling into a reserved parking spot. Mary stepped out first, the millionaire right behind her, his two turbaned bulldozers flanking them. Nobody looked panicked. Nobody looked forced. But that didn't mean a damn thing. They boarded, the stairs folded up, and in a blink, that jet was roaring down the runway and gone.

And I was left standing there like an idiot with my heart in my throat.

I didn't know where they were flying. I didn't know if she got on that plane willingly. For all I knew, she'd been grabbed at the table, walked out with a fake smile, and stuffed into a jet headed for God-knows-where. Back then, I had no playbook for something like this. Susan was back in Erie. I had no backup, no plan, and no clue.

The only person who might know anything was Harpo DelMonte. Harpo was head pit boss, a hometown guy out of tiny Erie, Pennsylvania — one of those dudes who made sure anyone connected to home didn't end up face-down in a dumpster behind Bally's. Susan used to rely on him, and now I had to.

I drove straight back to the casino and found him at his post. When I laid it out, Harpo didn't even blink — he knew exactly who I was describing. And that's when the situation went from bad to worse.

This guy wasn't some regular degenerate with a pocketful of tokens. He was Saudi royalty in everything but official title. Multi-millionaire. Oil money. Came through every couple of months with a smell of entitlement you could smell across the room.

My stomach tightened. If Mary pissed him off, hustling chips, he wouldn't drag her to security — men like him dragged women onto planes.

I didn't know if she went by choice or because she thought playing along meant staying alive. All the possibilities ran wild in my head:

Had he caught her?

Was she being taken somewhere she couldn't leave?

Sex trafficking?

Held for ransom?

Dead already?

Nobody knew. Nobody could even guess.

I waited. I stayed near the casino, checking in with Harpo every day, hoping she'd call his desk or walk through the doors looking pissed but unharmed. Nothing. No phone call. No message. No rumor. Just silence that stretched through days like chewing glass.

After a week of staring at walls and replaying every moment in my mind, I realized the only thing left to do was go back home to Erie. I didn't have the money or muscle to chase a Saudi jet across the world.

Before I left, I told Harpo, "If she shows up, hell, if she even breathes near a phone, call Susan's house. Don't wait. Don't think. Just call."

He nodded like he already knew the routine.

And I walked out of Vegas with the worst feeling a man can carry, not knowing if the woman he loved had vanished by choice... or been taken.

The drive back was torture. Hours of road with nothing but my head chewing itself apart. I didn't know if the woman I loved was alive, dead, or getting used like property by that sand-ni"er. By the time I rolled into Erie, I was running on fumes and dread.

I went straight to Susan's place, downstairs in Grandma DeSanto's house. I didn't tap the door, I beat on it like I was trying to wake the dead. Susan answered in a black negligee, looking like sin on legs. The DeSanto girls had that habit. More than once, one of them opened a door dressed like they thought they were auditioning for a late-night movie. But that's a whole different chapter.

I tried to get the story out — the airport, the limo, the jet — but the second I started talking, everything I'd been holding in just blew. My voice cracked, my knees damn near gave out. I told her I didn't know where

Mary was, who she was with, or if she was even still on this side of the planet. I told her I had nowhere to go now that I was back.

She didn't blink.

"Oh yes, you do, honey... you're stayin' right here. Come on in."

And that was that.

One thing I'll give Mary credit for — she must've bragged about me to her sisters and her girlfriends, because every time she and I split, or she wasn't around, I found myself... let's say, *welcomed*. I'm not proud, I'm not ashamed either. Life with Mary was a roller coaster, but no matter how many times we jumped the tracks, we always found our way back to each other eventually.

Sometimes it happened because it was easy, or because we worked like a smooth little crew on the hustle. Mary even did time for me when we got busted for the forged checks and stolen credit cards. I told her to flip on me. She wouldn't. She had that stubborn streak that made you want to shake her one minute and shield her the next. I honestly think I was the only man she ever loved straight-up. I was the only one her age she ever lived with, except Michael Farbo, and she only went out with him when we broke up to light my fuse. She usually went for older men with fat wallets. She wasn't stupid. She had something going on from childhood, something tied to her parents' split. Her father was a big name in Erie, running the Sports page at the Erie Times-News for years.

Susan brought me in, and that's when we actually got to know each other in every way you can imagine. This was way before she met and married Ray Ferritto. Trust me, once she married him, I kept my distance. No way

I was crossing that guy. Later on, Mary and I even babysat her kids when she had late-night work.

Susan showed me things about living that I wouldn't have picked up on my own. I still think the world of her, and I keep the signed copy of her book, *An Assassin Scorned,* like it's gold. I did a couple of favors for her, too. One of the biggest was right before I was headed to jail in Erie for the forgeries and the credit card mess Mary got hauled in on with me. I knew damn well I was going in. She was going through hell with a divorce from her second husband, Greg DiMichael.

The funny part was that I ended up cellmate with Greg in Erie County prison. Then he asked me to move in with Frank Fimonarri. That's a whole other mess!

CHAPTER 10
THE ABCS OF CRIME

I used to run through the ABCs of everything I'd done, like a messed-up catalog of a life that went sideways early. And even then, I knew it wasn't the whole list. Some letters needed stories under them, a little meat on the bone. Arsons were one of those.

I burned cars for insurance money for JR. That was a regular thing for us. One night, I had to burn a 1976 Cadillac Eldorado: Emerald green, white leather interior, white convertible roof. I begged J.R. to let me steal the damn thing instead and keep it. I told him I'd take it to another city and drive it. He shut it down. He said it had to be burned and found so that the insurance money would come through. So that was that.

And in the middle of all that, Peter Russell was on the lam. He'd lost a button off his leather coat during a score, and the cops had pulled a thumbprint off the button. They were hunting him because of it. One stupid button. One stupid print. And there was no way to talk your way out of that.

He was trying to lay low, couldn't do much, and needed some money. So he said, Timmy, let me burn the car with you. I'm like, Pete, I really don't need any help fucking doing this. And I really don't want to split the 500 bucks with you, but all right, what the fuck? Here we go.

So we went and took the pretty friggin car, and I had a burn spot out on the edge of Erie, not too far out because they had to find it. You had to make sure they found it so they could collect on the insurance. So drove it out there.

And then what you would do is roll the windows down, douse some gasoline on the dashboard, and a little on the interior. It wouldn't freaking take much. And then you pour gasoline over the hood, the top, the roof, all over the top of the outside. It doesn't splash it around.

Then you take a sheet and open the gas tank. You take the gas cap off, and you'd shove—first you dip. You dip the sheet in a little bit of gasoline and then shove it down the gas pipe. And then you wouldn't totally like put gas on the sheet. But you put a small stream on it as a fuse. And then you'd light that fuse, and you'd better run like hell because when that thing hits the gas tank, it's going to go.

I really didn't need any help, but Peter needed the money, so he came and helped. We went and prepped the car, getting it all ready along with the tail. Peter's got a head start on me already. I light the tail, and I'm running right after him, and both of us get back to the car. Peter beat me, and he goes, "Timmy, did you get the gas can?"

And I said, What gas can? I threw mine inside. It's plastic, it's going to burn up.

He goes, "Oh... I had a metal gas can. Timmy, it's got my fingerprints on it. You gotta go get that gas can!

"I gotta go get that gas can? I didn't leave the gas can."

He continues, "Timmy, you're younger than me, you can run faster, I got you."

So I go running back to the fucking Cadillac. By the time I get back there, flames are shooting out of the windows and the gas tank. I mean, the friggin' sheet has burned right to the gas tank, and flames are shooting out of the gas tank. It looks like the Batmobile. I freaking run around, I'm looking for the gas can. Fortunately, I trip over it, I fucking snatch it up, I friggin' start running. I don't think I got friggin' 15 feet away from this car when it fucking—oh yeah, when I came back, the electrical system was fucking melting through. So the alarm system was going off. The fucking high beams, low beams are flashing on and off, the friggin' horn is going off, there's a fucking alarm, friggin' siren going off, and then it fucking blows on me.

I get back to the fucking car, and he said, "Oh, Timmy, did you get the fucking can?"

I said, "I got the motherfucking can, you son of a bitch."

And he was grateful.

When JR made me burn the '76 Cadillac El Dorado... oh, that killed me. And we touched upon, I think, the arson of Susan DeSanto's house, so I was just going to add a little bit more to that.

So Susan DeSanto was going through a nasty divorce with her second husband, Greg DeMicheal, who was in prison with me. And he's the one who actually introduced me to Frank Fiminnari, which we've already covered. But Greg DeMicheal was the link to Frank Fiminnari.

But Susan was going through a nasty divorce, and she needed money, and she wanted to arson the house because she had an insurance policy on it, and she had a bunch of her ex-husband's tools in there that she wanted to fucking burn up. So she approached me and asked me if I would be willing to do it. And I told her, "Well, Susan, I gotta go to friggin' court in a few days from now, and I'm definitely going away for some time. I don't know how much."

But I said to myself, "Well, that might be the perfect cover, because if I do this, I'm going to be in jail." I said, "I'll do it like the night before I got to go to fucking court. So they're going to be looking for somebody on the street, and I'm going to be in the joint."

So, I agreed to do it with Susan. And I told her, "I don't know how much you're getting for the insurance policy." Then I said, "But if you get something, if it works out, you know, just take care of me. Just leave some money with my baby brother Michael," who worked in Erie at the time. He worked at the A.M./P.M. at 26th and State, right across from the stadium.

So I said, "If anything comes up, just leave it with him." So, a night or two before I had to go to court, I went to Susan's house, and I took an electrical cover off an outlet and sprayed ether starting fluid up into the wall at the electrical outlet, trying to make it look like an electrical fire so the wire would catch and they would suspect it was electrical.

Fortunately, they didn't even test for accelerants because it just looked like an electrical fire. But when I sprayed ether into the electrical outlet, it exploded inside the fucking wall. The force of it actually blew me over. It was an old plaster-and-lath type wall, and the plaster blew right off the fucking wall. The force of it really surprised me, almost fucking knocked me out.

But it was successful. It fucking torched the house. It all fucking took off.

Found out later that Susan had a girlfriend who lived right upstairs. Her apartment was upstairs, and her girlfriend was the manager of Dominic's restaurant.

Dominic's restaurant is where everybody went after they were done drinking all night long. It was one of the old, old all-night restaurants, 24-hour breakfast anytime. And Dominic's restaurant had the bomb for hangovers—they had a meatball omelet, which doesn't sound good until you have one. It was an omelet with meatballs. It was weird how many people put ketchup on their eggs; it had, like, mama's spaghetti sauce on the meatballs inside the omelet. It was the fucking bomb. And it didn't have American cheese; it had provolone and pizza cheese. It was a freaking bomb when you had a hangover.

I found out that her girlfriend was the night manager and always took the receipts home from Dominic's. And here she had a freaking bank, not an envelope, a bank drop bag. There was like 20 grand in cash under her bed in her apartment from Dominic's. Had I known that, I would have gone and robbed that before I freaking lit the house on fire. But as it was, her upstairs apartment didn't burn as bad as Susan's did, but it ended up burning the whole, the whole frickin' house, and she ended up collecting on it.

I finally got out. I was given an 11- and a half-month to 23-month sentence. In Erie County, they give you that sentence so that you don't go to a state prison. They give you one to two, you're going into a state prison. If they keep it at 11 and a half to 23 months, they keep you in the county prison. And that's where I had the good job of doing the laundry at night. It was really the best job you could get there.

So I got out of doing that bid, and when I got out, my mom let me move back into the house till I could get on my feet. And as soon as I get back to the house, I go up into the boys' bedrooms, our old upstairs bedrooms. Michael brought me up and said, *"Hey, I got something for you."*

I asked, *"What?"*

He goes into our closet and reaches into the back shelf. We always had this little stash spot. He reaches into the stash spot, pulls out the envelope, and hands it to me. I opened the envelope, and there were fifty, $100 bills in it.

He said, "Susan DeSanto stopped at work and gave me this about six months ago."

I said, "Well, thank you so much." She kept her word. She honored it. I did my part, she did her part, and she paid me off. We didn't talk for years after that. Really didn't see her.

But the day I got out of prison, I had five grand cash, which really helped. I went shopping, bought some new suits, and went out partying and had a great time.

So I'd say that would finish it up for arson season. Between Peter Russell and the '76 El Dorado and Susan's house, there were many, many more car arsons. I used to burn cars for the insurance money.

J.R. would meet me at a specific bar. He would have the keys to the car that needed to be burned. I'd go in, I'd have a drink, he'd leave the keys, and I'd go. I'd take the car, which was usually parked down the street somewhere, and I would burn it. It would have to be burned thoroughly enough to be sure it was totaled. But you had to do it in an area where they'd find the car.

You could not take it into the middle of the fucking woods and burn it and then have it not be found for six months or a year because that would defeat the purpose.

It took a little bit of balls to find a spot. I had a couple of good ones where the cars would be found, but you had enough time to get away. So that would be that.

So if we went down the ABCs, of course, I was a burglar. I was one of the best. Criminal conspiracy means only that two people discussed a crime. But that's all they could get anybody on for the armored car robbery. They never could prove the actual robbery. All they could get on the armored car robbery was criminal conspiracy, that two people spoke about a crime.

Drug dealing. I've hit all that.

Extortion. We would extort people.

Forgery was one of my better things. And I think I told you how I used to break into businesses on a Friday night, use their friggin check writer or check writing machine to do identical checks, and then hit every drive-through across the city of Erie. Which then leads to part of the identity theft under I. But I explained that I found a Pennsylvania picture ID when I passed out on a park bench and woke up to find one that looked like me. We've done that. We've talked about that already.

So then we come to the Gs, and this is where I came up with—for Gs—gambling, grifting, and getaway cars.

So first, gambling. People in Vegas love to say you need to get wiped out three times before the habit finally kicks you in the teeth hard enough to quit. I didn't need the reminder. I'd already gone past that number.

But the best gamble I ever made wasn't in Vegas. It happened because of a bunch of jockeys who ran at Waterford Park down in West Virginia. To get there from Erie, you had to take I-79 toward Pittsburgh, keep rolling past the state line, and eventually you'd hit Waterford Park. That track was a warm-up spot for horses headed to the Kentucky Derby. The real ones. The ones people later claim to have seen.

Every so often, one of those jockeys would call us and let us know if it was worth making the drive. The code was simple. If they said, "bet the house," you got in the car. No hesitation. You didn't pack a lunch or double-check anything. You just went.

So one day, we get the word: *bet the house.*

There were only four of us at the time.

It was still the late seventies, early eighties—just before everything went digital. You could still tilt the odds, but you had to be careful. If you dumped too much money too early, you'd drive the odds straight into the ground and ruin the whole thing. Timing mattered more than brains.

And I still remember the horse's name.

Trentonero.

Trentonero went off at 99 to 1, but only because the tote board didn't have room for a third digit. If it had, the number would've probably embarrassed everyone.

To keep that 99:1 alive, we had to wait until the last possible minute— literally a minute before post time. Four guys, each one ready to move fast, stick to the plan, and not look like we were trying too hard.

Because the whole game depended on looking ordinary until the exact second you didn't.

We waited right at the $50 window at the track, and right at a minute before post time, we had to act like we didn't know each other—the four of us. All you could do was $50 because anything higher would throw the odds off. So each of us went up and placed a $50 bet on Trentonero.

Sure as shit, that horse came flying in. For a $50 bet, each of us walked away with around five grand. Ninety-nine to one. Best gambling story I ever had.

But, as I said, you had to lose three times real big.

The following week, after we'd won the five grand, we were sitting at the bar. JR was running the sarsaparilla at the time, and another guy came over to tell us about a local track outside of Erie called Commodore Downs. You left Erie, headed toward Cleveland, maybe 15 or 20 minutes out, and you'd hit Commodore Downs. Still in Pennsylvania, right before the Ohio border.

We got the call that a horse was going off that had run in the Derby or had come in second place. Thought it was a sure thing. But this horse was running at Belmont, and back then, satellite dishes were coming in. They would beam the first race at Belmont to Erie, and people would actually bet on it as part of a trifecta.

So you would bet on the first horse at Belmont and make your bets on the first two races in Erie. Between those three races, if you picked all three winners, you would hit the trifecta. The odds could be incredible.

The guy gives us the tip: this horse is running at Belmont, sure thing to come in first. If we couple him up with every possible combination of the horses running in the first and second races at Commodore Downs, we could make a killing.

We went and put in every friggin' possible combination you could think of. We picked the horse first in Belmont, and in the second race in Erie, only five or six horses were running. We bet every combination with all five or six of those horses in combination with the top three horses running in the second race. We had every friggin' combination covered. There was no way we could lose this bet.

We got all our bets in, and we had all put thousands of dollars behind this. Same four guys that had won the week before at Waterford Park. We get all our races, and we have a stack of tickets like an inch thick. They were beaming the first race from Belmont, and man, we were ready to make a killing.

Here we go. Horses up the track, ready—boom—they're off. They're flying around the track. Oh yeah, there's our horse. He was out in front, winning by a mile. He rounds the bend, and then he starts dying. He gets beat right at the friggin' wire by a nose by another horse.

Our whole day lasted less than two minutes. We lost everything because we lost the first bet of the trifecta. That was one of the times I lost big.

Another time losing big was the first time: the college championship between Larry Bird and Michael Jordan. Bird was with Indiana, and Jordan played for North Carolina. This was right when the half-point spot showed up. That changed everything, because before that, you either got a one-point spot or a two-point spot. Once they made it a point-and-a-half, things got a whole lot trickier.

Long story short, I had Michael Jordan and North Carolina to win, but they had to win by more than a point and a half. They won, but only by one point. I ended up shooting my new color TV. So not only did I lose the five hundred I had on the game, I shot a five-hundred-dollar TV—that one hurt.

So that's the gambling. Believe me, I've lost more. I don't gamble anymore. I don't even bother with a lottery ticket unless it hits a billion. Maybe then I'll grab one.

Then there was the grifting. I just added this. In Peter Russell's chapter, there's a picture of a quarter, a nickel, and a dime stacked on each other. That was JR's grift. He figured out how to balance them. I worked out the physics so we could do it on command.

We'd walk into a bar, and JR would set the quarter, nickel, and dime right on the counter—boom, boom, boom. Then we'd start drinking. Eventually, someone would wander over, staring at the stack.

"Oh wow, that's pretty cool."

JR would shrug. "Yeah, right?"

Then he'd reel them in. "You want to try it? If you pull it off in three tries, I'll buy you a drink."

Everybody tried. Of course they did.

By the end of the night, we'd both have shot glasses lined up in front of us, and the whole bar would be doing this damn trick. Always remember, 'there's a trick to every trick and a hustle to every hustle.

So the trick itself goes like this. You park the nickel in George's nose on the quarter, like a little bike stand. You roll the nickel so George's nose catches it, and boom, it sits solid. Then comes the dime. On the back of the dime, there's a torch. You use that torch as your guide to line it up over the nickel. If you place it just right, one of two things happens — either the nickel twists or the dime twists.

I figured out why. On the flip side of that torch is Franklin Delano Roosevelt, and there's a dimple in his cheek. That dimple sits at a twelve-degree angle to the torch. That's what makes the dime twist or the nickel twist until it finds that groove.

Here's where the grift works. When people see the twist start, they panic and try to grab it, knocking the whole thing over. Then they lose the bet and end up buying you a drink. So the trick is: let it twist. Let it find that little groove.

But that was just the trick. The hustle was something else. We kept piles of change on both sides of us — one on my left, one on my right — depending on where the person stood. The key to the hustle was the nickel. You always kept a new nickel for yourself, one with nice, sharp edges so the dime would balance easily. And when it was time to pass the change to the mark, you slid them an old nickel with rounded edges. They'd never pull it off. You could drink all night for forty cents — a quarter, a nickel, and a dime.

But the best part? You have no idea how many beautiful women I picked up for forty cents a night. I'd always tell them JR made me promise not to tell the trick or the hustle to anyone... except the beautiful women of which you clearly qualify, young lady. Then I'd tell them everything. And plenty of times, I ended up going home with them.

I met more beautiful women for a quarter, a nickel, and a dime than most guys meet in a lifetime.

Trick, to every trick. Hustle, to every hustle. That's why they call it grifting.

In my book, the ultimate grifter was Peter. In Peter Russell's piece — I'm pretty sure I sent you the link, "Peter Michael Russell Erie Fugitive" on officer.com — that article is the best one written about him. It says he did a $27,000 burglary and a $65,000 burglary. But the way they wrote it, they make it look like that $65,000 was all cash.

It wasn't.

Forty thousand of it was cash. But the real prize was what they found inside. I didn't go in on that job — Peter went in. I handled the alarm system. When he got inside, he found a manila envelope with twenty-five bearer bonds.

You know what a bearer bond is,? It's a U.S. Treasury note worth ten grand. And right across the top it says, "Pay to the order of the bearer, $10,000." On the bottom, there are little tear-off tabs, perforated, one for every six months over twenty years. If you owned a bearer bond, you had to tear off the tab for that date and turn it in to your bank to prove you still possessed the bond.

So when we got everything home and started busting it up, that's when we realized what Peter had pulled out of that manila envelope—twenty-five ten-thousand-dollar U.S. Treasury notes.

None of that ever hit the press. Not one word. The news only ever said $65,000 was taken—no mention of the bearer bonds.

But we knew the heat was on those bonds. They were serialized. You weren't walking into any bank in America and cashing them. Those things were hotter than a two-dollar pistol.

So we get done, we're dividing the money up between the four of us. Everybody gets their cut, and then at the end there's this manila envelope with the twenty-five bearer bonds. JR hands it to me and says, "Take this and stash it in your apartment somewhere." He knew I was already keeping the reefer up there. I'm looking at him, thinking, Why do I get stuck with this? And it hits me all over again — I'm the youngest, so if anyone's taking the bust for this, it's me.

I asked him how the hell we were supposed to get rid of them. JR kept saying, "We'll figure out something." Meanwhile, for six months straight, the running joke was that I was going to be the idiot stuck holding the envelope forever. Those bonds sat in my place from winter into the following summer, and one day JR came in all excited. "I got it," he says. "I know how we're getting rid of the bearer bonds."

I told him the sooner the better because I didn't want that envelope in my house another minute. He goes, "We got something lined up at the Fort Erie racetrack." I'm like, what the hell could we possibly have lined up there? And he goes, "Oh, kid, this is going to be beautiful. I got a horse lined up that the owner is willing to sell and take the bearer bonds for."

I couldn't believe it. I asked him how we were supposed to pull that off. And he tells me I'm the one who's going to do it. "You're gonna dress up in one of your nice three-piece suits and play like you're some rich kid buying a racehorse because daddy told you to." I didn't think I was up for it, and JR kept pushing: "Kid, this is perfect. They'll never suspect you. You've got a baby face. Once you're dressed up, you'll pull it off."

There it was again — me holding the envelope and me doing the front-line work.

So we head up to Fort Erie, Canada. The racetrack is only about five minutes from customs after you cross the Peace Bridge. We get there, and JR really did have everything lined up. He had a horse trainer waiting and a truck with a horse trailer sitting ready to go.

Everything was set when we got there. We meet the owner of the horse, the one ready to sell. We show him the bearer bonds. He's all smiles. He hands over the paperwork, I sign it with the fake ID, and the deal is done. The guy is thrilled, drives off with the bonds, and I'm just relieved the envelope is finally out of my hands.

The second he pulls away, the trainer JR hired loads the horse into the trailer. We follow him as he drives a few rows over into the barns at Fort Erie. He parks, steps out, and another man is already waiting. This guy isn't wasting time — he's standing there with $150,000 cash. He takes the horse, loads it into a stall, hands over the money, and we drive off.

The whole thing took maybe thirty minutes. I was sweating bullets the entire time. I still can't believe we pulled that off. We turned those impossible-to-move bearer bonds into $150,000 cash. There was no way those bonds were ever going to be cashed in the States. They were too hot.

But for years after that, the joke stayed alive — I was always "the kid who got stuck holding the envelope."

So that closes the grifting part. Grifting is being a con artist, running parlor tricks, or pulling the long con, getting people to trust you and slowly taking their money. That's grifting.

The last G was getaway car driving. I drove plenty of them, but the wildest one came out of Youngstown, Ohio. That place made Erie look like a church picnic. Erie sat a hundred miles from Cleveland, Pittsburgh, and Buffalo. Youngstown sat about an hour from both Cleveland and Pittsburgh, which meant both cities fought over it for years. Same way the Steelers and Browns hate each other — it's not about football. It's turf. Always has been.

We got word on a card game down there. A Youngstown guy set it up for us, but he needed fresh faces. Nobody local could pull anything off in that town. Everyone knew everyone. Walk into a place, and half the room could name your uncles.

So it was me and another guy from there who had the intel with Peter as the muscle. JR came but stayed at a remote spot, like he always did. The plan was simple on paper: drive in, drop them right in front of the club, make sure the Pennsylvania plates were visible, let folks see strangers arriving. The plates weren't from my car — I had stolen ones. The car itself was stolen from Ohio, and we slapped Pennsylvania plates on it to muddy the trail.

I pull up outside the place. It looked like a regular neighborhood bar, but the card game was in the back. My job was to stop long enough for people to see the plates and two guys getting out, then keep moving. They were going to walk straight through the bar, push into the back room, pull guns, clean out the game, and go out the back door where I'd swing around to get them.

I had to take the car around the block, drop down this alley, and wait for them at the back door. The alley stretched about three hundred feet, roughly the length of a football field. And the damn thing was tight — maybe a foot and a half on each side of the car—a real squeeze.

I've said it before: one of JR's rules was always plan your getaway with right turns. You can take a right on red without drawing attention. So even in that alley, the plan started with a right turn. That was the setup.

I had scanners in the car. If calls started flying or shots started popping, we'd have to adjust fast. Any police call from the wrong direction meant the route had to change on the spot.

We went, and this alley wasn't doing us any favors—three hundred feet straight into a brick wall, a clean T at the end. You either went right or left. I planned the right.

I drop them at the front. We make sure someone notices the Pennsylvania plates before I pull away. That mattered. The place was a Cleveland-run club, and the second they saw those plates, they'd assume Pittsburgh was taking a swing at them. Nobody ever thinks of Erie. We wanted the heat aimed west.

They go inside, hit the back room, and sure enough, shots go off on their way out. They sprint out the door, jump in the car, and I floor it down the alley. I'm glued to the scanners, telling the guy next to me, "Listen to this, because I'm taking the right. That's the plan. I'm taking the right."

Then a call cracks through the scanner, saying units are coming from the right. And I'm already halfway into the turn — I mean, almost committed — when the guy from Youngstown starts yelling, "Left, left, left!"

So now I'm stuck mid-turn, basically pointed to the right but needing the left, and I have to swing it around like one of those old limousines. When you flip a limo, you nose into the intersection like you're making a right, take the whole width, then drag it around in a curve shaped like a question mark. That's what this felt like.

I had to make that move. I was actually turning right; I friggin' whipped it around, trying to make the left. I fishtail the fucking thing, the rear end of the car fishtails into the building. The T that we were going hits the fucking building, bumps me, bumps me straight headed in the right direction. I hit the gas, go vroom—taking off out of the alley, we go. The guy has the same quote that Peter Russell had when he first met me: "The kid can drive, the kid can drive." So that's the getaway car. And we got away with it.

That brings us to the H's: home invasions. We did home invasions. I told you about the one with the DeSanto, when the 80-year-old lady was there when she wasn't supposed to be. That turned out to be a home invasion. But we did home invasions when people owed us money for drugs. We would just walk into the fucking house and start taking stereos and TVs right in front of them if they owed us money.

Then I's: identity theft. I've already talked to you about how I found that one Pennsylvania driver's license, so that was gold falling in my lap. But how you had to do identity theft back in the day... now it's so fucking easy, you let your fingers do the walking. But if you really wanted to create a new identity back then, you had to go old school. But back in the day, there was only one way to rob someone's identity... You had to do it from the Grave! I would only do this in other cities, never in Erie, where I was born, but I had done it. You'd go to another city, hit their library. This was before computers and digitized records. You'd have to go through old newspapers.

And how you did that required time and research. There were no computers to let your fingers do the walking. You would have to go to a local library and look through microfilm of old newspapers from around the month and year you were born. You would have to look ideally for an infant or young child who died very early in life. From there, you would have to request a duplicate birth certificate, and this was via snail mail... no instant gratification or online documents. Then, once you received the birth certificate, you would apply for a Social Security card, because back in those days, you usually didn't have one until you went to work for a living. Step Three is what took a few balls...You would have to go to a local DMV (Department of Motor Vehicles) in the state where you were trying to create this identity. You would have to go in, apply, and take the written and road tests to get a legitimate driver's license. That's the pie'ce de re'sistance...once you had that, you could do anything as a totally new individual in the world...bank accounts, credit cards, loans...you were only limited by your imagination...and believe me... I had one of those! Frank Abagnale of "Catch Me If You Can!" fame had nothing on me, but I did produce a couple of identity thefts the old-fashioned way. That's how it worked.

Then J: joyriding—limos and boats. I used to borrow limousines. I worked at Rupp Limousine Rental, right across the street from my mother's house. All through 10th, 11th, and 12th grade, my job was washing limousines and hearses after school. But every once in a while, I'd borrow a limo, pick up my friends, and we'd ride around, party a little. I had to start returning people by 11 because I had to be back by 11:30, wash the limo, and make sure it was ready for the next morning. Midnight was the deadline, right across the street at my mother's house, or my stepfather would administer discipline.

You don't know how many people, every time I go back to Erie, Pennsylvania... just happened this weekend, somebody says, "Man, I remember when you used to pick us up in limousines." And last week, I was having lunch with a friend, Mark T. He said, "Murph, you were just a thrill seeker. It wasn't about the money. You had to feel smarter than everybody else, outthinking everyone." I said, "Mark, you hit it on the head." I was just a thrill seeker, Mark... that was the most concise synopsis of my life I ever heard, Mark. Of course, you saw it from a bird's-eye view... I could have saved thousands of dollars spent on counselors and psychiatrists had I just had lunch with you earlier, Mark! "Come on in, Tim... This is a safe house!" I will never forget that line, my brother... When I came banging at your door at two in the morning with sirens blazing down 10th street after me! Or the postcard from the Garden of Gethsemane... Or the Tao Te Cheng, my friend and Brother...

From life, lifelong friend, Mark T. ...

I saw it as I know I am a notorious "risk taker," which is close to a "thrill seeker," but not the same.

But the underlying motivation for both of us is the need to be seen as "smarter than the average bear."

You are VERY smart. No one can plan a heist like you can. It takes brains. It also takes know-how, skill, and nerves.

I'm like that too. I take on these larger-than-life projects to some degree to prove that I can make my vision materialize in spite of all the obstacles, and ESPECIALLY in the face of those who say it can't be done.

I think you do that too. When someone locks something in a safe, they are saying, "Nobody can get to this."

You and I are both interested in and motivated by proving those who underestimate us wrong. When we prove them wrong, we feel good.

I think my drive comes from being the youngest of five boys in a family of extremely bright people. I needed to prove to myself, and ultimately to the world, that I was just as good as my older, smarter brothers, but I did it in a different way than they chose.

I guess that your motivation comes from something deep-seated like that as well. There's a reason why we need to prove ourselves in the face of practically unrelenting opposition. I'm not sure exactly what it is, I'm guessing with myself.

But I know there's something!

Mark... You hit the nail on the head for the thing I couldn't put my finger on all my life! I don't know who I was trying to prove it to.... Maybe the world... Maybe no one but myself! That I could do it... Once I did it in my head... It was done! Then JR would tell me I had to watch it 3 times... Once I saw it 3 times... It was ours! We owned it! Thank God I only got caught for the stupid shit I did. No one was ever caught or did a minute because of me! ...the smart Irish kid that made the Italians so much money they couldn't afford to kill me...they wanted to...but they couldn't kill the goose that laid the golden eggs ... Thank God! And I do... Daily, but probably not enough, My Friend! And I count myself honored to be able to say that. Do you know that yours and Ellie's wedding was the first social experience I had in almost 3 years... I had been out for 3 days, I believe, in 1986... when you invited Laura and me to your wedding...Thank you, My Friend, for making me feel that there were people out here who still cared.

It wasn't about the money. It was the thrill, the adrenaline, the endorphins. Yeah, had to feel five moves ahead. That's what it was. Junkies got their dope, actors the stage, but no better feeling than pulling away from a score!

The other thing: how I lost my job at Rupp Auto Livery. I started 10th grade in 1974. Butch had just bought his first gray 1974 Cadillac hearse. Gray was beautiful—it hid dirt better than black. You splash a puddle on a black car, and it shows. Gray? It just disappears. I wanted to see this gray hearse in sunlight, so I pulled it out of the front door, looked around it, and walked the car. Beautiful paint.

I went back in through the garage door and had to cut it hard to fit it into its spot. Using my mirrors, swinging it in... suddenly, "Ah, fuck, I hit something." I stop, pull slightly forward, and back out into the driveway. I hop out, check the car—no scratch. I know I hit something, so I check the garage door jam—scraped. Look around the back of the car, nothing. I'm like, what the fuck did I hit? Walk to the driver's door—door hanging open. I go to close it... and the whole driver's door is caved in. Demolished. I couldn't believe it. I'm thinking, "This isn't a little scratch. I gotta call Butch." He's at dinner. Not a good time.

Then Butch comes down to the garage, stogie between his teeth. He walks in, looks around, sees the car—it's only six weeks old. I thought he was going to bite my head off. But he takes it all in stride. He looks at me and goes, "See, now that's why I told you not to be pulling these out into the driveway."

"Yes, sir, Butch," I said.

The only other thing he said was, "Well, that's what insurance is for." I found out later that he actually ended up making money off the insurance claim because he had a friend fix the door. So he profited from it.

Fast-forward two years. I'm a senior in high school now, really getting good at borrowing the limousines out the side door so my mom can't see me backing them out. There was a side garage door that led to a dirt road—

not much more than an alley, but it was a way out where my mom couldn't see me driving. I had to wait for Mrs. Rupp, the owner's mother, to go out on bingo night so I could take the limo out without her noticing.

One night, Mrs. Rupp is gone. I make my calls— "Hey, we're doing a limo ride tonight"—get all the cars washed, and pull the car I want out. It's sitting perpendicular in the main aisle, already lined up to go out the back door. Perfect. I changed into my cruising clothes so my mom wouldn't see. I go out the side door, get ready to close the garage manually—it didn't have an automatic opener, and I look up. Mrs. Rupp is home. Standing there, staring right at me.

I try signaling with my hands, trying to pull the limo around to the front so I can back it in. Her eyes are growing wider and wider. And then it happens: the 21-foot-long limousine I had backed out of starts taking off without me. I chase after it, almost reaching the half-open driver's door, but the door closes just out of my grasp.

The limo barrels down the driveway. I'm thankful it didn't clip all 13 of the front ends parked nearby; it very well could have. It hits a brand-new 1976 black Ford van, the flower van for the funerals. Head-on. And it drives the van straight through the concrete block wall on the other side. To this day, you can still see the perfect cutout of the van in the blocks where it went through. It was utter chaos.

I had to go home and call Butch Rupp again.

When he showed up this time, he wasn't calm like the first time. He starts going off on me, yelling, pacing, the whole show. He gets to the end of his tirade and says, "Well, how do you think you're gonna pay for this?"

I looked at him and said, "Well, Butch... isn't that what insurance is for?" It was the exact line he used on me when I wrecked the '74.

He went red. He was done with me. I handed over my resignation on the spot. That wrapped up the limo joyriding chapter of my life.

Then came the boat side of it. I learned later that stealing a yacht is an actual crime category, but I tucked that under joyriding. Down at the foot of the Erie docks, where my grandfather kept his tugboat, you had the marinas where people kept their boats. Back then, there was a beach bar called the Peninsula Inn. It used to be Sarah Coyne's place. My Grandma Murphy had been a partners with her. It turned into a big beach bar scene, right on the water. People drove there, sure, but plenty of them came by boat, dropped anchor and walked in through the sand.

I used to borrow boats. I'd take one from the dock, head across the water, and you had to run it out through the channel into the lake to get around the peninsula. You couldn't cut through the bay. I'd take a girl sometimes or bring my friends. We'd run the boat over to the Peninsula Inn, have a night, then cruise back and dock it again. Sometimes I even put gas back in it.

One boat I rigged with a toggle switch under the dashboard so you didn't need a key. All I had to do was hop on, flip the switch, and go.

That covered joyriding boats.

K was knowingly committing a crime.

L was larceny. Pretty much everything I touched had larceny tied to it.

M was mayhem, misdemeanors, and mischief. Motor vehicle theft fell under that one, too.

N was narcotic trafficking and night prowling. I hit both categories hard.

O was obstruction of justice. That came with almost everything I did.

P was pot dealing. We covered that already.

Q was Quaaludes. Back when Rorer 714s were running wild. JR went to prison once and handed me his collection book so I could keep taking payments for him and send the money to the joint. I'm going through the Q section and see "Chuckie Quaalude."

I'm thinking, who the hell is Chuckie Quaalude? It was Chuckie Nolf. I knew him. He owed JR. He was a heavy dealer. Quaaludes were his whole world. He was close with Sarah Coyne, and she let him set up a U.S. Army general's tent on the beach every summer. It was a round tent, about 30 feet across, and Chuckie treated it like his house.

We'd crash there for days at a time. Go home only to shower and change clothes.

Chuckie was so into Quaaludes he'd wake up at the crack of noon, pop a couple, and head straight to the water. That was his version of a shower. He'd climb out about the time the Quaaludes kicked in, drop down on the beach, look at his watch and say, "Flip me at two."

He meant it. He would be out cold, and we'd literally flip him over so he didn't burn on one side.

So one fine day at the crack of noon, Chuckie gets up an runs and jumps into the lake for his morning dip/bath... He dives in, comes up and screams...SHIT!!! I said, "What the Fuck?"... He said, "I lost my fuckin' teeth." You see, even though Chuckie wasn't that old...upper thirties...He had a set of uppers. We all went wading (Chuckie always had a following for the 'ludes), we're all looking for Chuckie's uppers... looked for hours... Nothing!

So the very next day...at the crack of noon... Chuckie, repeat performance...Chuckie dives in... he's down a little long... I start getting concerned... Then he comes up... Owww! He reaches down in the water... and pulls up his trophy... His uppers! He stepped on them in the water. He raises them triumphantly over his head... takes them and swishes them around in the lake water to sterilize them... then puts them in his mouth like nothing ever happened. So were the adventures of the "New Zoo Review" as we called Chuckie's general's tent!

S was for Strong Arm Robbery... One Friday evening, I was heading out to my father's house on West Lake Road... and I saw someone making a bank deposit drop just before midnight. So I follow JR's rule...watch it three times... So next Friday night I'm there, watching at 11:30... boom, 11:47, there it is... like clockwork... Let's see if the third time is a charm...next week... right on time!

So now...Game ON! I'm ready in place at 11:30... I found a great vantage point behind a garbage dumpster about 20 feet from the Night deposit slot, but out of the person's blind spot... I'm going to come running up from behind them and snatch the money bag. A car pulls up... Ready! The person gets out of the car...Get Set! They go walking up to the drop slot... GO! I go running up from behind... Wait... It's a Chick!... No time to flinch... I go for the gold!... Grab the bag, but she ain't giving it up easy... she's going to fight! I say I don't want to hurt you, lady, but I'm leaving with this bag! She struggles... she screams... but I finally wrestle the bag away and go streaking across the parking lot with it, like O.J. Simpson running through the airport for Hertz Rental Cars... Just then, a car comes ripping into the parking lot and nearly runs me down. I give him an O.J. move and barely sidestep the car and take off out of the lot... the guy jumps out of the car...

I had my own mess. He came after me, chased me down the block and into the park near 8th and Green Garden in Erie. He kept coming. I was worn out. I had glasses then, and when I leaned forward, they fell. I bent down for them, ready to pass out from how wiped I was. He stepped toward me. I reached into my pocket like I had a gun. I didn't. I told him one more step would be his last. He bought it. He turned around and went to help the girl.

I followed Green Garden up to the tracks and crossed them. Same tracks where Corporal Robert Owens died. I took them straight to the back of the Old Monte Club. Went upstairs, cut open the money bag, and the night turned into a party.

After that came the list. T was tampering, trespass, and theft. That covered most of my hobbies. U were unauthorized use of a motor vehicle and unlawful possession of a weapon. V was vandalism. W was weapons charges, and there were plenty. X never fit anything except maybe eXctasy...I tried it a couple of times...like no other drug in the world...truly Euphoric, maybe Euphoric recall... which is remembering past experiences in an overly positive light... yeah, maybe that's the story of my life. Y was the yacht job at the peninsula with the boats. Z was the religious zealot phase. I ran around like a holy roller for a while. I'm not like that now. Being a zealot should count as a crime anyway.

That was the ABCs.

CHAPTER 11

DOWN AND OUT IN NEW YORK

I've been transferred from Wende and then up to maximum security Attica. Had a fight to get my security changed to medium security. They put me in Attica because they deemed me maximum security due to an out-of-state warrant for a parole violation for crossing the state line from Pennsylvania into New York. I had to argue that and get my sentence reduced from three and a half to seven, to two to four. Then they sent me to Collins Correctional Facility in Hellmuth, New York.

I went down there and was only there for about three days when a man walked up to me in the prison yard and said, "Tony wants to talk to you."

I said, "I don't know no Tony."

He said, "Well, he's right over there in the corner. And I suggest if Tony wants to talk to you, you talk to Tony."

At that point, I figured maybe I should talk to Tony.

I walked over, and there was a little Sicilian man in the corner. He's got a half dozen bodyguards around him. I remember the scene, and I don't get close.

He said, "So you're Murph the Surf."

I said, "It depends, who's asking."

He said, "Don't get smart with me, kid. So you're JR's kid?"

That hit me hard.

I said, "Yeah, I'm JR's kid."

What shocked me was that JR was in a federal penitentiary in Lake Placid for the armored car robbery, and somehow, he found out where I was getting transferred to in the New York State prison system. He got word to New York City, and New York City got word back to Anthony Tony Cangiano.

This man ended up taking me under his wing because, within a couple of weeks, I became his lieutenant, the same way I had been JR's lieutenant. You couldn't talk to them until you talked to me, because they recognized I was the smartest person in the prison yard.

Tony and I built a near father-and-son relationship. Tony was from Sicily, a made mafioso capo, meaning he was a captain of his own crew.

He told me, I don't know if you remember the movie *The French Connection,* but in the movie, the last five or ten minutes are a gun battle. Tony Cangiano's brother was one of the real-life people killed in that real-life gun battle, the French Connection, when they busted all the heroin coming from Sicily through France into Montreal and then into New York.

Tony's brother was one of the men killed in that real gun battle in New York City. We forged a very tight relationship. He taught me two important rules.

The first one was how to be a tough guy.

He said, "Murph, being a tough guy ain't all that hard. Murph, 98% of the time, you live your life just like anybody else does. You go about your business and just live. Two percent of the time, you have to do what is required, when it's required, and how it's required. Then you're a tough guy."

I never forgot those words. Two percent of the time: what is required, when it's required, how it's required. Things were specific, and you'd better carry them out to a T.

We got close, and the whole time I was mourning Mary DeSanto's death. I learned of her overdose when I was in Attica and then got shipped to Collins Correctional Facility. My only objective was going to be getting back to Erie, Pennsylvania, and being judge, jury, and the angel of death in one night. I was going to find out who gave Mary DeSanto the drugs. I was going to find out, and I was going to kill them. I was fully prepared to end up doing life or die, and that was my only objective for getting out of prison.

I thought I knew who gave her the drugs. I thought it was Michael. I thought it was Michael Farbo because every time Mary and I broke up, he would swoop right in and start taking her out. So I thought it was him.

About a year after her death, I found out that Michael Farbo committed suicide by blowing his head off with a shotgun. I figured Mary DeSanto's brothers were probably there, standing by his side, helping him do it. I had some small bit of comfort thinking maybe that was handled. But this was before I learned he was dead.

So I was going to go back and take care of it. I was going to start going through drug dealers one at a time, the biggest dealers in Erie, and I would have gotten the answer.

About two months before I had to go to the parole board, Tony Cangiano and I were sitting on his bunk one night. He said, "Murph, Murph, I know what you're planning on doing, Murph, and I can't talk you out of it. But there's a saying back in my country, Murph." He was right from Sicily. "If you go out with vengeance in your heart, dig two graves, one for the person you're after and one for yourself, because that's where it might end up."

He let that hang for a second. Then he said, "Murph, do you think this is really what she would have wanted for your life? She wanted so much more for your life, Murph."

That was around the time I had been taking college classes. He said, "When you get out, go to college. Make something of yourself."

So when I got out, I went and got a two-year degree in robotics and automation, and I built a career as an electrical engineer off that two-year degree. I was grateful for Tony Cangiano.

There was one other thing after I got out. I believe it was 1986, some type of anniversary for the Statue of Liberty. It might have been the hundred-year anniversary.

Tony called me up from New York City because he had gotten out, and he asked Laura and me to come to New York City for the Statue of Liberty celebration. He had a yacht with about fifty people on it. It was going to go out during the Statue of Liberty celebration, and I'm quite sure it was a high-line affair. He said everything was taken care of, not to worry about anything, and that we just had to get up there.

I really wanted to go, but at the time we had Justin, and Justin was in a wheelchair, and we didn't have the care to take him. So, I ended up having to turn down his invitation. But I had a feeling he was inviting me up to

New York City for more than a casual party. I'm sure he would have propositioned me because he recognized how smart I was, and he appreciated me. I did a lot for him in the joint.

So that was Tony Cangiano. And that led to Christmas Eve of 1985. Tony had food brought in right from New York City, flown directly to the prison so we could make a decent meal, just like the scene in *Goodfellas* where they're cooking the meal. We didn't do that every day, but he had it lined up for Christmas. They brought real food in from New York City, authentic Italian foods, and we cooked all day.

On Christmas Eve 1985, there were about ten or twelve Italians from New York City. And then there was one smart Irish kid who made them so much money they couldn't afford to kill me. They wanted to, but they couldn't afford to. And then there were three Colombians who were invited by the Italians for Christmas Eve dinner, and that was because one of them was Pablo Escobar's nephew.

I do have a picture of them. There's a picture of three guys, Spanish-looking. You can tell from that picture. His nephew, Luis, is the furthest one to the right. The man in the middle—Sebastian, I'll remember his name—was the one who confessed to the same crime Pablo Escobar's nephew was in there for. That man had nothing to do with that crime. He confessed as a favor to Pablo Escobar, so he could follow his nephew through prison and guard him. He confessed to something he didn't do to stay with him. And the third man in the picture was like the Colombian sergeant-at-arms, the battle master. Those three were in there cooking dinner with us, too.

At the time, there was a huge snowstorm. It was Christmas Eve, and none of the buses from New York City could make it to the prison. They had buses chartered just for people visiting their loved ones from New York

City, bringing them into the middle of nowhere. Collins Correctional Facility in Hellmuth, New York—it was in the middle of absolute nowhere. And the buses couldn't get through. So nobody from New York City could make it. That meant no drugs were coming into the prison that night. No one had anything.

I was the only one who had drugs in the prison, because my wife Laura— she wasn't my wife yet—lived about fifteen minutes away and she was bringing me drugs regularly. Then Pablo Escobar's nephew, Luis Escobar, came up to me and said, "Murph, could you take care of me?" I said, "Sure, sure."

The next Saturday, Laura told me she had a knock at her apartment door. She opened it, and there was a little Colombian girl who didn't speak a word of English. All she had was a piece of paper with my name, Tim Murphy, 85C0177—which was my prison number—and a five-hundred-dollar bill. She handed it to Laura and turned and walked away without saying a thing.

Laura started getting me ounces of reefer. She would smuggle it in balloons, and she'd have to transfer it to me internally. I had to shove it up my ass to get it into the prison. So she would Vaseline up the balloons.

I was the only one on Christmas Eve night in the whole fucking prison who had a joint of reefer. We were just about ready to sit down and break bread together, and all of a sudden, these three Black guys came walking into the room, which was a big offense. They walk straight up to me because the one guy, the leader, Jay—this guy was a spitting image of Michael Spinks. Big, Black, dumb muscles and that's it. No brains.

He comes right up to me. His cube had been the cubicle next to mine for six months. One night, his cube was getting shaken down by the guards, and he slid a shank underneath my desk. I took the shank and hid it for him. I thought we were good. But in the joint, you're not good with anybody.

He walks up, and he said, "You got, and we want."

I said, "Well, there ain't nothing happening, Jay- Especially you coming at me this way. I ain't got a seed for you."

He said, "Oh, really? We'll be down in the fucking TV room at 7 o'clock." That meant I had to meet them down there to rumble, throw down.

I said, "Whatever."

And J said, "Whatever, whatever."

Then Nene, the sergeant-at-arms for Pablo Escobar's nephew, spoke up. He said, "Oh, excuse me. Does that go for anybody at this table?"

And J said, "Whatever."

And Nene said, "Whatever, whatever."

That meant it was on. Now we had a full-scale war between the Blacks, the Italians, and the Colombians. Everybody sent out their feelers right away.

Now I had to go get ready for battle.

I had to go put on my sweats and sneakers and make sure I was ready to roll. I went to my kid, Rosa, who was sort of my runner. I said, "You go get Patterson."

This leads into the next part of the chapter.

Kenny Patterson was one of the baddest men I've ever known. There's a picture of a poem at the end of this book that he wrote when he was in Attica. He had gone to Vietnam. He served in a search-and-destroy troop called the Widowmakers. He was the staff sergeant of the Widowmakers. He told me his job was that when they wiped out a small Vietnamese village, and it was over, he had to walk through and put a bullet in everyone's head to make sure they were dead. The poem lays some of that out.

ABC News 20/20 made a documentary in Attica about men who never had a parking ticket before Vietnam, went to the war, and came back stone-cold killers. We taught them how to kill, then dropped them back into society without rewiring anything. Patterson was one of them.

When he came back, he robbed a Jewish diamond store in the Diamond District in New York City. He got caught. He got seven years. He did the seven, made parole, got out. They alleged that in forty-three days on the street, he ripped off a million-and-a-half dollars from the same Jewish Diamond District.

He told me about the night he was holding down the diamond grinders, forcing them to open the safe. He had a gun to one guy's head. Something moved in his peripheral vision, and he said, "Timmy, in 'Nam, you didn't look to see what it was. You just shot." That's what he did. He fired left and hit whatever moved. Turned out it was one of the diamond grinders. Luckily, it didn't kill him. The bullet went through his cheek and out of his mouth.

He didn't kill the guy, but he got another seven years for it.

He was only out for forty-three days. He rips off a million and a half bucks and shoots somebody else. They throw him back into Attica, doing another seven and a half years. While he was inside, he went to college in the joint and got his degree in psychology. Four years. Perfect 4.0. He was another genius. That's why we hooked up the way we did.

ABC News 20/20 came in for that documentary about the guys who went to Vietnam clean and came home wired wrong. They only showed four interviews. Patterson was one of them. Before he went over there, he didn't have a parking ticket. Came back a killer.

So I told Rosa, "You go get Patterson." I got dressed for battle and went down to the TV room at seven. I stood in the corner with my back tight to the wall so I could see the whole room.

Patterson walked in, heading straight for me, staring me eye to eye. His hands were tucked under his arms. He walked right up, still staring. I said, "Patterson, don't give your back to this room." Meaning somebody could slide a blade in his spine. And he said, "If you blink, something's dying."

Right then, he shifted his arms, raised them a little, and I saw it. He had a shank in each hand, both of them tucked in under his armpits. Again, he said, "If you blink, something's dying."

Right on cue, Jay shows up. The Michael Spinks look-alike. Big, black, ugly muscle. Nothing else is going on upstairs. We met in the middle of the TV room. I said, "What's up, Jay?" He said, "I want, you got." I said, "Jay, if you came at me respectfully, I would've given you a joint. But not like this. You ain't getting a seed."

They started with the "whatever, whatever." Then boom, we went at it. Racking and cracking. We were on each other for maybe thirty seconds before the guards heard the noise and came in. Everyone scattered to the corners. I was in my corner trying to breathe. Patterson stood beside me, giving his back to the room again, like he didn't care who was behind him.

We all pretended the whole thing was a fight about somebody trying to change the TV channel. Guards bought it, calmed everyone down, and left.

I was trying to catch my breath. Patterson leaned toward me and said, "Timmy, you gotta get in close and hurt this motherfucker."

I thought, holy hell. I was never a boxer. I wrestled in high school. So I figured I'd try a leg takedown. Get him on the ground and tear him apart there.

Round two. We met back in the middle of the room, toe to toe. Ding, ding. I went for his leg, wrapping mine behind his. As I moved in, he caught me with a right uppercut that nearly took my left eyeball out. I was diving into it full speed. He came up with power. My eye blew up instantly. Felt like half a baseball.

But I managed to grab him anyway, and we hit the floor still fighting, racking and cracking, both of us trying to finish it. Guards come in again; we break it up and go to our corners.

Now I'm dying, I've had enough and am ready to call it a night when Patterson walks up again and says the words I'll never forget.... "Timmy, I got a news flash for ya! ... You ain't No Fuckin" boxer!" If I weren't close to death, I would have laughed. Then he got in my face, nose to nose, and said, "You've got to get in close to this guy and take a piece of him!" I had been ready to throw in the towel, but Patterson's words triggered me. Yes, that uncontrollable Murphy rage that had served me well in the past.

186

Round three. I went in and executed that leg take-down that Coach Renee Hayes had drilled me so many times on the Academy High School Lions' wrestling team… textbook execution…wrapped the leg…slammed him to the concrete floor… sleeper hold that JR had taught me wrapped both arms around his neck like an Anaconda snake…squeezing the life out of him. Then I saw my mark and remembered the words of Patterson… wanted to make him proud… "Take a piece of him!" So I bit a piece of his ear off and spat it in his face. Ding, Ding… Game, Set, and Match!

Within a few days, Jay had to enter himself into PC, Protective Custody… When you ask the Man to protect you in the joint because you are scared for your life. It wasn't me Jay was afraid of. It was all his little minions that had followed him because, after the fight, they all said to themselves, "That little white boy did pretty well against Jay. And a couple of them grew some balls for themselves and challenged his authority. That was it. He was gone.

Well, I got released in late May of 1986 and moved in with Laura and Justin because I did not want to return to the revolving prison door that awaited me in Erie, Pa. I started working day one for Julian "Butchie" Halliby, one of JR's old buddies. He actually wrote a letter to the New York State Parole Board on my behalf, stating that I had a job to come out to at Checker Cab Co. in Little Lackawanna, NY. That was huge in getting released. That and Laura writing a letter stating that I had a residence in New York State upon release.

Without those, I could have easily maxed out because the Parole Board doesn't like to take many risks, especially with out-of-state repeat offenders. When I moved in with Laura, she had taken in an 18-year-old girl to rescue her from the streets and to take care of Justin while Laura went to work at a local doctor's office. Laura had earned her GED and then went on to get her LPN, Licensed Practical Nursing degree, all while caring for a disabled son who required 100% care. Well, there were some awkward moments between the babysitter and me. We would be home alone during the day sometimes, and I know she used to hear Laura and me going at it at night. Hey, I had been down for years, and I was trying to catch up on lost time.

Well, she was barely 18, hot, and horny. She would sleep on the couch in nothing but her underwear, which left nothing to the imagination. She would hop up in the morning, everything bouncing and behaving, jump into the shower, and come out prancing in nothing but a towel. Then she would start asking me about prison, and I knew she wanted it. There was nothing to the imagination as she would flash and entice me. But I resisted, and it took all my might because I didn't want to screw things up with Laura, although I eventually would...

Patterson was released in July of that same year, just in time for the fourth. When he got out, he initially had to go into a halfway house, and technically, he and I could not have any contact being we were both on parole. But who follows rules? I would pick him up after I got done working for Butchie at Checker Cab. You see, it wasn't exactly a 40-hour-a-week job, like he wrote to the Parole Board. It was usually a few hours a day doing whatever maintenance the cabs needed. If there were a major repair on one of the cabs, I would work until the job was done. Sometimes days on end, sometimes into the night to get the cab back on the road. I didn't punch a time clock...I punched in on loyalty and gratitude for him writing the letter, so I always made sure those cabs were on the road, putting money into his pocket so he could put some money in mine. It was a mutual relationship, and Butchie liked having me around because I could fix anything. The God-given Murphy talent...take anything apart... put it back together... and make it work.

So I would pick up Kenny when I got out of work and take him to do whatever he had to do to satisfy parole. They were making him jump through hoops. I had to satisfy my own parole officer, who had a "Little Napoleon" complex. He was constantly exerting his authority on me…all five-foot nothin' of him, then sticking his hip out with his big man service revolver on his hip. Big man.

I loved Patterson. I owed my life to him. I would have never made it that Christmas Eve without him. So the best favor I could think of was to get him laid. He had been down almost 17 years, minus the 43 days he was out, so I knew he was due. So I talked to the babysitter who had a girlfriend who would come over to party when Laura was at work. I told them both to have a swinger party with the four of us … two ex-cons straight out of prison and two hot and horny 18-year-olds. They were all in.

The girls were waiting in the bedroom for us to come in. I sent Patterson in first and never walked in the room myself. I let Patterson have both girls to himself after seventeen years in prison. They were both only eighteen at the time. Patterson was forever grateful for that. He was very appreciative.

When he came out, he was happier than a faggot in boot camp. He said, "Timmy, you gotta do me one more favor. You gotta give me a ride."

I said, "Sure, I'll give you a ride."

He said, "No, this is a ride across the state."

I said, "What? Patterson, we're not supposed to… both of us are on parole. We're not supposed to be out of Erie County."

He said, "You gotta give me this ride, Timmy. Just one fucking ride."

He added, "It's almost Albany, clear across the state of New York."

It was like a six-hour ride. Then we took a left and went north. I said, "All right, Patterson, sure."

I gave him the ride. We were out in the boonies. I don't even know where I was. He was pointing and telling me where to go, and I was driving, Murph the Surf, as always.

We got out in the middle of nowhere—bumfuck, Egypt—and there was this old abandoned barn in the distance. He said, "Just wait here for me, Timmy."

So I waited. He walked out of sight, and I lost track of him. He was gone for over half an hour, going on forty-five minutes. I was starting to sweat. I wasn't supposed to be out of Erie County. I was sitting in the middle of nowhere in my car. If any cop pulled up, I was done. But I stayed. I waited.

After about forty-five minutes, he came walking up out of the barn. He had this little canvas military bag with him. He hopped in the car and said, "Okay, let's go."

We drove back. I didn't say anything. I didn't ask. I didn't want to know. I had given him the ride.

We got back to Hamburg, New York, to the apartment I shared with Laura. Nobody was home. It was just Kenny and me. He opened the canvas bag and started rooting around. I could hear there was a ton of jewelry and some cash in it.

Then he pulled something out and said, "This is for you, Timmy."

He handed me a piece of carved jewelry: a jade monk, about three inches high, standing on a black onyx base. The base was probably about two inches in diameter and an inch and a half thick, solid black onyx. Coming out of the base was a gold vine growing up and arching over the monk's head. On the vine were eight gold blossoms, and every other blossom had either a ruby or a diamond—four rubies, four diamonds.

This thing was probably priceless, but it had been buried for seventeen years. Patterson had stashed that canvas bag before he got arrested. Someone in his family owned the property back then, some farm way out there. While he was in Attica, they went belly-up, and the place sat abandoned. The barn shouldn't have even been standing, but somehow it was. He had hidden that bag somewhere inside—it looked buried to me because the canvas was filthy.

He said, "This is yours, Timmy. This is for the babysitter and her girlfriend."

I said, "Are you sure?"

He said, "Yeah. Don't worry. There's plenty more where that came from."

And he wasn't kidding. He pulled out diamonds like it was nothing. It was insane what he had hidden out there.

But I was on parole. And this piece was so identifiable it might as well have had a neon sign taped to it. I couldn't take it to anybody on the street. It looked like something you'd see behind glass with a security guard staring at you.

I had a problem, because my fence, Julian "Butchie" Halaby—JR's buddy—had just died. He was my guy. Without him, I was stuck.

Laura had a close friend, Robbie I., a jeweler who worked for the original Don Orlando Jeweler in Buffalo. Old-school operation. You had to get buzzed into the elevator on the seventh floor of the Franklin Building. Real deal people. Unmounted diamonds, serious clients.

Robbie liked me right out of prison. He was tight with Laura and one of the first people to throw me little jobs so I could get back on my feet—building a tool shed, fixing things at his house. He was a good guy. Still is.

He was the only person I could trust with something like this.

So I took it to him. I set the jade monk on the counter. Robbie didn't say a word. He went straight to get Don Orlando himself—Buffalo's top jeweler forever. They both looked at it, and Don offered me twelve grand on the spot.

Right there, I knew it was worth at least ten times that. Probably more. But I was on parole, sweating bullets, and I needed the cash. I said, "Give me the twelve."

I asked what they were going to do with it. Robbie said, "We're gonna cut it up."

I said, "You're not cutting that piece."

I told him the real move was finding a private collector. Someone with a stash of rare items who didn't care where it came from. Someone who paid for what they liked, no questions asked.

That's how I ended up getting rid of it.

Not long after that, Patterson stepped into another role—enforcer. Justin's father, Joe McHenry, wasn't paying child support. Years behind. Patterson overheard us talking one day about a hearing scheduled for Wednesday at nine.

He didn't say a word. He just showed up.

He sat in the back row of the courtroom, quiet as a shadow, watching Joe. Didn't nod to me. Didn't nod to Laura. Didn't even blink our way.

But we saw him.

And Joe saw him too, even if he didn't know who he was.

We walked out of the courtroom, and Joe McHenry was in a phone booth on Court Street in Buffalo. Right as we stepped outside, he was standing there on the phone. Patterson walked straight up to him, opened the door, and stood in the doorway so Joe couldn't move.

Patterson said, "Hang up the phone."

Joe hung up.

Patterson said, "You owe this lady some money. I suggest you better start making those payments next Friday. Don't make me come back and ask for another payment. And I better not hear anything on any Friday."

Laura started getting payments.

Then Joe screwed up and missed a few. Patterson found out. He called me and said, "Let's go bar hopping on Clinton Street." That was Joe's stomping ground.

We hit all the bars along the strip. We walked into the Pump Inn, a real dive, and there was Joe with his new wife. They were sitting in a booth.

Patterson didn't wait for me. He walked right up to the booth and planted himself at the end of the seat so Joe couldn't stand.

He said, "I thought I told you not to miss any payments, motherfucker. You're not getting out of this place without making this payment."

It started getting loud. I stood there without saying a word. I was just blocking his wife from getting up.

Then this guy came walking over—Chevy. Chevy had spent seventeen years in the joint with Patterson. We hadn't seen him walk in, but he saw the commotion.

He stepped up to the end of the booth and said, "Excuse me. Excuse me." Then to Joe: "You know what? I recommend that if you have a problem with this man right here, you settle that problem. Because no disrespect to you, sir, you might be a real bad. But I KNOW this man is really bad. And if you have a problem with him, I'd suggest that you settle it right now."

Joe took every dollar he had in his pockets and laid it on the table. I scooped it up. We left and headed to another bar.

Now we're drinking, and I don't even know what the issue was between Patterson and me, but we got into it. Bad enough that one of us had a little

.25 automatic out. I can't even remember the details. All I remember is going home afterward.

The phone rang. Patterson said, "I'm killing you in the morning, motherfucker." Then he hung up.

I didn't sleep much. I couldn't even remember what the fight was about.

In the morning, Laura called Patterson and begged him not to kill me. Thank God he backed off, because neither one of us could remember what we were arguing about.

JUST ANOTHER DAY

The sounds of the rotary
blades brings smiles and
grins to a few men in
need every now and then.
They look to the sky
with smoke ready in hand,
and hope in the heavens
that it can land.

The smoke is popped
and the bird comes in
with door guns blazing
and saviors with grins.
The few men run crouched
low and ready,
for they all know the shots
will come fast and heavy.

They sprint to the bird,
with their rifles firing,
in hopes of a chance to remain surviving.
Into the bird they all but one,
who spun and fell,
but somehow crawled on
his legs wet with the warm steady flow,
as his friends snatched him up,
and they were ready to go.

The bird lifted out in a low slow arc,
the men all smiled, they made their depart.
With one man wounded, eight still in tact,
the bird comes in with a hell-of-a-week

The wounded man off in no time flat.
The eight men are off and walking away,
wondering in their minds if they'll survive
Just Another Day.

                    by Ken Patterson
                    Vietnam 1966-1968
                    1st Bde, 101st Airborne Div.
                    2/502 Inf. (Widow Makers)

1

Kenny Patterson was a bad man, and I owe my life to him.

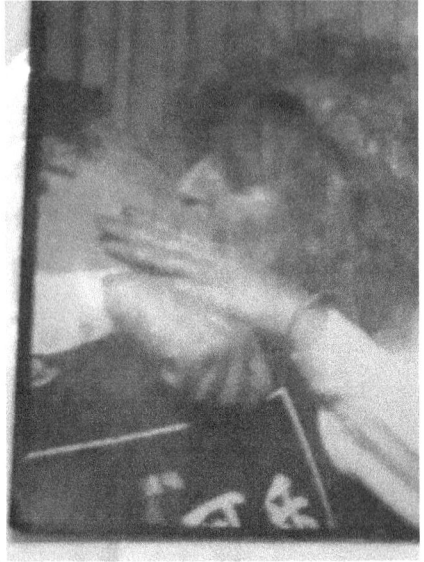

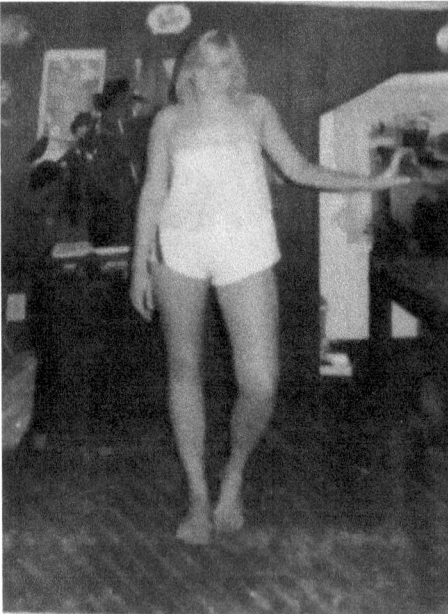

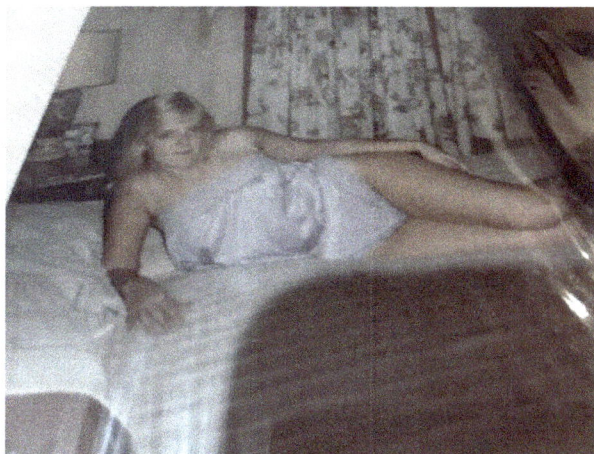

CHAPTER 12

THE COUNTRY CLUB

I was sitting in the Ol' Monte Club when this well-dressed young lady walked in, clueless about the kind of crowd she'd just stepped into. She'd had a few drinks already, got into an argument with her boyfriend, and bailed out of his car. Straight out of one mess and right into ours.

She said she was a secretary for the manager of a country club...and let slip that there was a spare key tucked behind the back entrance to the bar.

Elmer and I threw on Puma running suits and cased the place during lunch hour. We even sat down, ordered lunch, and charged it to an address at the country club, as we belonged there.

When it came time to do it, Elmer was out of town, so I went by myself. I went to the back door, felt around, and heard something drop into the dirt. Was that a key? It was.

I went in and cracked the safe: a few grand, plus some other valuables. On the way out, while passing the bar, I figured I could use a bottle of Black Velvet to celebrate. When I reached over the bar, I looked down, and a security guard was checking the bottles and glassware under the counter.

I caught him in the act of ripping off the place, and it startled him. He said, "You know the back door is open..." stammering because he knew he was caught.

I said, "I know. I was just locking up the place, and I'm going to check that right now."

I walked down the hall, hit that door, and took off running like a bat out of hell. It took him about thirty seconds before he realized I wasn't coming back. I had to run about a hundred yards across a spotlight-lit open field toward a tree line that led to the lakeshore.

Once the guard figured out he'd been chatting with the burglar who just cleaned the place out, he bolted through the back door and yelled, "Stop, or I'll shoot!" He wasn't bluffing either. I kept moving toward the tree line, and he shouted again, trying to sound official. I hit the trees, dove straight through, and only then learned there was a drop of forty or fifty feet on the other side.

I went tumbling down, bounced off a ledge, and rolled into a heap on the beach. Pain hit fast, and I could barely get upright. I didn't know if he planned to follow me down, so I dragged myself along with nothing but adrenaline and bad luck keeping me upright. I grabbed a piece of driftwood and turned it into a makeshift crutch, then hobbled down the shoreline for a couple of miles.

When I finally worked my way back up toward the streets, the first intersection told me everything I needed to know. Police radios. Checkpoints. A whole welcoming committee. This was back before cell phones, when you had to show up where you said you'd be or everyone assumed you'd vanished.

Funny thing is, one of the best partners I ever had was a woman. Year after year, I learned something simple: the women I worked with showed up. The men... let's say the attendance record told another story.

I moved away from the intersection and found a social club sitting out in the middle of nowhere. The parking lot had an old phone booth—perfect and awful at the same time. I went in, cracked the light so it wouldn't glow like a beacon, and called the young woman who was the second great love of my life. Sonny in *A Bronx Tale* says you get three. She was one of mine.

It was around two in the morning when I told her, "Deb, I need you to pick me up in this parking lot. There's a checkpoint right down the street." Then I gave her the plan: "Pull in, pop the trunk, and drive smooth through the checkpoint."

She handled it like she'd rehearsed it her whole life. Pulled in next to the phone booth, popped the trunk, and slid in, trying not to groan. She closed it, drove off, and rolled right up to the checkpoint. Calm as could be, she lowered the window and said, "Is there a problem, officers?" Meanwhile, I was in the trunk praying she didn't hit a pothole.

They made her switch on the dome light and checked the back seat. Nothing else. She eased on through like she'd done it a hundred times.

This girl—five foot nothing and maybe ninety pounds—had more guts than guys three times her size. We had a friendship, romance, love, and a fair amount of trouble mixed in. She even came all the way from Erie to visit me in a New York State prison before she moved to California. She was one of the best people in my life. Once I was busted in New York, most folks vanished. Maybe that wasn't the worst thing in the long run.

The final World Series of Rock was being held in Cleveland, Ohio on July 19, 1980 at Cleveland Municipal Stadium... And I was going to show Debbie a good time...

These were day-long events featuring 3 – 6 performers/bands and could only be scheduled when the Cleveland Indians played out of town for a few days...long enough to repair the damage to the infield and outfields. In 1974, there were three events, four in 1975 and in 1976, there were no events because of the extensive damage to the field in 1975. Aerosmith was the first band scheduled that year, but cancelled out when they were told that the fans wouldn't be allowed around the front of the stage because of the damage from the previous year. That put the kibosh on the rest of the season. In 1977, the season resumed with four shows. It was always a highly anticipated show as the lineups were always legendary, but it was also known for its drunkenness, drugs, and rowdy behavior. Back then, you could carry coolers right into the stadium, and there were no security checkpoints like today. If you had a ticket, you were getting in. The reason it was the final one was that the previous year, there were several shootings, robberies, and one fatality of those who waited outside the stadium overnight, as most of the seating was general admission for $12.50 a head. We weren't worried about any security issues...we had our own all-star lineup of our own to go with the incredible lineup that night.

So it was Debbie's Birthday weekend, and I was going to sweep her off her feet with my all-star lineup. First Big "Jimmy P. OR JP" and his pretty wife

Patty. JP was a bouncer in just about every one of Erie's toughest bar's from the Lower East Side Irish and Polish bars, to Little Italy's - P.P. Club, Sons of Italy, on and on. He was a big man 6, 3" at least 350 pounds... I used to feel bad for his wife; she was a sweetheart. We took JP's full-size Cadillac Fleetwood Brougham. Then there was the Birthday girl, Debbie and me. Then rounding out the lineup were Pearl Gryzbowski and Maxi Jordano ... two to would soon be infamous for some dramatic performances.

Pearl was only a few months away from pulling off the Halloween Mask Bank robbery in Erie, led by mastermind Leslie Hans. He had it down to a science. 4 people – stop-watch - 90 seconds in and out - military-like precision. One driver, lookout/scanner man, one man with the stop-watch and military assault rifle – holds down the front door and is the only one that speaks...He shouts orders for everyone to hit the floor and keeps the 3-ring circus under control. The other two actually walk in first, unannounced and walk right up to both ends of the tellers' counter and hop over to cover any teller that is going to make a stupid move for an alarm button. The ringleader comes in just as the two hop over the counter and announce that "This is a robbery, get on the floor!" to get everyone's attention for the split second to allow the two to get over and cover anyone willing or stupid enough to make a move. The stopwatch is clicked at this point, and time is ticking. Back then, with the technology as it was, you had at least 90 90-second response time before an alarm would go out to the alarm company and then to local police. The two wingmen would immediately start going teller to teller, cleaning out their drawers, with a gun pointed at the teller's head, directing them to leave the die-pack trip packs of cash, which would blow up an indelible die on a time release. The gun to the temple made the teller think a bit more clearly. When they met in the middle, they would jump back over the counter and make their egress without saying a word unless someone got out of line. They would exit and hop in the back seat with the money, and Leslie would be the last to exit the bank, hop in the getaway car, taking a right-hand turn out of the parking lot. They had alleged that Leslie Hans had masterminded and led over 70 such heists across the United States. Well, this time they thought it would be fun to take Pearl along for the ride since she was seeing Leslie's partner. Well, they would see how that works out in the future.

The other part of our party crew that day was Maxi Jordano, who was a knock-around guy on the streets of Little Italy. He wasn't a big guy in stature, but he was built stocky and solid and had been through the rough and tumble streets, but his summer would be in a couple more years.

The all-star stage lineup that night was incredible. It was Def Leppard's first concert back in the U.S. They were the warm-up band. Then J. Giles Band, which always got the crowd amped up with their one-of-a-kind harmonica jam band vibe. Next was Eddie Money who was a former New York City cop turned giant rock and roller … "Two Tickets to Paradise" and that's what I was hoping with "Little Debbie" she was like a little hot "Betty Boop" for real, a little doll, And last of the night the headliner was "Bob Seger" and the "Silver Bullet Band" I always thought was the quintessential Rock N Roll band … before everyone had "Autotune" built in Bob and the Boys rocked 'em best all night long.

So we drive up to Cleveland in JP's Caddy and get a hotel room. We can only find one double room with two beds. Pearl and Maxi decide they will crash on the floor. We had stopped on the way up and bought a Coleman camping cooler and a six-and-a-half-gallon. Then we went to the liquor store and bought two half gallons of light rum and a half gallon of dark rum because they didn't have another half of light. We took it back to the room, put the water container in the cooler, packed it with ice, put the three half-gallons of rum in the container and ordered room service for five gallons of Coke from the kitchen. They brought it up in ten pitchers on a room-service cart. So we were set with beverages for the evening.

Showtime comes, and we are off to the races with Coleman cooler and Rum and Cokes on ice for the night. JP and Maxi carried it right in through the gate. No questions asked back then. We make our way to some decent seats in the stands and let the music begin. Every band was electric, working the crowd into a drunken, drugged frenzy by the time the Nightcap Bob Seger and the Silver Bullet Band came on. During the set change, with roadies running wild to get the band set up, I hear these immortal words from JP... " I didn't drive a hundred miles to sit a hundred miles from Bob Seger! With that, the mountain arose and prepared to make a path. I looked at Debbie, who weighed all of about 90 pounds and said, *Whatever you do, stay behind him and hold on to his belt*. Well, JP arose and started clearing a path like Moses parted the waters. He marched right down the stairs onto the field and cleared a path for us, finally stopping about thirty feet from center stage. Oh man, what a scene. All of a sudden, JP turns around and says *Where's the Rum and Coke?* We all looked around and then looked back up in the stands, and there it was, all alone up in our seats, amazingly still there; no one had taken it. Oh well, an offering to the concert gods. No way were we going to try to retrieve it now. So the show goes on, and a good time was had by all.

We all head back and crash in the hotel room, JP and his wife Patty in one bed, Debbie and me in the other, and Pearl and Maxi get set to crash on the floor. Although Pearl wanted to join Debbie and me in our bed, she wasn't interested in me as much as little Debbie. Pearl would go both ways and was known to have nice little girlfriends whom she would entice into lesbian and bisexual relationships. I wasn't going to let her touch my Little Debbie and told her, "No Fuckin' Way! Stay on the floor, Bitch!" And that's a quote.

So we all have our spots and are trying to crash for the night. It was a Saturday night and it was a ritual back then to watch Saturday Night Live which was in it's prime with the original "Not Ready for Primetime

Players" which included the late great John Belushi, Dan Akroyd (The original Blues Brothers), George Coe (I gotta admit I don't remember him although I don't remember a lot from the 70's…the drugs were good back then), Jane Curtain, Garrett Morris, Laraine Newman, Michael O'Donoghue, and Gilda Radner (RIP). Bill Murray joined the cast in January 1977 after Chevy Chase got full of himself and left the cast halfway through the second season. It was all for the better because his exit allowed John Belushi to shine as he truly was the heart and soul of the "Not Ready for Prime Time Players." It was a tragic loss to the world that he took that fateful "Speedball" of heroin and cocaine and passed from this earth on March 5, 1982, in the Chateau Marmont in Los Angeles, California. Someone left a sign on his headstone one time, invoking one of his classic lines, which went… "He could have stuck around and given us a few more laughs… 'BUT NOOOOOOOOO!!!' "

We're all just about crashed for the evening when on the TV came a Public Service Announcement… A young, unfamiliar face came on the screen wearing a plaid hunter's cap and exclaimed, " Some people say what I have can be Werry, Werry, Sewious! I'm afwicted with Elmer Fudd diswease!" He went on and on, and initially, we thought it was a legit public service announcement. Back then, SNL used to mix these seamlessly into the show and were so good you wouldn't know if it was real or not until it got so outlandish you couldn't believe it. It started slow with a bit of a chuckle from JP … "Ha….Ha-Ha… Ha-Ha-Ha! … Who the hell is this guy?" Pretty soon we were all rolling with laughter so hard we couldn't catch our breath, to the point we were literally crying, the guy was so funny. It turns out that was the first night we all saw the comedic genius of Robin Williams doing stand-up comedy. Even though he had been doing his immortal "Mork" since the breakout comedy of "Mork and Mindy" in 1978, we had never seen him do impromptu comedy, which was pure genius and outrageously hilarious, always drawing uncontrollable laughter, as his mind was so bizarre that the average mind could only respond with uncontrollable laughter. That was the night we had the privilege of hearing four of the most powerful Rock N' Roll acts of the era and witnessing the advent of one of the true "Clowned Princes of Comedy" of all time. Another tragic parting of talent that burned so bright like a shooting star in John and Robin! May you rest in Peace, Boys... You made us laugh!

Little Debbie in the hot red pants- My Betty Boop with the heart of a Lion!

CHAPTER 13

ANTHONY "CY" CIOTTI

Cy Ciotti was the bona fide boss of Erie. He shared power with Ray Ferritto. They ran just about every racket in town and even shared bank accounts.

My brother-in-law once told me a story. Both he and my sister worked at PNC Bank in Erie. Terry said he'd have Cy Ciotti, Ray Ferritto, and Frank "Bolo" Dovisha come in once a month to get into a safety deposit box. Bolo was the one who was murdered later on. The three of them strolled in like they were checking on their own living room.

My brother-in-law was a shy guy, so timid that he avoided eye contact with anyone who might raise his blood pressure. He said, "I tried never to look at them. But now and then I'd have to look up, and every time I did, Ray Ferritto was staring me right in the eye." He said he'd snap his eyes back to the paperwork because it made him uncomfortable.

Cy was the boss of Erie. What family he was actually made out of is where the stories split. I always believed he was Magaddino. But the article, the UPI piece I kept, claimed he might have been Bufalino. That wouldn't shock me either. The Bufalino crew covered the east side of Pennsylvania. Still, I always leaned toward Magaddino, partly because J.R. answered to Cy. JR worked for him at the Cali Club and ran whatever jobs Cy sent his way.

Article:

New York, one of the U.S. Marshal's "15 Most Wanted Fugitives," tracked to South America and Asia for jumping bail on a narcotics conviction, was quietly arrested in a Manhattan hotel, officials said Monday. Anthony Dominic Ciotti, 56, of Erie, Pennsylvania, had been sought since May 1983 when he jumped $50,000 bail and failed to surrender to begin serving a 15-year sentence he received in Pittsburgh for a federal narcotics conviction, Inspector Robert Leschorn of the U.S. Marshal Service said. Charges included conspiracy to import and distribute controlled substances — synthetic heroin, marijuana, and cocaine.

Ciotti's close associate, Marion Parisi, 61, a private investigator from Coraopolis, Pennsylvania, was with him and was arrested and charged with harboring a fugitive. Parisi was later released on a $100,000 personal recognizance bond.

The two were quietly taken down by nine marshals during a stakeout in the lobby of the Sheraton Centre Hotel in midtown Manhattan late Sunday night, Leschorn said.

Although Ciotti, reputed to be a soldier in the Bufalino crime family in Pennsylvania, was considered armed and dangerous, he was unarmed at the time and did not resist.

"He was just a step ahead of us," Deputy Chief Marshal John Walsh said.

Ciotti had been moving around freely, traveling to Taiwan, Hong Kong, Brazil, and Venezuela. He had dyed his hair black, shaved his eyebrows and beard, and lost 35 pounds. He had been living quietly in Brooklyn with friends.

"It's over," the marshals said to him. They reported he looked "utterly amazed."

Both men were held at the Manhattan Correctional Center. Ciotti was set to be returned to Pittsburgh to begin serving his sentence.

Parisi faced arraignment and up to five years if convicted. Ciotti faced an additional charge of defaulting on his bond, also carrying up to five years. Ciotti already had four previous convictions for narcotics distribution. Parisi had convictions ranging from burglary to mail fraud.[2]

By William M. Reilly

Cy with his DiNobili   Mikey D', Tony Jr., Maynard Fergusen, & Cy

---

[2] *One of the U.S. Marshal's 15 Most Wanted Fugitives UPI Archives – March 25, 1985*

JR had been in our family since I was five. He knew my Grandma Murphy, my father Jack, and my oldest brother Jackie. Jackie's best friend was Dee Hientzel, and Dee's sister Dotty married JR when he moved to Erie.   So JR knew Grandma Murphy through the family and came to love her.

She ran the City of Erie through Prohibition with my Grandpa Murphy. My grandfather had a tugboat down at the dock that he modified by adding an extra gear set. During the day, he used all the low-end power to push the ore boats around. At night, he kicked that same engine into high-end speed and ran from Presque Isle to Long Point, Canada, and back in a single night, loaded with top-shelf Canadian whiskey—no rot-gut bathtub crap.

They brought it back to the west side of the docks, foot of Poplar, I think, right where the water pump house still sits. Some tunnels carried water and steam pipes up into the city, running under State Street. One of those tunnels came up right in the basement of Jack Paris' Steak House on 6th and State, which later became Sherlock's.

If you ever went downstairs in Sherlock's to use the bathrooms, there were two sets of doors chained and padlocked. Those doors led down into the tunnels. That's where they hauled all the booze from the water works into the basement of Jack Paris' Steak House.

After offloading, my Grandpa Murphy tied his tugboat up on the east slip, right where Rum Runners is today. The owner, Weed, still knows me through my grandparents. I was actually with her a few weeks ago, going over this same history.

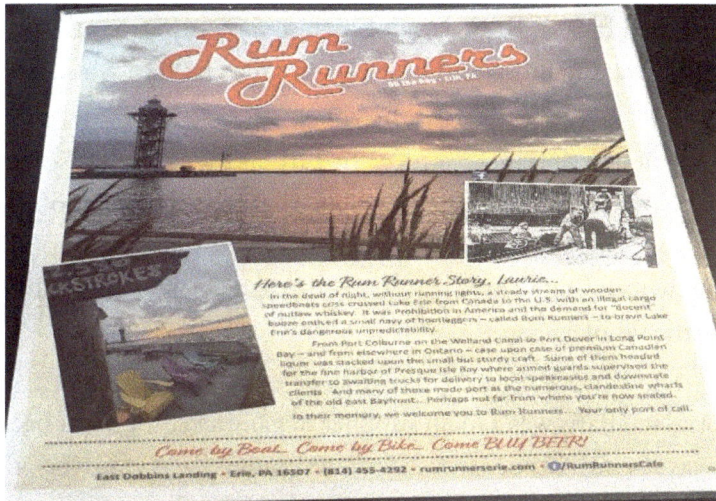

So my grandparents are the ones who supplied the entire City of Erie during Prohibition. Their Italian partner was Jack Paris, who was also my next-door neighbor when I was growing up at 314 East 32nd Street. Jack Paris got that piece of property as a gift for my grandma to build a house for her son — my father, Jack — so he could raise his kids there.

Every year, Jack Paris went back to Sicily for a month. When he came home, they threw a huge block party in our backyard. The whole block showed up. My father would hang a big sheet as a movie screen, and Mr. Paris would show all his vacation photos from Sicily.

There were tunnels running from under Jack Paris Steak House to under Isaac Bakers. Those tunnels actually still go up State, but access is limited now because they carry utility lines. Back then, you could walk underground right from Jack Paris' Steak House, past the Erie Police Station, to Isaac Baker's second floor, where my grandma ran her casino.

When Jack Paris died, he was living on the corner of Old French Road and East 32nd Street. I lived at 314 East 32nd, right across from Rupp

Limousine and Hearse Rental. Since high school, my after-school job was washing and waxing limos and hearses, so I knew how to wheel them.

When Jack died in the late seventies, the FBI raided a warehouse we always thought belonged to Pheasant Brothers, the pretzel and chip guys. But there was a private section of that warehouse. The feds started pulling out gambling wheels, one-arm bandits, roulette wheels, craps tables, card tables — the whole setup.

Turns out Jack Paris was a main supplier of gaming equipment back when Vegas was being built, and that equipment was moving through Cleveland, which had a big hand in the early Vegas days.

JR was tight with our family. He used to hustle pool with my father because they were both professional-level players, and my father used to shoot pool with Cy and JR back in the day. When JR got too hot in Erie, he'd go lie low with my brother Jack down in Meadville for days, weeks, sometimes months. Peter Russell and I did the same whenever things got tense in Erie.

It wasn't until Peter was going with Patty DeSanto that JR and Peter introduced me to Mary Ellen DeSanto. That's when I really started hanging around the neighborhood. By then, I was doing things with Elmer and "BJ," along with JR and Pete. Mary Ellen DeSanto was the first great love of my life, just like that line in *A Bronx Tale*.

I took her out to Vegas after a score. We lived with Susan out there. I got us a condo, and Susan moved in with us for a while. Then Susan went back to Erie. After a while, Mary and I broke up — and I still don't know how I'm going to handle that part in the book — but I came back to Erie crying at Susan's door. She was living in one of Grandma DeSanto's apartments on West 16th, underneath Uncle Vic.

218

I stood at her door, told her what happened, and said, "Now I don't even have a place to stay."

She said, "Oh yes, you do, honey. Come on in."

It was the sexiest line I ever heard from a woman. I stayed with her for a couple of months until I found another place. And those were two outstanding months. Let me make this clear — this was before she ever met Ray Ferritto. I never touched anything there once they met. He liked me anyway because he could tell I wasn't some beer-level dummy, and he was one hell of a burglar. I picked up a few tricks from him.

So that's how I came into the neighborhood.

And I told you how Cy kept Si Sittelli from killing me after I ripped off and wrecked his house. I told you the first thing out of Si's mouth was, "You are very fortunate that there are some very high people in this town who speak very highly of you... Or you would be dead right now."

I always figured it was JR getting word out from the federal joint after the armored car robbery: *Nobody better lay a finger on his kid.* That's what he called me, "the kid," because he always tried to protect my identity.

JR finally got out in '91. He didn't want to come back to Erie, so he went to his hometown in Lackawanna, New York. I'd been out since '86 and started working for Dunlop Tire Corp. in Buffalo. In '91, I met him every day after work at the Crown Club on Electric Avenue in Lackawanna — their version of the Ole Monte Club.

One day, we were sitting at the bar talking, and I said, "Thanks for smoothing that shit over with Si Sittelli... ripping off and wrecking his house because he was taking Mary out on the side."

He looked at me and said, "That wasn't me. That was Cy Ciotti. I was in the Fed joint and didn't hear about it until after."

I said, "Really?"

He said, "Not only did he know what you were doing with me with the scanners and silencers, but he really loved the old gal, too. She was just like Cy. A business person, but always helped people who deserved it."

I never got to thank Cy personally because by then I stayed out of Erie until I finished ten years of parole. When I was sent his memorial tribute, I was crushed. He was the only person in Erie I felt I owed anything to.

Nobody ever got caught when I set up the alarm system, supplied a scanner, or drove. Nobody did a minute because of me. That's why I never went back, even though my own family is still there.

I look forward to seeing Cy's son, Tony Jr., with Joe Salorino at Andy's on the 14th and at Rainbow Gardens on the 24th so that I can tell you more in person. I always have your back. You need to make it up to Buffalo one weekend so I can take you out, brother. *One Man Crime Spree*. Those weren't my words — that was Judge Penny Wolfgang, NYS Supreme Court Justice, after she read my FBI jacket before sentencing me. She looked at the file and said:

"Mr. Murphy, on paper, you appear to be a One-Man Crime Spree. Mr. Murphy... I hope you brought your toothbrush with you today, because you will be needing it where I'm sending you."

Three and a half to seven in Attica.

She illegally sentenced me as a three-time career criminal. My lawyer back in Erie, Elliot Segal, had gotten both my Pennsylvania felonies sentenced on the same day, so technically they only counted as one. That saved me. She had to reduce it to a two-to-four.

JR was the one who first introduced me to Cy Ciotti. He said, "You know who his grandmother is? Ethel Murphy." Cy turned around and said, "So you're the Million Dollar Baby's kid." I told him yes, and from that moment on, he treated me like I had a passport stamped 'approved'.

CY said he worked for the "Million Dollar Baby when he was young. He said he started out working at her card game on 7th and State, right across from the police station on the second floor of what would become the Isaac Baker and Sons Men's Shop, back when he was a kid in the fifties. He liked me right off the bat and started telling stories about how she had a pet monkey up at the card game.

Most of my dealings with him went through JR. That was the system. Cy kept it friendly, though now and then something came up where he handled it himself. He was a good man. One of the few I'd call a man of honor. Say what you do. Do what you say.

One time, JR called me to help unload some liquor at the Calabrese Club because friends from Pittsburgh were throwing a party and bringing their own booze—half-gallon bottles. I got it unloaded into the bar, and Cy was sitting at the end with his unlit DiNobli in his teeth. The other bartender still hadn't shown up.

This part belongs under the heading La Castro 50th Wedding Anniversary. And to be clear, it's L A, capital C A S T R O, not the LoCastro's in Erie. Janice LoCastro and her father, Lenny, former City of Erie Education Superintendent, whom I've known forever, once broke it down for me. I asked her, "What's the difference between the La Castros and the LoCastros?" She said, "We're the *low-class* Castros." She didn't flinch when she said it. The Pittsburgh La Castros were stacked with money, old money, the kind that never bothers to brag because the bank balance does the talking.

So these Pittsburgh La Castros wanted to throw their 50th anniversary party at Cy's Calabrese Club in Erie. People think everything in that world runs on cash. It doesn't. The grease is favorable. Always has been. Maybe Cy owed them one; perhaps they owed him. You never know the real scorecard. Either way, he said yes.

The day of the party, a step van rolled up behind the club, loaded with liquor. Not regular bottles either. Half-gallons. Of course, they brought their own, which meant Cy wasn't going to make a dime on bar sales. If you know Cy, you know he didn't love that. JR was bartending and, trust me, he wasn't expecting to unload a mobile liquor warehouse before the first toast.

I lived about a block and a half away, right around the corner. JR called me and said, "Unload the truck." No warm-up. Just unload the truck. So I dragged myself over and started hauling those half-gallon boxes out of the step van. Six to a case, but each one felt like it came straight from a quarry. I stacked every last one on the bar in the Calabrese Club.

JR pushed all the regular liquor to the back, and we lined up the half-gallons like we were stocking for a cruise ship. Cy sat in the corner with that DiNobli hanging from his mouth, not chewing it, just letting it sit there like a warning sign. He didn't raise his voice, but you could tell this was the last thing he wanted to deal with.

I finished unloading, then helped JR break down the boxes and get the bar ready. The other bartender never showed. Cy didn't twitch, didn't blink, but anyone paying attention could see the pressure building.

JR finally said, "Why don't you let the kid bartend?" Cy looked at me and asked, "Can the kid bartend?" JR said, "Yeah. He's got mixology papers from Vegas." Cy nodded. "Go put a suit on, kid."

I sprinted home, took a shower, threw on a suit, and got back just as things were kicking off. JR leaned in and said, "Don't fall for some Italian girl tonight and disappear for two weeks." I told him I'd behave. He raised an eyebrow like he didn't believe a word of it.

We finished setting up the half-gallons. Cy was still parked in the corner. JR said, "Pour them heavy, kid. These folks don't go home till the booze is gone." Cy cracked a small smile, which was his version of a green light.

Within an hour, the place turned into Studio 54 for retirees. People in their seventies and eighties were out on the floor moving to KC and the Sunshine Band. The DJ earned his money.

A while into the night, an older man came to the bar. He was dressed sharply, every detail crisp. And he had this brooch on his chest, the size of a doorknob. It looked like a diamond that could blind a truck driver. Fifteen carats, maybe more. I mixed his drink and watched him walk off. I looked at JR. He looked at me. I said, "That can't be real." JR said, "Oh, really, kid? Hold on."

Right then, another man stepped up, maybe mid-fifties. He wore a ring the size of—honestly—it looked like the knob from a kitchen cabinet. I made his drink too. Same thing. Polite. Calm. But in my head, I'm thinking, *no way these people walk around with a mortgage payment on their finger*. I looked at JR again. "Come on, that can't be real." JR said, "Oh, really? Take a look at the bathroom."

Both men were already heading toward it.

They had two bodyguards who looked like they were carved out of a quarry. One went into the bathroom first, checked every stall, and made sure the place was empty. The other stood at the door, blocking anyone from even thinking about stepping inside. I glanced at JR. He gave me that look and said, "Don't even think about it, kid. We wouldn't make it out of town."

I said, "All right, all right, message received." Those were the biggest pieces of jewelry I'd ever seen on people who weren't on a movie screen—wild sights.

The night kept rolling. People were laughing, drinking, and dancing. Right around midnight — the pumpkin hour — the front door opened, and this knockout blonde walked in. She stopped right inside like she owned the oxygen. White silk blouse, pink satin pants, spike heels. She looked like trouble in human form.

She paused, checked out the whole room, then her eyes landed on me. We stared at each other longer than made sense. Then she turned and walked straight into the DJ booth. I figured she must've been his girlfriend or someone he was trying to impress. Didn't give it much more thought.

A song later, the DJ cracked the mic and said, "I've got a young lady back here who wants to dance with the bartender."

JR looked at me. "Pretty sure she means you, kid."

So I walked out from behind the bar and headed to the booth. And there she was. Absolute Playboy material. Colleen McDonald. Unreal.

We hit the dance floor. One song turned into a bunch. When the party wrapped, we ended up at an after-hours spot—closed that place too. She came home with me, and JR didn't see me for a week.

When I finally showed up again, he just smirked. I said, "Hey, it wasn't two weeks."

He shook his head. "I knew it, kid."

The La Castro job was only one part of what tied me to Cy Ciotti. The other part was heavier. And this one took me years to understand because, for a long time, I credited the wrong man.

Back in the early '80s — '81, maybe '82, everything runs together, I ripped off Si Sitelli. Not my best move. He was taking Mary DeSanto out behind my back, and I went off the rails and trashed his place. Si wasn't the type to shrug something like that off. Word got around that he wanted me gone and not slapped around. Gone.

One Sunday, he called Jimmy DeSanto and me down to the club. Five of the hardest men in Erie were sitting there. Si opened with, "You're lucky. Some big people in this town think highly of you. That man came in from New York City to kill you." That's how the meeting started—zero warm-up.

For years, I thought JR somehow sent word from the federal joint, like a message that said, "Hands off the kid." He always protected me whenever he could, so that idea made sense. I stuck with that version for almost a decade.

Fast forward to '91. JR is finally out. He doesn't want anything to do with Erie, so he heads back to Lackawanna. I've been working at Dunlop in Buffalo, so we start meeting at the Crown Club after work just about every day.

One afternoon at the bar, I said, "By the way, thanks for smoothing out that thing with Si Sitelli. I never forgot that." JR looked at me and said, "That wasn't me, kid. That was Cy Ciotti."

I sat there stunned. JR shook his head and said, "He loved the old gal, too." Meaning my grandmother.

That's when the whole thing clicked. When I was five, JR came into our family through Dee Heintzel's sister Dotty. He knew my grandmother, my father, and my oldest brother. He knew the crew. JR was the one who first introduced me to Cy and said, "You know who his grandmother is?" Cy spun around, looked at me, and said, "You're the Million Dollar Baby's kid?" From that moment on, I was gold with him.

Cy had a history with my grandmother. She ran that card game across from the police station back in the 50s, upstairs from Isaac Baker and Sons. Cy worked there as a kid. He used to tell stories about that place, including the part about my grandmother having a pet monkey running around the card tables. That stuck with him. Loyalty's a strange thing, but when it's real, it doesn't fade.

When Si Sitelli wanted me buried, it wasn't JR who stepped in. JR couldn't; he was locked up. It was Cy. And that's why I always felt he was the only man in Erie I owed anything to, the only one I regretted not being able to thank. He wouldn't have taken anything from me, not his style, but offering is its own obligation. JR drilled that into me. Even if you can't pay a debt, you make the offer. Might save you a beating. Might save your life.

Cy had heat on him, too. They shut him down once over some liquor license mess and an old Pennsylvania law about how close a club could be to a church. The distance was short by inches. He had to fight to reopen. Typical Erie nonsense dressed up as regulation.

When the club got rolling again, Maynard Ferguson played there. Big name back then. Hot July night. They had the back doors open to let air in. Somebody tossed M80s out in the alley. Nobody owned up to it. Everyone inside thought it was gunfire. Half a dozen guys pulled guns. JR had his .45 — a general's pistol with a monster clip. The guy next to him pulled out a tiny .25. He looked at JR's gun, then his own, and quietly put his back in his pocket. A whole lot of macho energy in one room and not a single shot fired. That was the Cali Club.

Tony has more stories like that than anyone I know. But that one moment, Cy stepping in and saving my life, that's the one I still carry.

CHAPTER 14

RAY FERRITO "KILL THE IRISHMAN"

Ray Ferritto was the one who killed the Irishman, Danny Greene, in Cleveland, Ohio, on October 6, 1977. He came out of Erie, Pennsylvania, born and raised, and he hit the Great Lakes Rust Belt crime freeway the same way Jimmy JR Russell and I did. He headed west toward Cleveland and built connections in both Cleveland and Warren, Ohio. Warren was a heavy-industry town, close to Youngstown, which sat 60 miles from Cleveland and 60 miles from Pittsburgh. That whole stretch turned into one of the roughest corridors in the region.

Later, he pushed even farther and ended up in California, where he linked up with Jimmy "The Weasel" Fratianno. I've got plenty of clips of both of them on my YouTube channel, at least half a dozen. Fratianno was made in Cleveland and worked his way to Los Angeles, where he eventually became underboss and, for a short time, acting boss.

Ray met him in Chino prison. That's where they connected and built a friendship. When they got out, the bond carried forward.

They lived in the same apartment for a stretch, and that part is well documented in *An Assassin Scorned*. Jimmy "The Weasel" Fratianno is the one who brought Ray Ferritto in on the Danny Greene hit. Jimmy still had strong ties to the Cleveland family because that's where he got his button before heading out to Los Angeles. When Cleveland started drowning in problems with Danny Greene, they reached out to Jimmy for help. Jimmy reached out to Ray, knowing Ray wasn't even a hundred miles away, down the road in Erie.

Ray went to Cleveland first to negotiate the deal with the family. He wanted the job officially, not some handshake offer that vanished later. Cleveland agreed: if Ray killed Danny Greene, he would be made. They also promised him the territory between Ashtabula and Erie. Ashtabula sits right between Cleveland and Erie, so the offer had weight. Gambling and racket money from that whole stretch would be his.

Ray understood one simple rule: you don't stroll up to Danny Greene, and you don't slap a bomb on his car hoping for the best. Too many amateurs tried that. Ray wasn't cut from that cloth. His mind worked differently. Before he was a killer, he was a thief — a good one — and thieves know how to think around corners.

To locate Danny Greene's movements, Ray tapped the phone of Greene's girlfriend. He monitored her calls until he caught the detail he needed: a dentist appointment, exact time, exact place. Helpful information, but Ray still couldn't just wire Danny's car. Danny checked his vehicle before he stepped inside. Ray needed a different angle.

He bought a donor car and loaded TNT into the passenger door. When the day came, he waited until Danny went to his dentist appointment. Ray eased the donor car beside Danny's car. Danny walked out, heading straight toward his own door, with no idea that the real trap was sitting next to him.

The blast ended it. Ray Ferritto is the man who killed the Irishman.

As dumb luck would have it, or maybe the Cleveland mob set him up. When Ray pulls out of the dentist's parking lot in the getaway car, a young woman catches sight of him. She's either an artist or connected to the police in some way, but she sees enough to sketch him. Her drawing points straight toward Ray.

At the same time, the FBI picks up chatter on a wiretap they already have on the Cleveland crew. The tape isn't about paying Ray his cut. It's about putting a contract on him. Instead of honoring the deal for the Ashtabula-to-Erie territory, they decide it's cheaper to kill him.

Armed with the sketch and the wiretap, the FBI grabs Ray. They sit him down, play the tape, and ask the obvious question: why protect men who are planning to drop him? They spell it out — Cleveland wants him dead. This is late '77 into '78, and his choices shrink fast.

He takes the federal deal. He agrees to testify against the Cleveland mob, and they offer him witness protection and a new identity. To get the deal, he has to admit to four murders, all of which end up documented in the book and the film.

For those four murders, he gets a prison sentence of four years — a single year for each one. After that, he goes into the federal witness protection program. He lasts a year. Then he walks out of it and heads straight back to Erie, Pennsylvania, like nothing ever happened.

He has stayed on the streets of Erie for years. Eventually, things heat up with the Frank Bolo Dovisha murder. At that point, everyone with half a brain knows it's time to clear out. Same way, I cleared out when cops started killing themselves, and loan sharks turned up dead. When the city hits that level of ridiculous, you don't stick around.

Ray leaves. He moved to Florida with Susan DeSanto Ferritto, the older sister of the love of my life. He lives another couple of decades, close to twenty-five years, before he dies of natural causes.

Now, the thing people always ask is how Ray came back to Erie after testifying against Cleveland without being taken out. The explanation is spelled out right on the back cover of Susan's book.

Susan DeSanto Ferritto's book, An Assassin Scorned:

Back in the Day, as explained by Susan... Ferritto was arrested, along with four other men, for attempting to rob a gas station in Erie in August 1957.[19] Ferritto pleaded guilty,[20] and was sentenced to three to six years in state prison.[21]

In Warren, Ferritto met Ronald "The Crab" Carabbia and Tony "Tony Dope" Delsanter. Carabbia and his three brothers were all known as "the Crab," which was a play on their last name, and had become prominent in the organized crime scene in Youngstown. Delsanter was a made man in the Cleveland crime family. He managed the family's gambling interests in the Mahoning Valley.

In 1958, at age twenty-nine, Ferritto was arrested for burglary. He pleaded guilty and served three years of a three-to-five-year sentence. Once out, Ferritto spent some time in the Cleveland area, where he committed several burglaries with his childhood friends, Allie Calabrese and Pasquale "Butchie" Cisternino.

By the late 1960s, Ferritto had moved to Los Angeles, where he was associated with a group of Cleveland mobsters, including Julius Petro. In the forties, Petro avoided a death sentence on a retrial in a murder case. Ferritto and Petro were associates of Jimmy Fratianno, who was closely associated with the Los Angeles crime family. Likewise, Ferritto was trying to make a name for himself.

In 1969, Ferritto booked a flight from Los Angeles to Erie. He was driven to the airport by another burglar, originally from Cleveland. Accompanying the two to the airport was gangster Julius Petro. An accomplice wheeled the car into a parking garage spot at the airport. Ferritto waited for a plane to take off, put a gun to the back of Julius Petro's head and fired a shot, killing him. The jet engines muffled the single fatal shot. The murder resulted from a conflict with a well-known and successful bookmaker in Los Angeles who used Petro as muscle. Ferritto and his accomplice were likely candidates for the contract since they both also disliked Petro. Fratianno confirmed the facts of Petro's murder after Fratianno became a government witness in 1977.

Prior to the murder hit at the airport, Ferritto tried to plant a bomb in Petro's car. While assembling the explosive, Ferritto accidentally detonated the blasting cap, causing a minor injury to his leg. He opted for the *"one-way ride"* method of execution next. Petro's killing went unsolved for years until a dramatic turn of events began to unfold.

In 1971, Ferritto was convicted of burglary, this time with explosives. He was sentenced to fifteen years and incarcerated at the California Institution for Men in Chino, California. Fratianno was also doing prison time at Chino, and the two became friends. In 1974, Ferritto was released from Chino and returned to Erie. He started booking again and also worked for a vending company that was owned by a cousin. By that time, Ferritto developed a peptic ulcer severe enough to require partial removal of his stomach. To calm his nerves, he took handfuls of antacid tablets and even smoked marijuana.

In the 1970s, Danny Greene began competing with the Cleveland crime family for control of union rackets, resulting in a violent mob war. During this period, there were almost 40 car bombings in Cleveland and eight failed attempts to kill Greene. Finally, Cleveland family bosses Jack "Jack White" Licavoli and Angelo "Big Ange" Lonardo contracted Ferritto to assassinate Greene.

On October 6, 1977, Greene was at his dentist's office. Ferritto and Ronald Carabbia parked a car containing a bomb in the side door, next to Greene's car. When Greene started entering his car, Carabbia detonated the bomb and killed Greene instantly.

The two witnesses to the murder scene were Greg and Debbie Spoth. Debbie Spoth, the daughter of a suburban policeman, was a sketch artist who drew a fantastic likeness of Ray Ferritto for authorities. She took the sketch to her father, who, in turn, took it to the Cleveland police, who identified Ferritto from a police file.

When a search warrant was executed at Ferritto's house in Erie, police found the registration papers for the bomb car and arrested him. The search of Ferritto's house also turned up a copy of *Cleveland Magazine* with a picture of Greene in it. Upon hearing of Ferritto's arrest, Licavoli put out a hit contract on Ferritto. When Ferritto learned that the Cleveland family wanted him dead, he became a government witness and testified against his co-defendants in the 1978 trial. The State of Ohio indicted Licavoli, Lonardo, Ferritto, Carabbia and 15 other members of the Cleveland family for the Greene murder.

Ferritto also admitted responsibility for the 1969 killing of Cleveland gangster Julius Anthony Petro. He served less than four years in prison for both murders. Ray Ferritto left the witness protection program after one year and remained in Pennsylvania.

In January 1983, Ferritto and Magaddino member Anthony D. Ciotto found Frank "Bolo" Dovishaw, racket figure, dead of a gangland execution at Dovishaw's home [12]

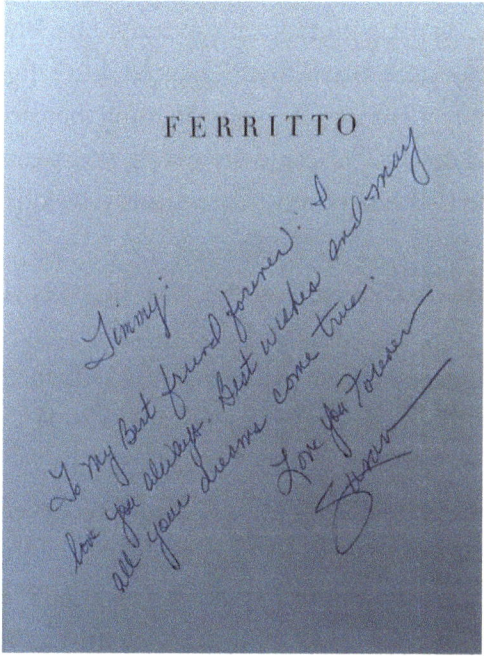

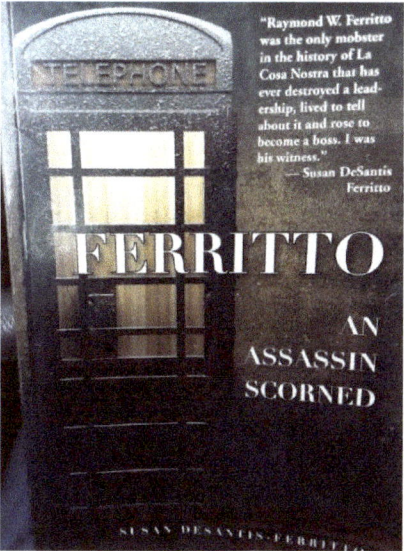

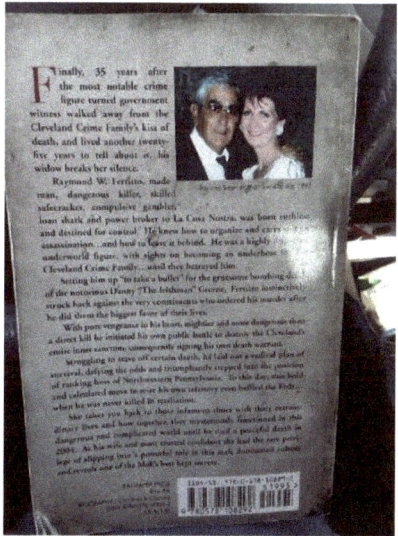

What baffled the feds was simple. Ray should've been a dead man. He knew it. Everyone knew it. Instead of hiding, he put together a plan that looked impossible on paper and took his spot right back here as the ranking boss in northwestern Pennsylvania. They couldn't figure out how he wasn't dropped in retaliation. The question hung there for years: how does a guy who flipped on the Cleveland crew walk the streets of Erie without somebody making that ninety-mile trip to finish the job?

Susan wrote it straight. She talks about how he takes you back through those wild years they lived together and how he somehow managed to function in that mess without ending up in a ditch. He kept moving through that world until he died a quiet death in 2004.

And the only reason he pulled it off was the Secret Seven. So secret, none of us knew who the other six were. But they were coming, and when that crew showed up, people stepped back. It was the "DeSanto" side, the Russell side, and one Irish kid who made them so much money they couldn't afford to take a shot at me.

But every time we heard somebody was in from Cleveland, we kept an eye on it. We'd make sure Ray was covered, wait it out, and once they were gone, things would settle again. And after Danny Greene was killed, things took a turn nobody expected.

Ray rolled over the whole upper tier of the Cleveland mob. He took down John Licavalli, the boss. Angelo Leonardo was the underboss. Angelo happens to be the cousin of my attorney, Leonard Ambrose, who represented me yesterday. And Angelo didn't just fold a little. He went all the way. He became a government witness and testified on all five New

York families during the 1985 Commission trials. Those trials brought down the heads of every family in New York City.

If you watch Kill the Irishman, Ray shows up by name in the last twenty minutes. They outline what he did. They mix a couple of points for the movie, but the backbone is accurate. The end of the film shows a map of the United States, with all the dominoes that fell after Ray killed the Irishman. Coast to coast. Cleveland, New York, Los Angeles, everywhere. That blast didn't just take out Danny Greene. It cracked the whole structure.

The Cleveland mob never bounced back to what it was before Ray Ferritto and Danny Greene. And the movie closes with the comment that if the Cleveland crew had known how much damage Danny Greene's death was going to cause, they would've let him walk.

That's the real punchline of the whole thing. The beginning of the end for what people call the Mafia in this country started with Ray Ferritto.

CHAPTER 15

THE MURDER OF FRANK "BOLO" DOVISHAW

When Bolo was killed, everything in Erie shifted. Frank "Bolo" Dovishaw wasn't some side player. He was Ray Ferrito's partner in the gambling rackets in Erie. Between Bolo, Ray, and Cy Ciotti, the three of them controlled every kind of racket running through the city.

I already told you how that worked, how those three locked down the streets. And this is where it ties straight into Bolo's own story, the one laid out in The Unholy Murder of Ash Wednesday.

The chapter below comes straight out of *The Unholy Murder of Ash Wednesday*, written by Dominic DePaulo. I'm not rewriting his work. I'm laying out the parts that matter to this story:

Detective DiPaolo arrests Anthony "Nigsy" Arnone, charging him with putting out the hit on Dovishaw.

"Erie was never safer than when the mob was in charge." I've heard that sentiment echoed by at least three generations of Erieites since I arrived here a decade ago.

The problem is that there never was a "family," no Cosa Nostra, no mob in Erie. There was a collection of local wise guys, wannabes, and career criminals, most of whom had the potential to be better than who they were. Some of them were born into crime. Some of them found it on the

239

playgrounds and on the streets. Most of them attempted to live up to the mystique of a rough and tumble Erie underworld.

Some of the guys who worked Erie's streets after World War II knew people, important people in the LaRocca family in Pittsburgh, and in the Licavoli crime family in Cleveland, as well as the Youngstown faction of the Pittsburgh crew. But none of those families set up shop in Erie. It was the 1950s. Manufacturing was king. Downtown was bustling and "the city was wide open," says former Erie detective and Magisterial District Judge Dominick DiPaolo.

DiPaolo and former Erie Times-News editor Jeff Pinski are co-authors of DiPaolo's memoir, The Unholy Murder of Ash Wednesday: The Stained Life and Rude Times of Mob Wannabe "Bolo" Dovishaw.

Because the city had no dominant crime family, an open market for gambling, theft, and sometimes drugs created a laissez-faire environment where criminals flourished, and cops chased their tails.

In 1954, Erie's Mayor, Thomas Flatley, was arrested alongside several people in his administration, top brass at the police station, and members of the city's crime syndicate on charges of corruption, abuse of power, and illegal gambling, to which he pleaded guilty to charges of conspiracy and violating his oath of office, leaving him to resign facing jail time and fines. In the decades that followed, many citizens of Erie suspected that their elected officials remained "connected" to local bookmakers and other conspirators, but none would go down in the sensational way that Flatley had.

The numbers racket was the primary vehicle for Erie's local brand of organized and sometimes disorganized crime.

This was before Pennsylvania sponsored its own lottery, and customers bet every day for a chance to win the 5 to 1 payout.

In local shops, factories, and pubs throughout the city, old ladies bet pennies, kids traded nickels, and laborers put down dollars on a chance to walk away with the daily take.

All they had to do was pick the right number, the last three digits of the next day's stock market at the closing bell.

Many played in the mid-twentieth century, but the game belonged to guys like "Bolo" Dovishaw.

Dovishaw lived in Erie's Little Italy. From his west side neighborhood, Dovishaw controlled the local gambling book, including sports betting and numbers, and became one of the most successful bookmakers in northwestern Pennsylvania.

Little Italy was Erie's only self-contained ethnic neighborhood in those days. Anything its inhabitants needed, a haircut, a butcher, a priest, and even a hitman could be found within the confines of the neighborhood's borders. Geographically, the neighborhood ran from the train tracks south of 12th Street to 24th Street, with an eastern boundary at Sassafras Street and a western front around Cranberry Street.

Future cops like Dominick DiPaolo and future criminals like Ceasar Montevecchio played together in Columbus Park as kids, they played baseball in the Glenwood League as teens, and, as adults, they chased and evaded one another on those same streets.

"There was no similar area on the east side," says Pinski. "Little Italy had its own public schools, its own church, its own funeral directors, its own stores. You never had to leave."

But in order to keep tabs on the numbers game and ensure that the East Side Italians and Polish kept their hands off their racket, guys like "Bolo" Dovishaw and his partner in crime, Ray Ferritto, had to leave the confines of the west side.

The city belonged to them, they believed. There was a business to run. Dovishaw had more than one hundred people taking bets for him. Maintaining a small army of criminals, one that included everyone from cops to kids, required a routine. It meant that every day, Dovishaw had to make the rounds and take the calls that would satisfy his ego and his wallet. Ferrito left the neighborhood for different reasons. He had the connections. He had skills that made him useful to people in Cleveland and Los Angeles. From burglary to murder, Ferritto carried out the wishes of "made guys," the kind of mobsters who provide cinematic lore and legacy. But they were interested in Ferritto, not his small-time gambling associates, not Erie. In that way, Ferritto was the most worldly of his Erie criminal brethren. He lived everywhere from Warren, Ohio, to Los Angeles. He did time in the California State penitentiary at Chino.

When the Irish Mob, led by Danny Greene, moved in on the Cleveland crime family of "Jack White" Licavoli and Angelo "Big Ange" Lonardo, it set in motion the machinations of a classic mob war. There were more than 40 car bombs in Cleveland in the early 1970s, several of which were intended to take Danny Greene's life.

Eventually, Cleveland called Ferritto to finish the job. And he did. Ferritto's legend preceded him in Erie. When he wasn't moonlighting for the mob, he partnered with "Bolo" Dovishaw. Who would dare challenge such a

242

dastardly dynamic duo? There, in part, lay the foundation of Erie's love affair with its mob. To the extent that various criminal elements competed for space in the city, they did so mostly under the radar of the media and police.

So, on the surface, the city appeared safe.

If one wannabe wiseguy steals from another's goods and cash that were the product of illegal activity, who was the victim to call? The police? It had to be handled internally, away from civilians.

If a group of kids mug a guy on his way to or from one of Erie's downtowns, second-floor gambling haunts, the guys in charge of the game would deal with it.

Mischief and mayhem were bad for business.

After Ferritto was released from Chino in 1974, he returned to Erie, where he and Dovishaw developed their routine. They were partners, and because their business required a routine, Ferrito usually knew where to find Dovishaw.

January 3, 1983, was like any other Monday for Erie's biggest bookmakers. They collected on the numbers racket, they stopped at Damore's pizza shop for a meatball sub because "Bolo" Dovishaw was a "fat pig [who] was always hungry," and they prepared for Monday Night Football. The Cowboys were playing the Vikings, Tony Dorsett was hot, and the action was going to be large.

Dovishaw dropped Ferritto off at his home at 6 p.m. so Dovishaw could get to his house and answer the phone. That's how the bets were made. Never in person. Only by phone. In those days, there were no answering machines.

That would only provide evidence.

Furthermore, old school analog guys like Dovishaw and Ferritto were probably averse to such technology. If the phone rang too many times, the call could be transferred to another number. If Dovishaw didn't answer, one of his associates surely would. An hour after Dovishaw dropped off Ferritto, Ferritto called Dovishaw to check on the action for Monday Night Football. But the call got transferred to their underlying. Dovishaw was nowhere to be found.

Did he run off with his gypsy stripper, Chastity? He wouldn't trade money for that kind of action. Did he get pinched by the local cops or even the feds? The FBI had been hunting La Cosa Nostra for more than a decade, but usually big players in big cities, not little connected numbers guys in nether regions like Erie. In part, the focus of the federal government on the Italian mob allowed for challenges to power like the one Danny Greene tried to carry out in Cleveland or the kind of coup "Whitey" Bulger executed in Boston. But there was no "family" in Erie.

As Ferritto searched for Dovishaw, becoming at once more concerned and more angry by his partner's absence, he decided it was time to head to Dovishaw's house on West 21st Street.

The house belonged to Dovishaw's mother. She was deceased. Dovishaw had lived there alone. He also died there, alone. Ferritto searched the house and found his friend and associate bound in the basement, his hands tied with the belts of his mother's dresses, which were still hanging on a rack downstairs. "Bolo" Dovishaw had been shot once behind the ear, on his knees, execution style.

The sordid tale of the events that preceded Dovishaw's murder and the investigation that followed is the subject of The Unholy Murder of Ash

Wednesday. It is "a cop's memoir." Connecting the characters introduced, dug up, and put away in this story of old Erie crime creates a roadmap that leads from Erie's dark past to its darker present.

Erie may never have had a mob umbrella under which to hide on rainy days. But today's disorganized criminal enterprise, steeped in drugs and searching for order, makes the organized crime of old a nostalgic ride with some familiar faces. Readers of DiPaolo's story, as told to Pinski, are sure to recognize many of the people and places in the book. They might even find themselves within those very pages.

Jim Wertz can be contacted at jWertz@ErieReader.com, and you can follow him on Twitter @Jim_Wertz.

Dominic DePaulo had a front-row seat to it all. He was an Erie police detective, and he happened to be on duty the night Ceasar Montevecchio pulled the Louis Nardo burglary that led to the murder of Corporal Robert Owen and kicked the whole mess into motion. Looking back, it felt like the city hit a pressure point. One bad move after another, and everything started sliding at the same time.

When Bolo finally got taken out, that was my cue. I didn't need a memo. It was time to get out of town before I ended up as background noise in the same story. I didn't deal with Frank "Bolo" Dovishaw directly. I knew the guy well enough to nod and keep walking. Everybody knew he moved with Ray Ferrito and Cy Ciotti. That part wasn't a secret.

The part that shook people was how it happened. Bolo was killed in the basement of his mother's house. She had already passed, but he still lived there. It was a Monday night. There was a Monday Night Football game on. Ray had dropped him off so he could start taking calls for the bets tied to that game. They had a phone setup that was fancy for its time. If Bolo

245

didn't answer within a set number of rings, the call jumped to another associate who would take the action.

That was the routine. And that's precisely the night it all stopped.

So, Ray drops off Frank "Bolo" Dovishaw at his mother's house so he can be in place before the Monday Night Football action starts coming in. Routine stuff. Midway through the game, Ray calls to check the numbers, see how the bets are coming in. No answer. He tries again—still nothing. After a few rounds of that, Ray's irritation kicks in.

He figures maybe Bolo took off with his girlfriend. She danced under the name Crystal and worked at Partners, which is still standing in Erie. Ray thinks maybe the two of them slipped off together.

He drives over to the house. Walks in. The first floor is quiet. No movement, no sound. He checks the rooms, but nothing. Then he heads down to the basement. That's where he finds Bolo.

He's tied up with belts taken off his mother's old dresses. She kept piles of her clothes in the basement, and whoever came in grabbed what they could and bound his hands and feet. He'd been executed. Straightforward and cold.

They killed him to get the keys to his safety deposit box. That's where the gambling receipts were kept — Ray's cut, Bolo's cut, Cy's cut. They'd make monthly deposits. I already told you my sister and brother-in-law worked at the bank where those deposits were made. They saw everything come through.

The setup had been tight for years. That night, it blew apart in one move.

The setup behind Bolo's murder points straight to Niggs Arnone. He ran Arnone's Bakery over in Little Italy, right on 18th and Cherry. That place was legendary. They made this pepperoni ring bread that could knock out your hunger in one go. You could live on it for a week if you had to.

Niggs wasn't just rolling dough; he was running angles. His sister happened to work at the same bank where Bolo kept his safety deposit box. So Niggs put together a plan that, for Erie, was pretty slick.

They rented a safety deposit box as close to Bolo's as possible. Practically neighbors in the vault. But they couldn't just stroll out of the bank with whatever was inside Bolo's box — too risky, too obvious. They needed his keys. That's why Bolo was tied up the way he was.

Their plan depended on getting those keys and walking into the bank like nothing unusual was going on—no alarms, no mess, just a quiet swap in the vault corridor. For a bunch of guys who spent most of their time around bakeries, bars, and backroom card games, it wasn't a half-baked idea at all.

They moved everything from Bolo Dovishaw's safety deposit box into the box that Nigsy Arnone's sister had rented. I don't know whose name they used. It sure wasn't hers, so maybe it was under Niggs's name. They shifted the contents over and chipped away at it whenever they felt like it. I can't say I witnessed any of that, but the whole thing is laid out in The Unholy Murder of Ash Wednesday.

The nickname "Ash Wednesday" came from the mark on Bolo's forehead. It looked like he'd just walked out of church after getting ashes. Erie loved a nickname, and this one stuck.

There's plenty more in that book, but this chapter isn't about retelling DePaulo's work. It's here to show how wild things were in Erie at the time. The place was a minefield. You had cops turning up dead, crooks turning up dead, and nobody was sure who was on which side. Trust was worth less than a burnt cup of diner coffee.

Ray Ferrito's finding the body only made the night stranger. He called Cy Ciotti. Cy came over to Bolo's mother's house, and the two of them called a cop they knew wouldn't slap cuffs on them right away. Ray had already confessed to four murders. He wasn't exactly the guy you'd expect to call in a dead bookie. Anyone else would have hauled him off before he finished the sentence. But he made the call, and for once the world didn't tilt sideways on him.

That whole scene was the breaking point for many people. You could feel the walls sagging. Anyone with half a brain started packing or already had one foot out the door.

And here's the twist life threw in. At Bolo's funeral, Ray Ferrito met Susan DeSanto. Cy Ciotti introduced them in the funeral home. They traded numbers, grabbed coffee, and before long, they were married. Funny how death and love can pass each other in the same hallway and barely nod.

CHAPTER 16

THE SCORE OF A LIFETIME

There are many pieces to this story. Whenever you're involved with something like this, you never have the whole picture right up front. You only get things in bits and pieces. Things are on a need-to-know basis, and very few people need to know. And you only need to know your piece of the puzzle. It took me many years to find out all the pieces to this puzzle because I came in really on the tail end of it.

It all started one Sunday morning. I got a call from Jimmy JR Russell, my mentor and mastermind, to go pick up Monk—Gary "Monk" Montgomery—and take him wherever he wanted to go. At first, I thought we were going out for a drink. I went and picked up Monk. He got in the car; I had a 1979 Cadillac Eldorado, black-on-black with a chrome roof and a mirrored sunroof. This was in 1982. The car was a few years old, but it was still the hottest car we'd seen anywhere we'd pulled in.

The first thing Monk said was, We've got to go pick up Ragu. Ragu was his girlfriend, Brenda Damasi. She was called Ragu because that's Italian— an Italian knockout—and she was going with Monk at the time. Ragu, like the spaghetti sauce. That's why we called Brenda Damasi "Ragu."

She was a knockout, no doubt about it. We went to pick her up, and then Monk told me to pick up my girl. I went and picked up the love of my life, Mary Ellen Desanto, and we took off. He told the girls to pack an overnight bag; we'd buy the rest there.

When I first picked up Monk, he only had one rather large suitcase. I popped the trunk, he threw it in, and I never looked inside. Then we had to pick up two other passengers. One was Maxi Giordano, a local Little Italy muscleman who had been a knockaround guy forever and was well known in the neighborhood. You didn't want to mess with Maxi. He wasn't big in stature, but he was built like a brick shithouse. The other person we had to pick up was the Tutsoon.

Tutsoon is Sicilian slang for what we'd call today a mulatto—somebody who's half Black and half white. That was Wendell. It took me a long time to figure out how Wendell fit into the puzzle, but toward the end of this escapade, I discovered that Monk and Wendell had been cellmates in Western State Penitentiary in Pennsylvania for several years. Cellmates get tight—after all, you're entrusting your life to another man. That was Wendell's part in the puzzle. I don't think he was actually involved in the Armored car job... I think he was covering "Monks" back... that goes for Maxi too... I think they were just Monk's security.

It was a Sunday afternoon in Erie, Pennsylvania, and the blue laws were in effect. You couldn't get a drink of alcohol in Pennsylvania before they repealed the blue laws. Monk wanted a drink, so we had to head up to New York State to find one. I was familiar with that run because, throughout high school, the drinking age in Pennsylvania was 21, while in New York it was 18.

We ran up to New York and started on a Sunday afternoon at Peak 'n Peak Resort in Clymer, New York. Usually, it's a ski resort in the wintertime, but in the summer, it has full resort amenities.

We started at Peak 'n Peak just to get a drink. While we were sitting there, Monk told me we had to go to Westfield, New York, and then to Barcelona—Barcelona Harbor, right on Lake Erie. That was amazing for me because it had been a rendezvous point for Grandma and Grandpa Murphy when they were trying to evade Eliot Ness. Besides Erie, it was the only navigable point from Canada to the United States. There's still a stone lighthouse there today, right on Route 5 along the lakefront.

I knew exactly where we were going and how to get there. We drove from Clymer to Barcelona, right on the Erie waterfront. Once there, we went into a bar that today is called *When Pigs Fly Barbecue*, though I don't remember the name back then. The owner was originally from Erie and had replicated the Peninsula Inn—the PI in Erie—down to the smallest detail. The PI had been a beach bar originally owned by Sarah Coyne, where I used to borrow boats at night to take friends and girls over, party all night, and bring the boat back.

He had recreated the back of the PI at *When Pigs Fly*, complete with tiki bar, bonfire pit, and volleyball courts. You could walk from the tiki bar right down to the lakefront with your drink. It was a little slice of heaven.

So we went there, and it didn't take long to see what had to happen. We walked in and met someone from my past through JR—Westfield Jimmy. He was a made *mafioso* lieutenant with the Magaddino family. He owned a hotel right on the New York–Pennsylvania line and controlled the gambling in Erie. Everything flowed through him — CY Ciotti, Ray Ferrito, and Dee Auditori, who owned the cigar store in Erie. They all sent their money up the ladder through Westfield Jimmy.

That was the original job Jimmy JR Russell had in Erie: he was the carrier between Erie and Westfield. So, when we showed up, and Jimmy recognized me, that became Monk's introduction. And it made sense why JR sent me.

Monk still had to kick up money to Westfield Jimmy and, through him, to the Magaddinos. Magaddino was dead by then, but the rules didn't change. You paid for the privilege of doing work...

At that point, Monk went to my trunk. I stayed put. I found out later he took sixty grand in cash and kicked it up to Westfield Jimmy. That handled the business. And really, it was "JR's" tribute...Old School!

From there, we were on a straight party run. We bar-hopped along Routes 5 and 20 — Dunkirk, Fredonia, every small bar on the strip — all the way to Buffalo. Drinking, laughing, and drifting from place to place.

We rolled into Buffalo on Route 5, and the skyline hit me. That's when I fell in love with the town. You'd pass Hoak's restaurant and Foit's, which JR's family ran, both right on Lake Erie. Once you hit those spots and saw Buffalo lit up at night, it did something to you. Nighttime hid the smokestacks from Bethlehem Steel. It gave the city a cleaner look.

So we hit Buffalo, and Monk comes up with the bright idea that we have to go to Canada. I tried talking him down hard. I said, "Monk, we're messed up. We're going to get pulled over the second we hit that border. Look at us. And look at this car. It's a walking billboard for trouble."

Didn't matter. Monk had it in his head, and there was no moving him. So fine — we head for the Peace Bridge.

We cross over, reach Canadian customs, and I swear I didn't even have the car fully in park before the officer points us straight to the customs building. No hesitation. Just a sharp wave: pull over, doors open, everyone out. They were ready to tear my car apart, and the six of us were marched inside for questioning.

It was before everything went digital. Back then, when you walked into customs, they handed you a pre-printed index card, and you filled out your basic info. That was it. So the six of us filled out our cards one by one, pretending we looked like ordinary Sunday travelers instead of absolute idiots.

And after we finish filling everything out, we're stuck there getting grilled by a Canadian customs officer. He's flipping through all six index cards, tossing little questions at us — middle names, addresses — just poking for cracks.

Then he hits the big one.

"Have you ever been convicted of a felony in the United States?"

Silence.

Not a breath.

It was a full Mexican standoff. Nobody wanted to be the one who blinks.

Then the Tutsoon pipes up from the back, "Felony? For what?"

That was it. Game over.

The officer switches into reject mode. Boom, boom, boom — all six of us denied and kicked back to the U.S.

We're walking out toward my car, and Monk is on fire. He's tearing into the Tutsoon.

"For what? *For what?* What did you think they were gonna do, go alphabetically? Start with the A's — armed robbery, arson. Move to the B's — burglary. Hit the C's — criminal conspiracy. *For what,* you idiot? I should kill you right here."

I'm trying to calm him down. "Monk, relax. We need to get out of here."

We all pile into the car, I drive back over the bridge, and I tell him, "Let's just grab a hotel in Buffalo. We'll sleep it off and try again in the morning."

That's precisely what we did. Monk rents a couple of rooms, and we crash. We were hammered. We had no business going anywhere near a border that night.

The next morning, I take us over the Rainbow Bridge. Smooth as silk. No one even looks twice.

Now we're in Niagara Falls, Canada. Clear sky, warm day, and Monk wants the best hotel in town.

Right at the base of Clifton Hill is the Fox Head Inn Sheraton, still a Sheraton today, though I'm not sure it still carries that name. Back then, it had top-floor balcony suites facing the Falls—three of them.

Monk walks in and says he wants those three suites for a week. Cash talks, and he had plenty of it — all U.S. hundreds — so they handed them over without blinking.

We split up:

Monk and Ragu take one suite.

Mary and I take the second.

Maxie and the Tutsoon take the third.

So now we go sightseeing for the day. We hit the Falls, walk up Clifton Hill, and do the usual tourist loop. That evening, we head to the top of the hill where there's a bar called Rumors. Back then, it was a straight-up dance club. Today it's Kelsey's, a steak place, but the bones of the building haven't changed.

At that time, Rumors was packed with U.S. teenagers — nineteen was the drinking age in Canada, so half of New York State treated the place like their personal playground.

We walk in and start partying. The place has to hold 300, maybe 350 people. And Monk decides to buy the bar a drink. I look at him, thinking, *this is precisely why JR wants eyes on you.* He's drawing heat for no reason. Too late. He already waved the bartender over.

It's around 12:30 at night. Monk has no clue about Canadian last-call rules. In Canada, one o'clock hits, the lights come on, and they grab the glass right out of your hand.

Monk goes off again. He's shouting about buying the whole bar a drink, and now they're cutting him off. I tell him, "Monk, relax. You're lighting yourself up like a billboard."

I finally talk him down. "Let's just go back to the hotel. Tomorrow I'll hit an LCBO, buy a whole bar, set it up in the suite, and we'll run our own show." That calms him enough to call it a night.

The next morning, we get up and start moving again. More sightseeing. More partying. Clifton Hill has everything — Ripley's Believe It or Not, Guinness World Records, wax museums, whatever you can imagine. The place feels like a tiny version of Vegas.

That's why I kept going there a few nights a week once I moved into my beach house in Sherkston Shores, Ontario, 30 years ago! —less than a half-hour's ride. I still go. I'm known up there as "Murph the Surf, Robin Hood to the homeless."

I don't walk past anybody sleeping rough without slipping them a Canadian twenty. I like the look in their eyes when they realize someone is looking at them. The homeless talk, and word gets around. They know me by name.

So we're partying that night, and we get up the next day and do it all over again. That night, we head out, and the Canadian last call comes. We already know the drill. We head back to the Foxhead Inn Sheraton and go to our room. We had set up the bar in Maxey's and Wendell's room because the two couples didn't want to be bothered. So that room became the bar.

I'm mixing drinks for everybody, and we're having a good time when Monk starts up again. He says he didn't pay three hundred bucks a night to sit in a room and drink. This was when a regular hotel room was thirty-nine ninety-five, and these Foxhead Suites were three hundred a night. He wasn't letting that go.

He says he spent that money to sit, look at the falls, and drink. So he tells Maxie and Wendell to take the couch out onto the deck. The couch in the suite. These two start wrestling with it, looking like the Three Stooges minus the talent. They can't get it out the door. I finally tell them how to do it: stand it on end, flip it out the door, balance it on the railing, swing it, and drop it on the porch. They finally listen. Boom. The couch is on the deck. They bring out a few chairs, and now Monk is satisfied. We're out on the deck with our drinks, staring at the falls.

This turns into the nightly setup. We go out, we party, we come back to the room and keep it going. Part of Monk's ritual is the radio. He's got it locked on 800 AM because CKLW—the Big 8 out of Detroit—comes in across Lake Erie. Detroit to Buffalo to Niagara Falls. Nice clean signal on a clear night. Monk insists on catching the Detroit news.

One night, he finally gets what he's been waiting for. The news guy comes on with something like, "Pistol-packing punks rob the Royal Oak Armored Car Depository outside Detroit, Michigan, getting away with $3.2 million cash." They give all these details. At the end, the announcer says one of the robbers wasn't short on humor. He was heard yelling, "Don't worry, honey, we're only shooting a movie," as bullets flew.

Monk starts pounding the table, yelling, "That was me. That was me."

So this is a piece of the puzzle that took me years to sort out, because I didn't know any of it at the time. I put two and two together later and figured they were involved, but the details didn't surface until years afterward.

I believe this entire score was set up by Leslie Hans, a master bank robber who pulled off the Halloween bank job in Erie, Pennsylvania, with Pearl Gryzbowski. It took a while before they caught Leslie. He was alleged to have robbed over seventy-five banks. But this job was different for him. I believe he had the information and went to JR for help setting up the details.

The setup went like this: the Royal Oak Armored Car Depository was outside Detroit, and JR negotiated a contract with them to film a "movie" in their parking lot. He posed as a film producer and actually had a signed agreement allowing him to shoot there. So the armored car depository let the so-called film crew drive right into their lot and set up equipment. These guys were there all day, setting up like they were straight out of Southern California with camera gear and all that. The place let them in without a second thought.

Another piece that didn't click for years was something JR showed me months before this. He had a picture of an outdoor 240-volt AC electrical receptacle. He showed me the configuration and asked if I could get some male plugs that would fit the female receptacles.

At the time, I was working in a machine shop, so I told him I could come up with something. He needed six. I found six plugs that matched the configuration and handed them over. It was months before the robbery.

Later, I found out what they were for. The "film crew" had brought all this movie equipment, including six Kleig lights, the big spotlights they shoot into the sky at Hollywood openings. A Kleig light is basically a welder's arc with a reflector behind it. Look into one, and you'll fry your retinas. It's the same effect as staring into a welding flash.

They had six of them set up as part of their so-called lighting plan. And they plugged them straight into the outlets on the spotlight posts in the armored car depository parking lot. They were literally running those monsters off the depository's power.

JR also had something.

The armored cars are offloading their cash into these rolling laundry baskets along the dock. Everyone's busy unloading. They wait until one basket is complete, then they hit all six Kleig lights at once. The blast of light nearly blinds the dock workers and the armored car guards. The six bandits are wearing their sunglasses that snap to pitch-black as soon as the arc hits. They grab the basket loaded with the $3.2 million, throw it into the getaway vehicle, and take off.

While they're speeding out, they have to smash through the gate. Monk swears a hot security guard was working the booth. As they burst through the gate and bullets start snapping past them, Monk yells out the window, "Don't worry, honey, we're only shooting a movie."

He hears the whole thing reported on CKLW that night, and he's riding high on it. The next morning, he wakes up in a different mood. Now he's paranoid. Now he's convinced someone is on their trail. He keeps saying, "They know we got it. We've got to move."

Then he tells me, "Go tell the girls to spend all the Canadian money. We have to go back to New York City and disappear in the crowd."

I tell him that if disappearing among millions of people is the goal, we can hit the QEW and be in Toronto in under two hours. Even back then, the place was huge. He doesn't care. He's fixed on New York.

"Go tell the girls to spend the money. We're checking out. We're leaving," he says. Then he adds, "And Timmy, you and I have to take a walk to your car. Just you and me. Not Wendell, not Maxie, not the girls."

So Monk and I walk back to my Caddy. He tells me to pop the trunk. I open it, and his suitcase is sitting there like it has its own gravity. Thing has to be around thirty-six inches long, almost thirty across, and thick enough to hide a family of raccoons.

He opens it. That was the first time I saw what he had inside. There's $365,000 in cash and a .45 automatic. That's after he'd already given Westfield Jimmy sixty grand. Monk grabs a stack of hundreds, ten grand, hands it to me, and says, "Stash this. It's yours. Don't tell the other two."

Right then, I figured he was ready to cut Wendell and Maxie out if they had even breathed wrong. The whole moment felt like that scene in *Goodfellas* when De Niro hands Ray Liotta his stack. Same tone. Same energy. I took that ten grand, shoved it down my pants, and didn't take it out until I found a safe place.

We head back to the hotel. We had already told the girls to spend all the Canadian money. We expected them in the lobby. We check out. Still no girls. Now Monk's jumpy again. I have to talk him down. I tell him they're shopping. They could be anywhere.

We walk outside onto Clifton Hill, look both ways. Then we spot them across the street with about ten people around them. Everyone's laughing. We don't see the joke. We cross over, walk up, and ask what's going on. They can't even talk. They're just pointing up.

We turn around and look up at our suite. Two Chinese hotel workers are trying to shove that fold-out couch back into the room. Every time they push, the thing springs open and knocks one of them sideways toward the railing. They're yelling at each other in Chinese. The whole crowd is cracking up. We stood there for half an hour watching it. By the end, there had to be fifty people gathered, laughing their heads off.

I finally got my Caddy. I spin it around and pull up. Our little crew piles in, and I head up Clifton Hill. Monk thinks I'm taking him back to the border and on to New York City. No chance. My gut didn't like that plan. We were all still keyed up and laughing, and that's when I made the move. I hopped on the QEW toward Toronto before Monk even realized what I'd done.

The second he saw the Toronto skyline, he froze. He'd never been there. No idea how big it was. Once he got a look, he started to like the idea. So we grabbed a hotel on Yonge Street—spelled Y O N G E—billed as the longest street in the world, how they figure that out, no clue. But they've got a giant sign about it down at the harbor. I saw it again this past summer while visiting my Canadian ballet artist.

We checked into the King Edward Hotel. Monk, of course, wanted the best rooms they had. Then we started going out on Yonge Street every night. Back in the late seventies and early eighties, that street didn't sleep. Bars, music, crowds—everything running till sunrise. Even with last call at one, there were enough private and underground spots to keep the night alive.

One place on Yonge Street stood out: the Zanzibar, one of the oldest strip clubs in Canada. Still standing today. I drove by it this past summer to confirm. Monk loved the place. He started hiring dancers nonstop. He was throwing money around like it was Monopoly cash. The girls in our group were hanging out with us, drinking, laughing. We got known fast. Monk spent thousands in there every afternoon.

We stayed in Toronto for weeks—three, almost four. Then Monk started getting that itch again. He wanted New York City. I finally convinced him: fine, we'll go. But we'd drive all the way across Canada first, then cut down into New York from the east.

So, we headed out along the St. Lawrence Seaway and stopped in Montreal. Gorgeous city. The only problem was that none of us knew French. Back then, it felt more French-only than bilingual, at least in some areas.

We ended up staying in Montreal for a few weeks. Then Monk started getting restless again, so we packed up and headed out. I drove east across Quebec and crossed into the northern tip of New York State, near Lake Placid. Nothing around us but trees, mountains, and the kind of silence that makes you question your own decisions.

We dropped down through Albany and kept going until we hit New York City. That turned into almost a month. Monk paid Ragu's rent, mine, and Mary's through Western Union. Every so often, we would send forms back home so nobody got tossed out. That whole stretch felt like one long, strange vacation that had no business happening.

Eventually, we had to go back to Erie and pretend we had everyday lives. Coming down from all that was rough. After we got back, things shifted. Monk started getting suspicious of me because he decided I knew too much. JR tried to calm him down, told him not to worry about "the kid," but Monk never fully relaxed.

Then there was the other problem: "Si" Sittelli. Si never liked me after the whole break-in and everything that came with it. He blamed me for what happened with Mary DeSanto. The only reason he didn't take me out was that CY Ciotti stepped in and shut that down. Instead, Si stuck me running the Uthmann Chor club. He trusted me with the money because he knew I wasn't stupid enough to dip into his till. But trust ended there.

He still wanted me gone. Eventually, Monk and Si Sittelli joined forces and tried to put a contract on me. That whole mess led straight to the seventh secret member, Cosimo Farbo, ending up dead.

CHAPTER 17
THE MISSING SEVENTH - COSIMO FARBO

Cosimo Farbo, and I'm pretty sure he was a distant cousin of Cy Ciotti. Cosimo was a rock of a man. Built from years of concrete and brick work. Solid, steady, and not someone you wanted to test. He also ran a place in Erie called the Cypress Shop. They'd drive down to Florida, dredge cypress logs out of swamps, haul them back, and he'd slice them into slabs. He turned those slabs into furniture—heavy pieces with a shine that looked like you could dive into it. He coated everything in polyurethane and made it look easy.

Cosimo was part of us.

So, all hell had been breaking loose in Erie, Pennsylvania, really since the bells rang in 1980. The decade had rolled in with everybody talking big, hoping the country would shake off the recession and the oil mess from the 70s. People my age, early 20s, thought the future was wide open. The theme they pushed for the new decade was "It's 1980. Why wait!"—like a commercial for optimism. It got loud fast.

New Year's Eve 1980, the Monte Club was packed. Midnight hit, and the whole joint was flying from the vial of LSD-25 we'd scored. That vial came from an associate whose crew actually marched onto a military base in full uniform, in military vehicles, and forged orders claiming they were transporting "liquid gold" to another base. Nobody stopped them. And that one vial lasted our group all the way through to the next New Year's Eve, when we threw the toga party.

The place was charged. Downstairs in the bar, upstairs in the private dance hall—stage, dance floor, seating for maybe a hundred if you squeezed them. We didn't squeeze; we jammed bodies in until the walls sweated. A couple of hundred easy, and almost all of them were flying. I walked around with a tincture bottle and an eyedropper, selling hits for five bucks. Drop it on their tongue and watch their eyes blow open.

The stuff was pure. Government pure. Processed by CIA chemists who were probably the same Nazi scientists we smuggled out of Germany before they ever sat in front of a Nuremberg judge. The same "experts" who thought nothing of drugging American citizens for fun and research. Nobody cared about long-term effects, least of all us. The government didn't care. The prisoners they tested on didn't get a vote.

And the CIA didn't stop with prisoners. They even dosed their own people. Not so different from what we pulled the following year when we dumped it into the Asti Spumante and Lambrusco at the party without warning a single guest.

The togas lasted about an hour that night. The decade was young, and everyone wanted a new high, so we started dropping the LSD directly onto our customers' eyes on request. It hit fast. People felt it within minutes, and by the twenty-minute mark, they were gone. The battle cry of the night—and honestly, the first few months of the new decade—was "It's 1980. Why wait?" And we didn't. We charged straight into the decade like nothing could knock us off course. The irony was brutal because the storm nearly ate us alive by year's end.

The other reason people in my generation thought things were finally turning upward was the rush of new technology. Color TVs were finally in reach for regular folks. VHS and Beta were fighting it out like two drunks in an alley, and nobody knew which one was going to win. Then came the big one: video games. Pac-Man, Galaxian, Space Invaders and Asteroids created whole new worlds for a crowd that had been raised on the 60s and blasted through the 70s. All it cost was a quarter.

Nintendo, Atari and Namco were wrestling for the top spot in this new marketplace, but the one machine that caught me hard in November 1980 was Battlezone. It had new software in a new cabinet and felt like slipping into another identity. Battlezone was the first three-dimensional wireframe game, and that hooked me immediately.

Battlezone lets you sit in a tank, staring out across a desert through a small viewport. It was the beginning of the first-person shooter. Now the whole gaming world runs on that view, but back then it felt like something stolen from the future. I still remember the first night I played. I went through four rolls of quarters—forty bucks in one hit, trying to get good at it. I stayed hooked for years. Anytime I saw a Battlezone machine, I fed it quarters. That's how my 1980 started.

But by November of that same year, everything started to unravel. It kicked off on November 25, 1980, with the Luis Nardo robbery— $550,000 in jewels, coins, gold, and silver. That led to the stolen ring I'm convinced I saw on David Grassy's finger one night at the Uthmann Chor Club. Grassy was the nephew of Mayor Louis J. Tulio.

Then December 29, 1980, hit: the murder of Erie police corporal Robert Owen hit.

After that, the city felt like it was shaking apart. You didn't know who was dirty, who was dangerous, or who was pretending to be either one. Trusting anyone felt like volunteering for trouble. Erie turned into something sharper and meaner than anyone expected.

While all that was happening, I kept moving reefer. There was a point where you couldn't find a seed of marijuana in the entire city without it passing through my attic first.

I controlled everything coming in and out of the city for the most part. As the months rolled through 81, 82, and beyond, we hit a point where the last bale of reefer we received looked like Acapulco Gold. It had that gold color, looked like it was worth a fortune, but once you smoked it, it was dirt weed. We figured it had been sprayed with paraquat by our own government down in South America, because High Times kept running stories about how the government was spraying paraquat to wipe out marijuana crops. Instead, it ended up poisoning the people who smoked it. We didn't have any other supplies, so we sold it anyway. It was all the town had. Things went dry fast. People got desperate.

It was around the time after I had robbed "Si" Sittelli's house. Even though I had worked for him, opened his club, brought in bands and made him money, he still wanted me gone. After the armored car robbery later in 82, and JR getting arrested and imprisoned for it, Gary "Monk" Montgomery—whom I had taken out of town right after the job—started getting nervous about me, too. He figured the kid knew too much. I believe Sittelli and Monk were plotting to kill me.

Their plan wasn't complicated. They knew I was the one running the reefer in town. They knew there wasn't a single bag left to be found. So Monk walked up with an offer: he said he had a line on fifteen pounds of marijuana at three hundred dollars a pound. Great price. Suspicious price.

Ever hear something that sounds too good to be true? That was the moment I should have listened to my own alarm bells. But I needed a product. My customers wanted supplies, and I had nothing. So I agreed.

I needed 4,500 dollars for the 15 pounds. I didn't have it, but I knew Cosimo "Richie" Farbo—really Cosimo, but he went by Richie Farbo—always had cash from his legit business, the Cypress Shop. I went to him and asked to borrow the forty-five hundred, so I could make the deal with Monk.

On the day of the deal, we were supposed to meet at the Ole Monte Club, where everyone gathered. JR was there playing chess for $1,500. His opponent put up the cash, and JR put up his Walther PPK… "His James Bond gun." They were playing a best-of-three match for it.

We were waiting for the ride to show up. The ride Monk was waiting on was Big Steve. I had only met Big Steve once, down at Waterford Park in West Virginia, at the racetrack where we hit the biggest score of my life on "Trentonaro" at ninety-nine to one. So, we waited for him to show up.

JR didn't know about the deal until that moment. I told him, and he said something was off. He told me he didn't like it. He told me to give Cosimo his money back. I said I already had it. He repeated himself. I told him I could handle myself, that I had my piece, and I could go for the ride and pick it up. He told me again, and this time he didn't soften it. He told me to get Cosimo, who was sitting at the bar.

Cosimo came over while JR was still playing chess. JR ordered me to take the money out of my pocket and hand it back to Richie Farbo, which I did. I didn't like it, but I did it. JR handed the money back to Cosimo and said his kid was out of the deal. If Cosimo wanted to go through with the deal, he could do it himself.

Cosimo wasn't thrilled, but he walked back to the bar. I went over to him and told him if he still wanted to go through with it, and if he got the product, I would move it for him and split the profits after his forty-five hundred was paid back. That appealed to him.

We waited. It was almost an hour before Big Steve showed up with Monk. They expected me to take a ride with them, with the forty-five hundred, to pick up the reefer. I didn't find out until six months to a year later that the plan was to take me on my last ride. The forty-five hundred was going to be the payout for Big Steve to kill me.

But the plan changed when JR pulled me out of it. They took the forty-five hundred from Cosimo and said they'd be back in a couple of hours to deliver the reefer.

A couple of hours turned into a few hours. Then it dragged into the night. By midnight, we were still at the bar, drunk and waiting. It was apparent it was a rip-off. I tried to talk to Cosimo, but he was drunk and furious. He wanted to go out behind the Ole Monte Club and talk.

We walked out back, and he gave me the worst beating of my life. He beat me up and down the back lot and both "Bocce Courts." He was a rock of a man, a bricklayer, a cement worker, and even though he was probably twice my age, he handed me a beating I still remember. Inside or outside the joint, he would've kept going. He probably would've killed me if something unexpected hadn't happened.

A truck pulled into the back parking lot. Two guys jumped out with baseball bats. One of them was my younger brother Patrick. He had a feeling I was in trouble, and he and a friend—either Casey Bartlett or Chris Green or Joey Clemente, one of that crew—were driving around looking for me. They showed up at the exact moment they were needed. They came at Cosimo with the bats, which was the only thing that was going to separate him from me.

They pulled me into the truck, and we got out of there.

After a couple of days of recovery and JR talking to Cosimo, we agreed the whole thing had been a setup from the start. JR believed they wanted me dead.

At that point, Cosimo wanted his money back. The only place he thought he could get it was Waterford Park, West Virginia, because that was the only place we had any line on Big Steve. So, Cosimo and I went down there. We stayed a couple of days, looked everywhere for him, and found nothing. We came back to Erie.

That weekend, I was at the PP Club partying. I walked out around three or four in the morning, got in my car, and started driving across West 18th Street toward my father's house, where I was staying at the time. I hit a bump, and the car suddenly lurched right, smashing into a parked car. I was so drunk I just backed up, straightened the wheel, and kept going.

I went another block or two, hit another bump, and the car pulled right again, hitting another parked car. I was lit and just wanted to get home, so I kept going. I probably hit twenty cars across the city every time I hit a bump. Each time, the car jerked right and slammed into whatever was parked along the curb.

In the morning, when I sobered up enough to walk outside, I checked the car. Someone had cut the right front tie rod. It had been sawn almost three-quarters of the way through with a hacksaw. When I hit the first bump, it snapped, which is why the car kept shooting to the right. It was apparent someone was trying to kill me.

I replaced the tie rod and got the car functioning again, but the right front fender was demolished. And I had left a trail of wreckage across Erie without even knowing it.

So Cosimo Farbo still wanted his money, and he decided to go down to West Virginia himself. He had a girlfriend, a young girl named Kathy. I can't remember her last name now, but I knew her. She was my age, and we'd become friends through two of my female friends who were horse trainers. They kept their own horses in stables and boarded others. I dealt pot to them, and because of their connections at Commodore Downs outside Erie, they were valuable to me. They knew what horses were running, which jockeys were hot, and now and then, they gave me solid tips. In return, I gave them a break on their weed.

They were the ones who introduced me to Kathy, a pretty blonde girl who ended up having an affair with Richie Farbo. Cosimo — Richie — was married with kids, even though most of them were grown by then. But he took Kathy with him down to Waterford Park, West Virginia, to look for Big Steve.

Down there, I don't know if they ever crossed paths with Big Steve or not. But on the drive back, going through the mountains of West Virginia and Pennsylvania, someone had cut Cosimo's brake lines. His brakes failed. Their car went over a steep embankment and down a mountainside. Cosimo died instantly. Kathy, that beautiful young girl, was torn up badly in the wreck and spent months recovering.

Someone wanted Cosimo dead, and they made it happen. It dragged out for a while, the way these things often do, and nobody ever solved it. But anyone with half a brain could see it tied right back to that drug deal.

I regretted getting Cosimo involved from the moment I heard the news. JR warned me from the beginning. He said the deal stunk, and he didn't want me anywhere near it. I went ahead and got mixed up in it with Cosimo anyway.

You learn from mistakes. But sometimes the lesson comes too late.

Hindsight is 20/20. I see it now. Back then, everything felt like separate incidents, nothing tied together. But as the years went by and little pieces of the puzzle drifted in, it got obvious. They wanted me dead because I knew too much about the armored car robbery, and "Si" Sittelli never got over me "raping his house," as he liked to call it. He felt I'd violated his place, even though he used me like an indentured servant, and I turned his club, the Uthmann Chor Club, into a money maker.

He still wanted his pound of flesh. If Cy Ciotti hadn't stopped him, Sittelli would've come for me himself. Instead, he leaned on Gary Montgomery. Gary had his own reasons. I knew too much about the armored car job, and that made me a problem for him, too.

So, looking back, no mystery remains. They were going to take out the smart Irish kid who'd made them a pile of cash. They didn't care if they were killing the golden goose.

That's the truth of it.

When I laid out the photos — the three Russell brothers, the two DeSanto brothers, and me — that made six of the seven, and it hit me that the seventh needed to be there too. One of the biggest regrets of my life sits right in that missing spot.

Cosimo was a tough guy. Tough son of a bitch. And he should've been in that lineup.

CHAPTER 18
THE LAKESIDER

The Lakesider was a strip club on the Lackawanna–Hamburg line, right on Route 5. Jimmy Russo owned the place. He and Jimmy JR Russell grew up together in Lackawanna. They were so close that when they got in trouble with the law, they gave each other's names. Russo would claim he was Russell, and Russell would claim he was Russo. Their friendship stuck for life.

When I first started driving JR down to Buffalo, it was mainly for the Monday Night Football tickets. That's how it all kicked off. Every time I drove in from Erie, the first stop was always the Lakesider. Russo's place became my landing point. Once I got there, I could figure out everywhere else we needed to go. It turned into my home base.

I became good friends with Jimmy Russo. We got close enough a couple of times that, when we came down to do scores, we ended up taking the whole safe and needed a spot to crack it open. Russo gave JR the location of the spare key for the Lakesider's back door. There were stairs in the back that led to the second floor, where he kept rooms for dancers to rent. They'd entertain whoever they wanted up there. One of those rooms was always available to us. More than once, we broke open a safe in that room.

Time moved like it always does. Things happened, people scattered, and I lost touch with Russo when I went to prison. JR got out in '91, and he passed in October '93. Over the past 5 years, I worked at Dunlop Tire as a plant electrical engineer.

After work, I'd pick up JR. Whatever small errands he had, I took him. Sometimes we just parked ourselves at a barstool and had a couple of beers. He only let me have a couple, then he'd run me off like a cranky older brother. He'd point at me and say, You've got a wife and kids, get your ass home. He meant it. He cared about my family.

He died in October '93. At the service, I turned around, and there stood Jimmy Russo. He looked at me and said, Where have you been, kid? I said I'd been on a bit of vacation, Jim, and now I had a family and tried to keep things straight. He told me I should stop in anyway and have a drink.

The Lakesider sat right on my way home from Dunlop Tire. Back then, we were all squeezed into a mobile home in Hamburg, New York. Five of us. Laura, Justin, John, and little Lauren, who was only a toddler. Russo kept saying, Stop by for a drink sometime.

So one time after work, after JR died, I stopped in Jimmy's place. I sat there having a couple of drinks, minding my business, and Jimmy came out from the back room. I went to pay my tab. His bar manager, who'd been there forever, was working the bar. Jimmy told her, "If this man ever tries to give you money, his money's no good here." He wouldn't let me pay for a drink.

I said, *"Jimmy, you don't have to do that."*

He didn't care.

It wasn't exactly helpful for a marriage when you can walk into a strip club and drink for free. Anyone with a pulse can figure out that's not the straightest path to domestic peace. But for a couple of years, I stopped into the Lakesider pretty regularly, had a few drinks, and never paid a dime.

I'd do Jimmy a few favors here and there, because that's how things worked. You didn't keep score on paper, but you kept score.

Jimmy had this little cement mixer for his horse farm out in Angola. He had horses, and he also bedded horses, so the place always needed something fixed. The mixer needed a drive motor and a drive gear. I found the parts, ordered them through Dunlop Tire's spare parts room, picked them up after work, and brought them to Jimmy. I put everything on the mixer myself. It ran fine again, and he was thrilled.

Then he had another job. Since he had that horse farm, and Dunlop was scrapping a conveyor, he wanted it. Dunlop was going to junk it, but even getting scrap out of that place took a circus of signatures. You had to get a formal scrap pass and go through the head engineer, who was my boss, for total production.

I did the whole thing anyway. Got the scrap pass. Had one of Jimmy's guys drive a truck to Dunlop. We loaded the conveyor on the truck, and he hauled it to the farm. We assembled the whole thing out there and turned it into a bale conveyor. He could throw bales on it and send them straight to the second floor of the barn. Jimmy loved it.

Everything was favors back then.

Just like the favor when JR first came home in '91 from the armored car robbery. He worked at A-Light or Astrolite, and the owner was Scrunch.

It was the first day I ever met Scrunch. My first stop after JR got out. That's where he landed after the armored car robbery, fresh from the federal joint in Lake Placid. I met him at Scrunch's place, the A-Lite Lounge. That became the hangout by default.

Those first couple times, we just sat there and talked about old times, had a few drinks, nothing complicated. Then one day, Scrunch was cussing at this meat slicer in the back. The thing wouldn't run. I told him I'd take a look. I grabbed my meter from the car, checked the motor, and found it was shorted.

I wrote down the specs of the motor — frame size, horsepower, amperage, all the electrical numbers. Dunlop Tire had a graveyard of used motors in a corner of the plant. Some were junk, some were fine. I dug around and found one that matched. Getting it out the door was another story. Getting anything out of Dunlop without paperwork was like smuggling the Crown Jewels, but I managed to slide the motor into the back of my car and get through the gate.

I brought the motor to the A-Lite Lounge, rigged it up, rewired everything, and got the slicer running. From that day on, Scrunch treated me like I was his personal electrician.

Little favors, that's all it ever took to lock in loyalty with certain people.

Jimmy Russo was the same way in his own lane. He wasn't an angel, but he had lines he wouldn't cross. If a woman wanted out of stripping and dancing, he'd actually help her. He'd give her a room upstairs for free, let her stay long enough to build a little money, and leave the life. He didn't broadcast it. He just did it.

What really set him off in the late 80s and early 90s was the mess across the border. The strip clubs in Canada were basically a pipeline. The Canadian French Connection ran girls from Montreal to Toronto to Niagara Falls to Fort Erie, right down to Buffalo's doorstep. They moved the girls like chess pieces. The minute a girl felt settled, or someone local tried to help her, they shipped her to the next city. It was human trafficking. Russo couldn't stand it.

1996 rolled in, a few years since JR died. A lot had happened in that time. The lawsuit for Justin — the one JR set in motion through Joe Monahan — finally paid out. With that money, Laura and I started hunting for a new place. We found one that looked like it was built to show off.

A ranch in West Seneca. Three thousand square feet, four bedrooms, five bathrooms. The basement wasn't even part of the listed square footage, and that space alone could've been another house. It finished the whole thing. There was an L-shaped bar, a regulation 10-foot pool table, and the works. When we bought it, the sellers had six pinball machines down there. They wanted to keep those, which was fine. That basement could hold seventy-five people and a band without anyone tripping over anyone else.

We were a few steps away from closing on it. The final paperwork had to be done at the Erie County Courthouse on Delaware Avenue in downtown Buffalo. So, we're there at this big table — our realtor, our lawyer, the sellers, their people, the usual lineup. Everyone flipping through stacks of documents like it's a parade of signatures.

Down the room, there's another group gathered around a table. It's a crowd, not a small one. I look over, and there he is: Jimmy Russo. He looks up. I look up—no nod, no smile, just a quick lock of the eyes that said plenty.

So we keep going with the paperwork. At one point, I catch Laura watching something behind me. Her eyes shift, and I can tell it's not the mortgage documents grabbing her attention. I turn around, and Jimmy is standing right behind my chair.

"Timmy, I gotta talk to you."

I tell him I'm in the middle of signing my life away. He doesn't care.

"Timmy, out in the hallway. Now."

So I excuse myself from the table, and Jimmy and I walk out of the room, then out of the courthouse. He looks like someone who hasn't slept.

"Timmy, this is killing me."

I ask him what he's talking about.

"I'm here to sell the Lakesider," he says. "Been dealing with this guy for almost a year. Thought he was American. Thought he was the buyer. Turns out he's just a front for someone else."

The real buyers? The fucking Canadians running the strip clubs up north. Jimmy didn't want to sell to them. He was ready to walk away from the whole deal, but he couldn't run the Lakesider day to day anymore. The grind had worn him down.

"Timmy," he said, "why don't you take over the place? I'll hold the paper on it." Meaning, I wouldn't even need a mortgage — make payments to him every month.

I was floored. "Jimmy... I'd love to, but I'm still on parole. Ten years of parole and probation from Pennsylvania after getting out of New York. No way I'd get a liquor license."

"I'll hold the paper for that too," he said. That's huge. Taking on someone else's liquor license liability is no joke.

I shook my head. "Jimmy... if I do this, I'll be down the hall next year in divorce court. I've got a family. Three kids. A wife. I can't do it."

He was disappointed, to say the least. We finished our closing, and I moved into the new house.

About a year later, I ran into Jimmy again. He finished the story. He'd sold the Lakesider to the Canadians. When the papers were signed, they suggested one last drink at the club before handing over the keys. Jimmy agreed.

From the courthouse to the Lakesider was less than fifteen minutes. By the time they pulled up, the Canadians had already hired a construction crew. They were ready to demolish the place.

Jimmy opened the doors, poured everyone a shot. They clinked glasses. Then the top Canadian nodded to the crew. The demolition started right in front of Jimmy. A lifetime flashed before his eyes. That, he said, killed him too.

He had wanted me to take it over. I could have taken the Lakesider for nothing, just on my word. I don't know if Jimmy Russo is still alive, but that's the story of the Lakesider; he was a good friend to both JR and me... And he was a good man.

CHAPTER 19

FLY UNDER THE RADAR!

That was taught to me in many ways long before JR. All the way back to Grandma Murphy, when I was six years old, every Sunday after church, we would visit Grandpa and Grandma Murphy, and ever since I gave her that nickel that she taped up on a plaque in her kitchen, she would whisper things to me. When she did, I knew to listen. She did things with me that she didn't do with any of her grandchildren. I was the only one, I believe, who slept over at Grandpa and Grandma Murphy's house at 415 German Street, Erie, Pennsylvania.

She took me to wade in the fountain in Perry Square... Not named after My Grandpa Perry but for Oliver Hazard Perry, who led the Brig Niagara against the British in the Battle on Lake Erie in the War of 1812, "If a Victory is to be gained, I will gain it...!" "We have met the enemy, and they are ours!" These are the type of things she would whisper... so splashing in the fountain, two other kids were starting to fight. I was going to break it up. She said STOP! I did. And then she whispered, "See who wins." I was surprised at first, and I'm sure Grandma wouldn't let anyone get hurt, but it taught me...Wait...Observe. She would say, "You have two ears and only one mouth...That's so you listen twice as much as you talk." This is at six! She then took me shopping at the Boston Store when it was in its heyday, like Miracle on 34th Street. She took me to the toy floor, and just her and I walked down the aisles, and she told me I could have whatever I wanted. I don't know if it was entirely my choice, but I picked out a very lifelike "Tommy Gun," and she didn't discourage me at all as I tested it out all the way home to my house in Grandma's gold Cadillac.

When I came into the house with my new toy, my mother was livid, I could tell, but Grandma was standing right behind me, and Mom didn't say a word, but you could cut the tension in the air. Even at six, I could sense it. A few days later, while I was at school, that "Tommy Gun" mysteriously disappeared, and I already told you of the ride from Academy High School to Ashtabula, Ohio - Traffic Court. All the way to her, driving her Cadillac across the country to California Naval Base Hospital, and get her Boy Out! I'm sure with a roll or two of Benjamin's that would choke a horse!

Grandma had power long after prohibition ended, as I pointed out about her running the card game right across the street from the City of Erie Police Station: Seventh and State Street; Second floor of what would become the Isaac Baker Men's Store.

She also taught me positive things like," When You're Up in Life... and you can give someone a hand up... Do it! And don't ask for it back right away...if you can afford it. They'll think about it more than you will...Unless You Need It... Then the longer they've owed you, the more willing they're going to be to pay you back... No matter what..."

But the best evidence of GrandPa and GrandMa Murphy's far-reaching power long after prohibition was over is this picture, which I will repost here. Note: My Grandfather was named Perry M. Murphy (I believe Michael... I'll have to check with my brother).

In the picture showing my father receiving the Navy Bar, the list of attendees includes Mr. & Mrs. John C. Murphy Jr. and Mr. & Mrs. John C. Murphy Sr. My father was not a Jr. My Grandpa Perry was not John C. Murphy Sr., nor does it mention Grandma's first name, "Ethel Mae." Also of note is County Commissioner Thomas Fatley, who would later become the Mayor of the City of Erie with Grandma's help and then be convicted and removed from office for taking kickbacks from gamblers like Grandma Murphy's card game right across the street from his office, but he never mentioned Grandma, You either owed her money or she had some dirt on you. Either way, she had you!

ERIE VETERAN HONORED—The air medal Tuesday evening was presented to John Charles Murphy, Jr., AMM2/c, USNR, at the Erie Naval Reserve Armory "for meritorious achievement in aerial flight as radioman of a torpedo bomber plane in Night Torpedo Squadron Ninety attached to the U. S. S. Enterprise." Participating in the ceremony were, left to right, County Commissioners Thomas W. Flatley, Dell Darling, Comdr. T. K. Dunston, representative of the U. S. Naval Reserve, 4th District headquarters; Commissioner Fred Lamberton, Mrs. John C. Murphy, Jr., John C. Murphy, Jr., Mrs. John C. Murphy, Sr., John C. Murphy, Sr. (Times photo.)

Some of the fellows in Barracks "C" turned seve pools couple of evenings ago. *I was the 'co*

Thomas Flatley, who became Mayor, Navy Officer, Mom, Dad, Grand Ma and Grandpa. Dad was NOT a Jr., as Grandpa was Perry M. Murphy, but Grandma Murphy had enough power to change what was in the Erie Times-News to protect Grandpa from being in the U.S. with no documentation, while getting Her Son's Hero Welcome at Home from the USS Enterprise. It was over 10 years after Prohibition ended, and in another decade, the mayor would be removed from office after admitting to receiving kickbacks from gamblers... but would never name Grandma.

So I was well primed for Jimmy JR Russell and his many rules and "Lines to Live or Die from," I learned to listen...I know it's hard to believe today... I used to be the quiet one... But he schooled me well, and the roots of his organization were under Stefano Magaddino, who controlled out of Niagara Falls, New York, USA. To "The Arm" of Buffalo, NY. But far beyond the international border to Hamilton, Ontario, to Toronto, to the doorstep of Montreal, Quebec, which was controlled by Stefano's cousin, Joseph Bonanno, and his Caporegime Carmen Galiente, who together led "The French Connection." But Magaddino's territory in the United States extended from Buffalo to Erie, PA, to the doorsteps of Cleveland and Pittsburgh, all the way into Youngstown, Ohio, and beyond to Las Vegas and Los Angeles.

He controlled this vast region for five decades, longer than any other La Cosa Nostra Boss ever. What he preached is "Fly under the radar," "Don't attract attention to yourself." It was John Gotti's downfall; he forgot this basic rule. Once he became "The Teflon Don" and attracted the limelight, it made old-time Sicilians cringe. It was only a matter of time... That, coupled with "Kill the Irishman" Danny Greene and Ray Ferritto, was the beginning of the end of the La Cosa Nostra in the United States.

Another key to Stefano Magaddino's mantra was "Always have a visible means of support" and "Plausible Deniability," meaning have a job to cover other activities... and I always did. One of the best examples of this in Buffalo was the Laborers Union Local 210 which provided "Show and No-show jobs" all the way into the 1990's when it was brought down by former Local Business Manager Ron Fino who was an informant to the FBI from 1973 to 1988 and brought down the long time "Visible means of support" for many Magaddino family members as well as associates. "The Undertakers' "death in 1974 and the exposure of Local 210 severely weakened but never destroyed the Buffalo Mob.

I always maintained a visible means of support to present plausible deniability before and after serving three prison terms. As I said from day one from being released here in New York, I had a job with Butch Halliby and Checker Cab Co. Then I went to work at Laura's girlfriend, who they would tease me with a "me'nage a' trois" when I was in the joint, her boyfriend had a business "VanCrafters" would customize vans and would do handicap modifications to Vans. I learned these skills and started my own business doing handicap modifications to vans and houses called "Access-N-Able Inc."

I then worked for a custom machine builder, D.A. Griffin Corp., building state-of-the-art machines, including a CNC/XYZ positioning table interfaced with a 5-kilowatt Spectra-Physics CO_2 laser, while attending an Associate's Degree program in Robotics & Automation at Erie Community College (NY). With this in hand, I was hired as a Contract Controls Engineer at Dunlop Tire Corporation, as they were undergoing a $200 million expansion of the Buffalo, NY, plant, and was subsequently hired full-time as a Plant Electrical Engineer from 1989 – 1996 ...Flying under the Radar.

"JR" had been released in 1991, and I would pick him up after work or sometimes during lunch. I would hop out of work, run to pick him up in Lackawanna, zip back to my good friend Greg D's, who used to own the "NightCap" just down the street from Dunlop... within beeper distance of the plant. They would have our lunch waiting for us. I would eat and leave JR running my tab until I got out at 5 o'clock, then come and pick him up again and bring him back to Lackawanna on my way home to my family. He would only let me have two beers before sending me home. Sometimes it would be two at every stop along the way home.

When JR was released, he had hundreds upon hundreds of United States Silver Dollars. He used to love silver. We needed a way to get rid of these without attracting attention. We came up with these little cardboard display cards for silver dollars. There was room for 10 in 4 rows in a pyramid shape... 4, 3, 2, 1 at the top... perfect.

We loaded up the silver dollars and made up football pool square charts for bar patrons to buy squares for a chance to win 10 silver dollars. It was a huge hit and provided JR with an untraceable cash flow, usually a lot of dollar bills. We had a route of bars all the way from Tonawanda to North Buffalo, Downtown, and South Buffalo, all the way back to little Lackawanna, NY, that provided JR with a steady income, and I would always help him out if he needed anything. I owed the man my life.

After" JR" passed on October 10, 1993, the day after my birthday. I left Dunlop Tire Corporation in 1996 to go to General Motors Corporation - Harrison Radiator Thermal Division in Lockport, NY, another layer to flying under the radar. General Motors required me to complete my Bachelor of Science degree, fully paid for via Empire State University, another layer.

General Motors gradually spun off the Thermal Division in Lockport to become Delphi Thermal Systems... yet another layer on the resume. Delphi was almost autonomous from GM for ALMOST seven years.

There was a little line buried in the fine print of the GM/Delphi spin-off agreement that stated if "Delphi Thermal Systems was solvent for a period of seven years," General Motors would be free and clear of providing any Union Pension Retirement Benefits and could walk away from workers and their families that had worked a lifetime for them, when Delphi Thermal Chairman J.T. Battenberg pulled the trigger and declared Delphi Thermal Systems bankrupt, weeks before the agreement would have been finalized. It caused panic at Delphi and GM, and both offered Salary Early Retirement packages to thin out the herd of overhead fat among old timers milking the system.

They offered it to any employee with 10 or more years of seniority. I had 12 years, 6 months' severance pay to leave. I was the first to raise my hand, took my $40 grand in pay, along with over $100 grand in pension.

I really had no idea what was being deducted from my pay over 12 years of service. I took this and started another business, "Data-N-Able Inc.," sound familiar? Data-N-Able was a Barcoding / Manufacturing Information Systems Corporation. I went back to my former boss at Dunlop Tire and gave him a sales pitch to implement barcoding systems at Dunlop, which was jointly owned by Sumitomo Rubber and Goodyear Tire. I installed all their barcode/manufacturing information systems over the next five years... Another layer! I also ended up going back to Delphi Thermal Systems and designed, engineered, and installed all their Barcode/Label Error-Proofing Systems – "Plausible Deniability!"

After JR passed, I continued to "Fly Under the Radar" and "Always have a Good Plan B," and in 1996, I purchased a Summer Beach home in Sherkston Shores, Ontario, Canada, for the family, just 20 minutes over the Peace Bridge in Buffalo. Follow the South Shore of Lake Erie in Canada, which we would call the North coast of Lake Erie... You follow the coast on their Route 3 until you come upon a little slice of heaven right outside Port Colborne and the Welland Canal.

Sherkston Shores was always my plan B. If things ever got too hot in Buffalo for any reason at all, 20 minutes across the international border of the Peace Bridge, I had a residence where I could go, collect my thoughts, and think of an exit strategy if I needed one.

I also had a stash that I had given Laura to take care of her and the kids in the event I had to make an "Irish Good-bye" and "Go Surfin'" "Murph the Surf style ... No witnesses! Gone in 30 seconds! This is what was ingrained into me... from the beginning... Break the Rules... And the

Rules will Break You! And if I could ever follow Grandma Murphy's words of wisdom to offer a hand up, I would and did many times!

I always remembered her parting words to someone she had given a hand up to: "Never call in your marker." She would part the debtor with the words and orders... "Take Care of Your Family!" She would say this to small businessmen she helped start in business, like "Cy and Blackie," in their first Hot Dog Cart. She made sure anyone she ever helped took care of their family first. And in the long run, that hand up was paid off when Cy saved my life with just a look in the eye and a nod of the head. What goes around comes around, and Grandma Murphy's logic bore out in saving her Grandson's life decades later.

She never knew – Or did she?

Timothy P. Murphy – Fly Under the Radar Resume

Over 35 years of progressive experience in Electrical Control Systems Design and Engineering with a demonstrated proficiency in successfully leading multiple major multi-million-dollar capital projects and implementing automated control systems. Managed all phases of various projects, including cost estimates, project planning, purchasing, and organizing task assignments. Experienced in the generation of control hardware specifications, control panel designs, schematic wiring diagrams, including PLC, HMI, SCADA, SQL, and SSRS programming and integration.

Have developed state-of-the-art manufacturing information systems using 1D & 2D barcode labeling and reading to provide real-time information to the office desktop for quality assurance and production management. Also, over twenty years of experience in custom machine building and hands-on troubleshooting of electromechanical machinery. Proactive in work habits, excellent inter-personal communications, attentive to detail, responsive to change, conscious of cost, quality, & schedules.

Proficient at programming and interfacing with the following hardware, software, devices, and systems:

- <u>Automation SCADA Software</u> - GE iFix, Cimplicity, Plant Edition, AB RS View32
- <u>PLC Programming</u> - Allen Bradley Control Logix, SLC500, Siemens, Modicon, GE Fanuc
- <u>HMI Touch screen</u> - Emerson / GE Viewstations, Quickpanel, AB, Proface, Xycom, & Industrial PC's
- <u>Servo Systems</u> - Allen Bradley, Emerson, Indramat, Ormec, Delta, AC & DC drives
- <u>Barcode Scanners</u> – Honeywell, Handheld Products, Welch Allyn, LaserData, Data Logic, Barcode Printing - Loftware Labeling, Printronix, Intermec, Sato, Zebra
- <u>Ethernet Networking</u> - Local Area Networks (LANs), routers, switchers, wireless, Ethernet
- <u>Lasers</u> - Precision measurement and sensing, industrial cutting, welding, marking & training. Automatic Controls-Hydraulic, pneumatic, temperature, robotics, vision, sensors, & actuators.

Summary of Employment [COVERING HOLES IN TIME]

May 2015-October 2023   IMA LIFE North America Inc.

Control Systems Engineer   2175 Military Road Tonawanda, NY 14225

Programming SCADA systems, HMIs, PLC's, SQL databases, SSRS Reporting, Virtual Machines, Ethernet Network Designs and integration for custom built state of the art Freeze Drying machines for the pharmaceutical industry.

Jan. 2008-May 2015   Data-N-Able Inc.
145 Pinewood Drive   , West Seneca, NY

Owner / Project Manager / Sr. Controls System Engineer

Developed Manufacturing Information System, interfacing PLCs to HMIs, barcode scanners & printers. Networked plant floor equipment to server computers and leading site SQL and Oracle databases. Integrated system processes into the intranet website to report real-time work in process, quality assurance and scheduling data. Utilized Virtual Machine Technology to enable information flow throughout the manufacturing processes. Developed a cloud-based Inventory Control System, interfacing UPC databases to utilize an Android-based application to scan barcodes through smartphone devices.

Jan 2000 - Dec. 2007   Sr. Manufacturing / Controls Engineer

Delphi Thermal Systems   Lockport, NY

Utilized 2D DataMatrix barcodes to serialize every part produced, tracking labeled products for quality control throughout manufacture, testing, and shipping. Installed and commissioned all new production equipment, including Braze furnaces, radiator core builders, clinch machines, & mass spectrometer leak test machines. Familiar with Lean manufacturing, IS09000, QS 9000.

Oct. 1996-Dec. 1999   Project Engineer / Controls Engineer

General Motors Corporation (Harrison Radiator/Delphi) Lockport, NY

Managed installation of $12 million automated aluminum & stainless-steel brazing systems utilizing Vacuum braze furnaces, de-oiling, and heat-age processes. Developed automated material handling systems, interfacing automatic load trucks to conveyor systems and process equipment. Supervised all union skilled trades and outside contractor labor through successful project start-up and commissioning. Tuned complex multi-zoned furnaces, PID process controls. Wrote PLC programs for production machinery, which included self-diagnostic messaging for increased uptime and ease of maintenance, and troubleshooting.

June 1989 - September 1996   Plant Electrical Engineer

Dunlop Tire Corporation   Buffalo, NY

Installed and maintained automatic tire production equipment, including tire building and curing presses. Programming and troubleshooting of tire test equipment, including Tire Uniformity Optimizers (TUOs), automatic balancers, and X-Ray machines. Redesigned and programmed automatic material handling and conveyor systems. Supervised union skilled trades/maintenance workers in daily troubleshooting and managed outside contractors in capital project work.

1987-1989 Flex-O-Vit USA - Engineering Technician - Angola, NY

Contracted to redesign and retrofit Industrial abrasive manufacturing equipment, including 13 ovens, high-pressure stamping presses, web processing, and cutting equipment. Engineered and programmed new control panels to NEMA standards. Built a new control panel for the grinding wheel destructive test machine.

1985-1987   D.A. Griffin Corporation   Electrical Technician, West Seneca, NY

Custom machine building of automated production equipment for various industries, including automotive, heat exchangers, welding, and assembly. Built a laser welding/heat treating system utilizing a CNC servo-controlled positioning system. Built, wired, and programmed all types of PLC-controlled custom-built equipment.

1983-1985   Snap-Tite Hydraulics - Maintenance Foreman- Erie, PA

High-pressure hydraulic valve machining and assembly. Supervised second shift maintenance of all production machinery. Responsible for all troubleshooting of electrical and mechanical repairs.

1978-1980   VanDekamp Frozen Foods   Electro-Mechanical Maintenance   Erie, PA

Frozen food production and packaging - Responsible for troubleshooting all electrical and mechanical repairs of food processing equipment, including mixing, flash frying, freeze & packaging machinery.

1976-1978   Buffalo Molded Plastics, Mold Maker Apprentice

Akron, Ohio

Served two years in a mold-making machinist apprenticeship program, studying blueprint reading, technical math, and machine shop theory. Learned to operate all types of machine tool equipment, including CNCs

---

Education

2001-2005   Empire State University of New York

Bachelor of Science   Concentration - Automated Manufacturing / Information Systems Technology

1986-1989 <u>Erie Community College</u> (AAS) Automated Manufacturing

Buffalo, New York,   Associate of Applied Science - Concentration-Robotics Technology

1985-1986 Consortium of the Niagara Frontier (In NYS DOC Prison) <u>Daemen / Canisius College / Niagara University</u> - Amherst, New York Liberal Arts Studies – 32 credits

Letters of recommendation and references are available upon request.

<u>Awards received</u>

<u>2004 InfoTech Niagara Buffalo Emerging Technology Awards</u> - Manufacturing Information Systems utilizing 2D bar-coding for real-time production information/quality tractability to the office desktop.

<u>2005 Delphi Global Excellence Award</u> for Manufacturing Information Systems Label Error Proofing System using Lean Manufacturing Principles for Zero defects to the customer (General Motors).

OUR SUMMER PLACE – SHERKSTON SHORES – ONTARIO

THE CROWN JEWELS – MURPH THE SURF STYLE
INTERNATIONAL CURRENCY

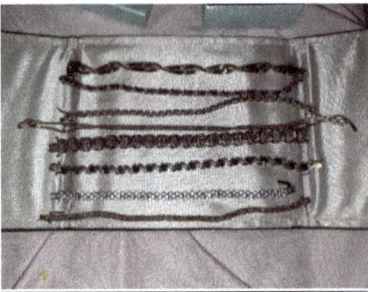

These are actually the three Fallsview Balcony Suites we stayed in after the Royal Oak Armored Car Depository Robbery.

"To think I did all that!"

THE REAL REASON I FLEW UNDER THE RADAR!

THE REAL AND ONLY REASON IS...

BUT FOR THE GRACE OF GOD!

To Any and All who wish to share your side of any "Murph the Surf" story, Good and Bad... (I'M A BIG BOY)

Go to "Onemancrimespree.com and enter it in so it can be in the Next adventures of "One Man Crime Spree" ... To be continued...

Dedication

To those who came before:

Beginning with My Great-Great-Grandfather Murphy, one of the lone Survivors of "The Charge of the Light Brigade," I do this to preserve my family lineage in writing, so it is never lost!

Calvary Cemetery – 3325 West Lake Road- Erie, Pennsylvania

Perry M. Murphy 11-17-1885 - 06-12-1969 {Grandpa}

"Chief Engineer – Great Lakes Tugboats"   "Rum Runner" Irish Tenor – Piano Player – Once sang with Chicago Philharmonic Orchestra – Fantastic Irish Joke and Story Teller.

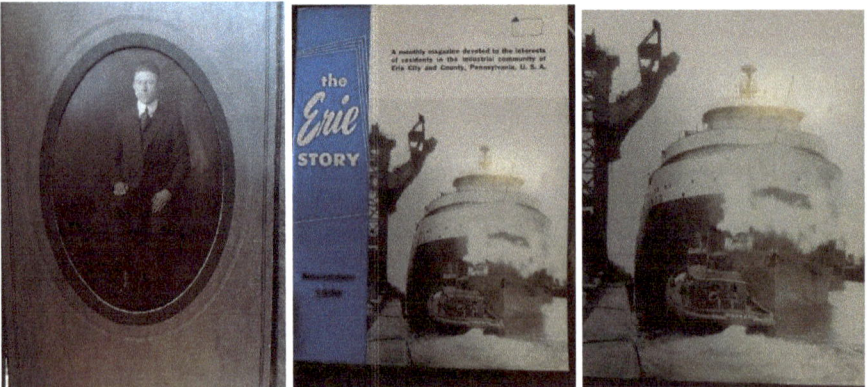

Ethel Mae Murphy 05-??-1903 - 09-26-1979 {Grandma}

"The Million Dollar Baby" of Erie, Pennsylvania

Picture w/ Jackie 25th Wedding Anniversary Aug 10, 1947 [Aug 10 1922]

Marriage certificate for Perry/ Ethel married in Ripley, NY, July 10, 1922. Ethel's dad was Charles Mae Ohs from Sweden, now of McKeesport, Pa. Mom was Margaret O'Dare from Pittsburgh, Pa. Ethel lived at 618 Kelly Ave, Wilkinsburg, Pa.

Perry's dad was John Murphy, who lived at 402 Parade St., Erie, PA, from Desoronto, Canada (which is across the lake from Oswego), now in Oswego, NY, and Helena Healy from England.

Perry lived at 304 West 2nd Erie, PA, and was an engineer (When searching Ethel's last name comes up as Oks)

{Murphy Plot - Dad, Florence Barczak, Grandpa, Grandma}

Jeremiah might be middle to John Murphy Perry's Dad.

[per Patty (Kohler, our 1ˢᵗ Cousin?)]. Uncle Bill Kohler (My Godfather – married to my Father's only sibling), My Aunt Rose Marie (My Godmother)

In Dad and Uncle Bill's Ash Hauling Hearse.

[Male Icon] John Jeremiah Murphy

{Great Grandfather} 1859 – 1929

{Loretto Rest Syracuse, NY}

Born in Canada (English) in 1859 ...[Female Icon]

Helena Healy Murphy {Great Grandmother}

{It may well have been Helena Healy's Father that rode in "The Charge of the Light Brigade"}

John "JACK" Charles Murphy {Father}
26, August 1924 - 06, September 1992

United States Navy Veteran- (Sea Warrior) USS Enterprise, Aviation Machinist – Second Class– Ribbon bar of the Navy Unit Commendation awarded for his outstanding Heroism.

W -80.15799 N 42.09699 Calvary Cemetery Erie, PA

S/W Corner East of Fence Rd. East of the 2nd water spigot.

Aunt Ruth Krill {Mom's Older Sister} 2 rows west.

Donna Mae Krill Murphy Barczak {Mother}

26 June 1927 – 01 April 2012

{Mom and Joseph Barczak- "Mr. B" (2014) with Johnny}

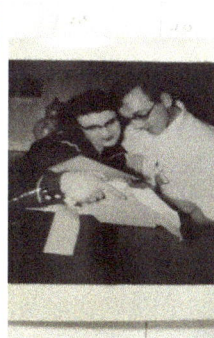

The most fantastic Mother in the World! Bar-None! She saved her family from ruin. Incredible housewife...Could do anything around the house. She taught me basic electricity when I was about 12. She taught me how to rewire a lamp and basic wiring since she worked at Erie Resister during WWII. Then, to put food on the table for seven children, she worked full-time at General Telephone Company, Loblaws, and Hills Department Store while raising all of us. We never missed a meal! Thank you, Mother! I'm sorry for the pain I caused you...I never really knew until I had a Son, John Michael Murphy, who strayed!

(The Murphy kids - Judy, Margie, Diane, Jack, Tim, Pat, & Mike)

(The Murphy Boys - Surf, Trevor, Dad, Pat, Jackie, & Mike)

*The **Denial's** [GrandMa Krill Snyder's] {Mother's Mom}. Came from Ireland to Canada because immigration was closed to the Irish.*

{William and Edna Krill – Mom's Parents}

Then came over between Chicago and Milwaukee, then to the industrial Gem of the Great Lakes. Erie. Her brother, Aden Denial, ran the Riverside Hotel in Cambridge Springs, PA, for nearly 40 years [and wintered in Florida, where he ran a snowbird hotel].

I was at the historical society in Cambridge Springs and reviewed the payroll records. Uncle Aden's name was the first on the record after the Colonel [owner].

John Perry "Jack" Murphy <masterofcrude@gmail.com> wrote:

Grandpa Murphy has NO birth certificate. His baptismal certificate is on file at St. Mary's Church, Oswego, NY

~~~~~~ ***Both sides of the family were illegal***~~~~~

John Michael "Casey Russel" Murphy {Son and Father}
21, December 1989 - 26, December 2016

Lakeside Cemetery – Section J - 4810 Camp Road Hamburg, NY Dual-Diagnosed – Bipolar Disorder - Drug Addiction Overdosed – Fentanyl in the Cocaine – Member of the "27 Club" Brian Jones, Jimi Hendrix, Janis Joplin, Jim Morrison....

John was 27 years old for 5 days only because I would not allow the doctors to test for brain dead or body temperature until after 12:01 AM on December 26, 2016. NO Way was Christmas Day going on his headstone! I informed the doctors of this... and they agreed they were very busy until after 12:01 AM.

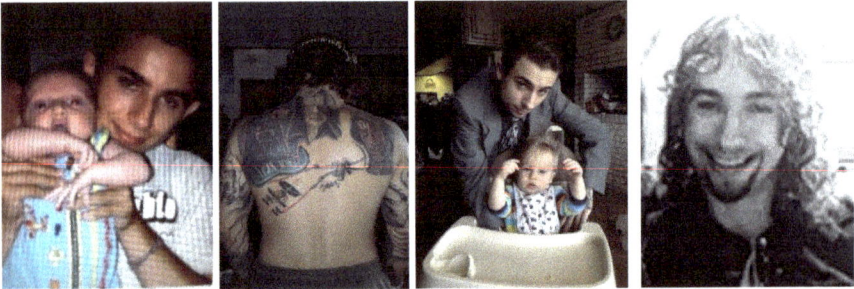

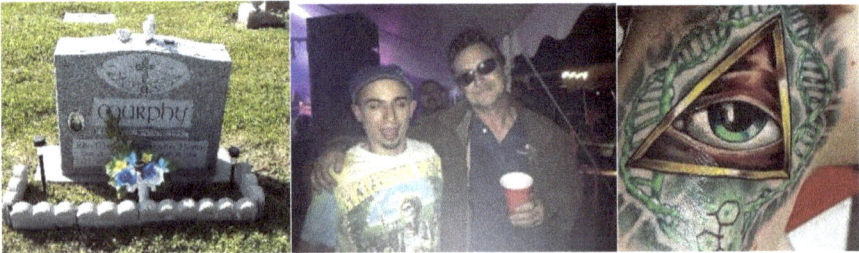

~Michael Charles Murphy {Baby Brother}

14 February 1963 – 11 June 2018

*United States Navy Veteran- (Sea Warrior) USS Virginia, USS Stump –
Sonar Technician – Many Letters of Commendation for his technical
knowledge and skill*

Otis Elevator – Elevator Constructor/Troubleshooter - 28 years

Wintergreen Gorge Cemetery in Harborcreek Township,

Erie County, Pennsylvania

(Mom, Joe B, Michael)   (Michael, Patrick, Tim... Visiting in the Joint)

~~~~~~

*Laura Lynn Sorce Murphy {Wife - Twice}
29, September 1959 - 23, May 2023*

*Married 1ˢᵗ time April 15, 1989 - Southtowns Christian Center Married
2nd time May 14, 2005 - Southtowns Christian Center Licensed Practical*

Nurse – Buffalo General Hospital – Our Lady of Victory Hospital – Lackawanna, NY.

Medical Biller – University of Buffalo Neurosurgery Co-Leader of an Amazing group of "Specially Abled" Christian Worshippers called Shepherds Troupe out of The Tabernacle in Orchard Park, New York.

She was a fierce advocate for the Rights of the Disabled as she fought for her son, Justin Thomas Murphy, to have care, dignity, and a life.

Lakeside Cemetery Section J - 4810 Camp Road Hamburg, NY

Mary Ellen "DeSanto" {The First Great Love of My Life}

16(?), August 1963 - 10, March 1985

Overdosed – [Set's] (1)-Doriden and (2)- Codeine #4. Received a letter from my Mother on the 3rd day in NYS DOC. March 15th, 1985 "Beware the Ides of March!"

The Last Christmas together at Dad's house – Mary Ellen and Tim

James P. "JR" Russell {Mentor – Partner - Father}

13 February 1936 – 10 October 1993

*Mastermind, Genius, Master Thief, Grand Master Level Chess Player,
Pool Hustler*

~~~~~~

Robert J. "RJ" Russell   { Partner - Friend}

22, October 1939 – 16, May 2016

United States Marine Veteran, Restaurateur, Businessman

~~~~~~

*~Peter Michael Russell - Erie Fugitive { Partner - Best Friend}
09, August 1950 – 30, November 2019*

*Staged his own Suicide and got away with it for over 10 years – Then he
did it again!   " IN THE WIND, BRO! "*
I was by each brother's side when they left this earth – Partners!

*The Russell Boys
Bobby "RJ," Jimmy "JR," Peter "DR"*

Adam Thomas Murphy – {Only Male Heir Grandson}

*Son of My Only Natural Born Son – John Michael Murphy Born to
Mother Sarah Shipston - 28 January 2012 - The only Male Blood Heir to*

the Murphy Name- And thus any proceeds which would come from this book in any format, including film and/or Mini-Video Series...From His Pappy Murph!

Adam Thomas... Always remember to take care of your Uncle Justin "UNC" Murphy...

You will be the Only One!